TEACH YOURSELF BOOKS

SWEDISH

This book is written primarily for those wanting to learn Swedish privately. An English reader should have no great difficulty in acquiring a working knowledge of the language as both the grammar and vocabulary are comparatively simple. Closest attention is also paid to pronunciation.

"Dr. McClean's work is not only up-to-date and very comprehensive; it is also based on sound teaching method."

The Linguists' Review

TEACH YOURSELF BOOKS

SWEDISH

A GRAMMAR OF THE MODERN LANGUAGE

R. J. McCLEAN, M.A., DR. PHIL.
Examiner in Swedish to the University of London

TEACH YOURSELF BOOKS
ST PAUL'S HOUSE WARWICK LANE LONDON EC4

First Printed 1947
Second Edition 1950
Third Edition 1969
Second Impression 1971

Third Edition Copyright © 1969
The English Universities Press Limited

ISBN 0 340 05825 0

PRINTED AND BOUND IN ENGLAND
FOR THE ENGLISH UNIVERSITIES PRESS LTD
BY HAZELL WATSON AND VINEY LTD, AYLESBURY

PREFACE

The present volume has been written primarily for those who wish to acquire a knowledge of Swedish by private study. This has made it necessary to be rather more explicit on minor points than would otherwise have been the case, and to devote special attention to pronunciation. In Part I every endeavour has been made to describe the sounds of Swedish as clearly and simply as possible. It should be carefully studied before any of Part II is attempted, and constantly revised, so that when the student hears Swedish spoken, he may know what to listen for and how to correct his own pronunciation. Since Swedish is a tone language, students will do well to avail themselves of every opportunity to hear it spoken. Students living in or near the large ports will almost certainly be able to get in touch with Swedish seamen, either through the local Swedish Seamen's Church or the nearest Swedish Consulate.

The phonetic script adopted in Part I is much the same as that found in French and German books used in English schools, with the addition of a few symbols to represent those sounds that are peculiar to Swedish. Students who have never met with phonetic script before are urged not to be deterred by it, but to take the little trouble needed to understand it. Once it has been mastered, it will prove an invaluable aid to correct pronunciation.

Little need be said of the way in which the remainder of the book should be used. Obviously the grammar in each chapter should be learned before the vocabulary, and the vocabulary must be memorized before the exercises are attempted. Constant revision is strongly recommended, and too rapid progress should not be attempted, as it only leads to disappointment. Anyone who masters the contents of this book in six months has every reason to be satisfied with his achievement.

A vocabulary is given at the end of the book, and this should facilitate revision work. For further study the dictionary recommended is W. E. Harlock : *Svensk-engelsk ordbok* and the *Engelsk-svensk ordbok*, compiled by Kärre, Lindkvist, Nöjd and Redin, both published by Svenska Bokförlaget, Stockholm. Those who wish to work through a more advanced grammar after they have finished the present work, are recommended to get Im. Björkhagen's *Modern Swedish Grammar* and *First Swedish Book*, published by Svenska Bokförlaget, Stockholm. Further particulars of grammars and annotated texts will be found in an article entitled " Swedish Studies " in *The Year's Work in Modern Language Studies*, Vol. VIII, p. 243, Cambridge University Press, 1938.

My best thanks are due to the Senate of the University of London for granting me permission to include some passages from recent examination papers in the translation exercises at the end of this book. Messrs. Carl Gehrmans Musikförlag, Stockholm, have allowed me to reproduce the music of Stenhammar's *Sverige*, and Messrs. Albert Bonniers Förlag have allowed me to use and adapt a short passage from *Socialiststaten och nutidssamhället*, by the late Professor Knut Wicksell. To them, as also to Mr. Åke Lamm of the Swedish Ballbearing Company, Luton, who very kindly compiled specimens of commercial letters for inclusion in Chapter XXIV, I tender my cordial thanks.

In the final stages of preparing this book for the press I have been privileged to consult Dr. Asta Kihlbom, Director of the newly founded Swedish Institute in London, on a number of difficult points, and her expert advice has been extremely valuable to me. Lektor Im. Björkhagen, Äppelviken, has very kindly looked through the section on pronunciation and suggested some improvements, and I owe a number of corrections to students attending the British Council's summer school at Malung, Dalecarlia, in July, 1946. In conclusion I have to acknowledge the great help I received from my wife as a living " work of reference " on Swedish usage ; also from my former colleague Mr. J. Bithell, M.A., who has kindly read through the proofs and given the book the benefit of his extensive knowledge and experience.

London, July 1947.

PREFACE TO THE SECOND EDITION

In the preparation of the new edition I have revised the text throughout and have tried to incorporate as many as possible of the corrections and improvements which teachers and students have been kind enough to suggest. I am particularly grateful to *Fil. lic.* P. Brandberg, Lecturer in Swedish at University College, London, for his valuable suggestions.

An alphabetical list of contents has been added at the end of the book; and it is hoped that this will enable the reader to find any section quickly.

London, August 1950.

PREFACE TO THE THIRD EDITION

The text has again been revised throughout and further corrections have been made. Students should note that the prices given in Exercises 18 and 23 were those prevailing in 1947.

London, February 1969.   R. J. McCLEAN

" I am learning Swedish so that when the war is over I can get to that blessed land for a short respite, as I like their brand of democracy, which is based on good manners."

—the late Hendrik Willem van Loon,
a great Dutch-born American.

Greenwich, Connecticut,
Thanksgiving Day, 1943.

INTRODUCTION

Swedish is a Germanic language closely related to Norwegian and Danish; in fact educated Swedes, Norwegians and Danes can usually understand each other and read each other's languages without difficulty. Though historically Swedish belongs with Danish to the East Scandinavian language group, at the present time it is closer to Norwegian, especially the Norwegian *Landsmål*. Both are tone languages[1], in contradistinction to Danish; and since the introduction of the recent spelling reforms in Norway there is much greater resemblance between the two languages in orthography. On the other hand Swedish spelling gives a more accurate picture of the pronunciation of the language than is the case with the other Scandinavian languages. Norwegian and Danish have many consonantal assimilations which make it difficult to form an idea of the pronunciation from the written word. Swedish is much more consistent in this respect. There are, it is true, certain consonantal letters which are mute, e.g. in *djup* the *d* is not pronounced, in *hjärta* the *h* is not pronounced, and in *ljus* the *l* is not pronounced; but, compared to Norwegian and Danish, there are very few such "mute consonants."

An Englishman will not find it very difficult to acquire a reading knowledge of Swedish. The grammar is comparatively simple, as English and Swedish have developed on similar lines. There is not the elaborate declensional system that confronts the student of German, though there is a certain amount of difficulty involved in mastering the plural formation of Swedish nouns. In many cases the plural can be deduced from the form of the singular. Thus a word like *blomma*, disyllabic and ending in -*a*, must have the plural form *blommor*; and similarly a word like *oxe*, disyllabic and ending in -*e*, must have the plural form *oxar*.[2] But no one can tell at a glance how the plurals of *bord*, *fisk* and *park* are formed; these are words, the plural of which

---

[1] See § 68.

[2] There are a few exceptions to these rules among the neuter nouns.

has to be learnt individually. Another difficulty is gender : though there are a few rules for recognizing the gender of a noun from its meaning, in most cases it is impossible to deduce the gender of a noun when it stands in isolation. Yet immediately it is used with the article or an adjective its gender becomes apparent. Through the coalescence of the old masculine and feminine genders Swedish now has only two genders, the common and the neuter, as against the three genders of Icelandic, the Norwegian *Landsmål* and— to go further afield—German. The student should note the gender of every noun as he comes to it. Another section of the grammar deserving of special attention is the verb, though as regards endings there is little difficulty, since they have been much reduced, as in English. The conjugation of a Swedish strong verb is very similar to that of its cognate— if there is one—in English or German ; the conjugation of the weak verb is governed by definite rules which can easily be acquired. One of the most difficult chapters in the Germanic languages is prepositional usage. Special attention has been paid to this in the present book, and an attempt has been made to give a good selection of prepositional phrases in common use.

As regards vocabulary, Swedish does not present any great difficulty to the English student. Many common words are very similar in the two languages, e.g. *man* and ' man,' *fisk* and ' fish,' *hus* and ' house,' *horn* and ' horn,' *hund* and ' hound,' *båt* and ' boat,' *bok* and ' book.' Owing to Swedish sound changes other cognate words are not quite so easy to recognize, e.g. *ord* and ' word,' *under* and ' wonder,' *tacka* and ' thank,' *hjärta* and ' heart,' *hjälp* and ' help,' *bjärt* and ' bright.' Students familiar with the dialects of Northern England and the Lowlands of Scotland will have the advantage of being able to recognize the meaning of many more words. Thus the Lancashire man, with his ' tooth-wertch, belly-wertch and head-wertch ' will easily guess that the Swedish *tandvärk* means ' toothache ' and *huvudvärk* ' headache.' When it is raining ' cats and dogs ' in the North, the inhabitant of Cumberland says ' It's fair silen doon,' using a dialect word *to sile* meaning ' to strain, to pour through a sieve.' Similarly in Swedish *sil* means ' a strainer ' and *silregn* is rain that is falling as heavily and continuously as if it were poured through a sieve. Many such examples could be quoted from Scottish dialects. To take a few : ' braw ' and *bra*, ' bairn ' and *barn*, ' murk ' and *mörk*, ' to greet ' and *gråta*, ' neb ' and *näbb*, ' rowan ' and *rönn*. And even an expression like ' to go aince errand ' has its equivalent in the Swedish *gå ens ärende*.

An Englishman who knows German has an enormous advantage in learning Swedish, as there are a great many loan words of Low German and High German origin in the Swedish vocabulary, and many compound words are modelled on German originals. Words of Low German origin in Swedish are : *herre, fru, jungfru, adel, mästare, gesäll, lärling*. Examples of High German loan words are : *glans* (Glanz), *plötslig* (plötzlich), *gruva* (Grube), *hytta* (Hütte). Derivative suffixes were also taken over from High German, often via Low German, e.g. *-bar, -het, -inna, -eri, -era* ; thus *fruktbar, frihet, furstinna, röveri* and *barbera* may be compared with the German *fruchtbar, Freiheit, Fürstin, Räuberei* and *barbieren*.

Further, the vast majority of compound and derivative words in Swedish can be equated with German words, e.g. *snälltåg* (Schnellzug), *riksdag* (Reichstag), *huvudstad* (Hauptstadt), *rådhus* (Rathaus), *skadeglädje* (Schadenfreude), *verktyg* (Werkzeug), *stenrik* (steinreich), *viktig* (wichtig), *färdig* (fertig), *likgiltig* (gleichgültig), *erhålla* (erhalten). Thus the student who knows German well and has acquired a basic Swedish vocabulary will often find that, by translating a compound word from German element by element, he can produce the correct Swedish word. But it must be admitted that this method is not free from pitfalls. The writer recalls that, when travelling in Sweden in his student days, he once asked a railway official where he should ' *omstiga*.' The question elicited the required information, but he afterwards learned that the correct Swedish word for ' change ' is *byta*, even when changing trains. Enough has been said, however, to show that students with a knowledge of German can make it carry them a long way in Swedish.

In the present work occasional references have been made to survivals of older usage. Though the book is principally intended for private study, it is hoped that these historical notes and the excerpts from London University examination papers may prove useful to university students taking Swedish as an examination subject.

CONTENTS

PART I
THE SWEDISH SOUND SYSTEM

PART II
GRAMMAR

PART I

THE SWEDISH SOUND SYSTEM

THE SWEDISH ALPHABET

Swedish makes use of the following letters. For the phonetic transcription of the pronunciation of these letters see below:

A	a	[ɑ:]	K	k	[ko:]	U	u	[u:]
B	b	[be:]	L	l	[ɛl]	V	v	[ve:]
C	c	[se:]	M	m	[ɛm]	W	w	['dɵbbəlt ve:]
D	d	[de:]	N	n	[ɛn]			
E	e	[e:]	O	o	[o:]	X	x	[ɛks]
F	f	[ɛf]	P	p	[pe:]	Y	y	[y:]
G	g	[ge:]	Q	q	[ku:]	Z	z	['sɛ':ta]
H	h	[ho:]	R	r	[ær]	Å	å	[o:]
I	i	[i:]	S	s	[ɛs]	Ä	ä	[æ:]
J	j	[ji:]	T	t	[te:]	Ö	ö	[ø:]

(*Note the order of the last three letters when referring to a dictionary*).

a, o, ŭ(short), å are called back vowels.[1]

e, i, ū(long), y, ä, ö are called front vowels.[1]

b, d, g, j, l, m, n, r, v are voiced consonants.

p, t, k, f, s are voiceless consonants.

---

[1] See § 4.

CHAPTER I

PRONUNCIATION

1. Although Swedish spelling is more consistent than that of Norwegian or Danish, the same sound is sometimes spelt in more than one way and the same letter is made to represent more than one sound. Moreover, Swedish contains several sounds which have no exact equivalents in English.

2. *Phonetic Script.* In order to overcome this difficulty, and to give the student an accurate account of the pronunciation, use will be made of a simple system of *phonetic symbols*, consisting partly of the ordinary letters of the alphabet, and partly of special characters, when no letters to represent the unfamiliar sounds are available. In this system each symbol represents *one sound only*, and each sound is always represented by the same symbol.

3. *Quantity.* The system also affords a simple means of indicating long and short vowels. When placed immediately after a vowel, a colon (:) indicates that the vowel is long ; when no colon appears, the vowel is short, thus [man] *man* ' man ' ; [mɑ:n] *man* ' mane.'

VOWELS

4. Vowels are produced by vibrations of the vocal cords, the resultant voice sound being modified mainly by varying the configuration or shape of the oral cavity. This is done by raising the front, back or central portion of the tongue towards the palate ; in addition, the lips may be rounded and protruded to a varying extent. According to the part of the tongue that is raised we speak of *front*, *central* and *back vowels* ; according to the degree of raising we speak of *high*, *mid* and *low vowels*. If in the articulation of a vowel the lips are protruded and rounded (as in whistling) we speak of *rounded vowels*. English has only back rounded vowels (e.g. in *bought, boat, boot*) ; but Swedish

has both back and front rounded vowels. The degree of rounding may vary. The terms *tense* and *lax vowels* indicate that the muscles of the tongue may be taut or slack during their articulation. In general Swedish vowels are tenser than the corresponding English vowels.

Swedish vowels may be long or short, as in English. The vowels of unstressed syllables are always short.[1] Short vowels are usually more open than the corresponding long vowels, i.e. the gap between the highest point of the tongue and the palate (roof of the mouth) is wider. The Swedish long vowels are pure vowels as in German and Scottish and not diphthongs as in Southern English (cf. the Scotsman's pronunciation of *oatcake* with that of the Southern English speaker). The student should guard against any tendency to diphthongize the Swedish long vowels by keeping the tongue in the same position throughout their articulation. With one exception there are no diphthongs in Standard Swedish, and even this is only heard in a few colloquial forms.

LONG AND SHORT VOWELS

5. *Rule.* A vowel is long in an open syllable (i.e. one not ending in a consonant) or when followed by a short consonant,[2] and short before a long consonant, before double consonants and before a group of consonants.[2] When a vowel which is long in accordance with the above rule comes before a consonant group in inflected forms of words, or in derivatives or compounds, it usually remains long, e.g. *leva* ['le`:va] 'to live,' *levde* ['le`:vdə] 'lived,' *levnad* ['le`:vnad] 'life'. But sometimes before a genitival *-s* it is shortened, e.g. *hav* [hɑ:v] 'sea,' but *till havs* [hafs] 'to sea '; *liv* [li:v] 'life' but *livslängd* ['li`fslɛŋd] 'length of life.'

FRONT VOWELS
[i]

6. The Swedish short [i] is a high front vowel and is

---

[1] Stress is indicated in the phonetic transcriptions given in this book by placing ' before the stressed syllable, and tones (see § 68) by placing ` or ´ after the vowel. Phonetic transcriptions are placed in square brackets.

[2] See § 35.

closer than the English *i* in *sit*; Swedish *sitt* [**sit**] 'sit'
is pronounced like English *seat* with the vowel shortened.
When long it is closer than the vowel in English *seen*, and
tense; the tongue is so close to the hard palate that it ends
with a fricative sound [j], i.e. friction is caused by forcing
the breath through the very narrow opening.

Examples: *flicka* ['**fli̱ˈk̲k̲a**] 'girl'; *sitt still* [**sit stil**] 'sit
still'; *vit* [**viːt**] 'white'; *fri* [**friː**] 'free'; *bi* [**biː**] 'bee.'

[y]

7. This vowel is a rounded [i], i.e. the tongue position is
that for [i] but the lips are vigorously rounded and protruded, so much so that they form a kind of funnel, but with a
very small opening. When long the vowel ends with the
fricative sound [j].

Examples: *rygg* [**ryg**] 'back'; *mygg* [**myg**] 'midge';
vy [**vyː**] 'view'; *syn* [**syːn**] 'sight, view.'

[e]

8. Short close [e] does not occur in Swedish; the vowel
is always long [eː] and is close and tense. The student
should try to prolong the vowel in English 'pin,' keeping
the tongue muscles tense.

Examples: *ben* [**beːn**] 'bone, leg'; *ren* [**reːn**] 'clean';
ek [**eːk**] 'oak'; *vet* [**veːt**] 'know.'

[ø]

9. This vowel, also, only occurs long. It has the same
tongue position as [eː]; but the lips are rounded and
protruded. It is approximately the vowel of French *peu*
lengthened.

Examples: *söt* [**søːt**] 'sweet'; *röd* [**røːd**] 'red.'

[u][1]

10. In stressed syllables this vowel is always pronounced
long. It has a slightly higher tongue position than [eː], and

[1] Although this is a front vowel, it falls into line with the back
vowels in its effect on the pronunciation of a preceding *k* or *sk* (see
§ 33 and § 59). This is because it was at one time pronounced with a
more retracted tongue position, nearer to that of the cardinal
European *u*.

the lips are rounded and protruded but not so much as for [y]. As the articulation of this sound finishes, the lips come so close together that they almost meet, producing a momentary bilabial fricative. (Practice blowing slightly through almost closed lips). As this is one of the most difficult sounds in Swedish, the student should use a mirror to verify the lip position and mouth opening. Every opportunity should be taken to listen to a Swedish speaker and imitate his pronunciation.

Examples: *hus* [hu:s] 'house'; *ful* [fu:l] 'ugly'; *nu* [nu:] 'now.'

In an unstressed syllable this vowel is shortened, becomes more centralized (i.e. comes nearer to the position for ə) and loses its friction.

Examples: *bukett* [bu'kɛt] 'bouquet, bunch of flowers'; *som du vill* [som du vil] 'as you like'; *musik* [mu'si:k] 'music.'

[ɛ]

(11). When short this vowel is practically the same as in English 'best'; but the student should try to give the sound a crisp, clean-cut quality. The long vowel is somewhat tenser.

Examples: *bäst* [bɛst] 'best'; *häst* [hɛst] 'horse'; *äta* ['ɛ`:ta] 'to eat'; *läsa* ['lɛ`:sa] 'to read'.

[œ]

12. This vowel only occurs short. The tongue position is that of [ɛ] and the lips are rounded, though not so much as for [ø] or [y]. The opening is about twice as large as for [y]. The quality is approximately that of *eu* in French *neuf*.

Examples: *född* [fœd] 'born'; *nötter* ['nœ`tter] 'nuts'; *höst* [hœst] 'autumn'.

[æ]

13. This vowel only occurs before *r*, which gives it an open quality, practically the same as that of the vowel in Southern English 'carry.' It occurs both long and short.

Examples: *här* [hæːr] ' here '; *bär* [bæːr] ' berry ;'
värk [væerk] ' pain '; *märk* [mæerk] ' notice.'

[a]

14. This sound only occurs short; it is a low front
vowel and is heard in the Northern English pronunciation
of *man* or in the French *la*. A Southern English speaker
should isolate the first element of the diphthong in *my*,
drawing the corners of the lips slightly apart.

Examples: *man* [man] ' man '; *katt* [kat] ' cat.'

THE CENTRAL VOWEL

[ə]

15. This sound, which is sometimes called the ' neutral '
vowel, is produced by raising the central part of the tongue
to about half the distance between the lowest and highest
positions. It is like the vocalic murmur heard in the first
syllable of English *address* or the second syllable of *sofa*, but
a little closer and further forward, i.e. nearer to [ɛ]. Like
the corresponding English vowel it only occurs in unstressed
syllables.

Examples: *beslut* [bəˈsluːt] ' decision '; *dike* [ˈdiˑkə]
' ditch.'

BACK VOWELS

[ɑ]

16. Swedish [ɑ], which is always long, is like the
English *a* in *father*, but is accompanied by slight lip rounding. It is a low back vowel.

Examples: *dag* [dɑːg] ' day '; *fat* [fɑːt] ' dish.' Care
should be taken not to exaggerate the lip rounding, as this
sounds vulgar.

[ɔ]

17. This sound, which only occurs short, is like the
English vowel in *awe* when shortened and accompanied
by more lip rounding.

Examples: *kopp* [kɔp] ' cup '; *slcˑt* [slɔt] ' castle.'

[o]

18. This sound, which is nearly always long, is somewhat closer than the English *awe* ; if the latter is pronounced with increased lip rounding, the desired quality will be obtained.

Examples : *å* [o:] ' river ' ; *skål* [sko:l] ' bowl.'

[ɔ]

19. This vowel is like the English *oo* in *book* but with much more lip rounding and a very narrow lip opening ; it occurs both long and short. When it is pronounced long and in a fully stressed position, the cheeks are momentarily distended owing to the pent up breath-stream being checked by the narrow lip opening, and as the articulation of the sound finishes, the lips come so close together that they almost meet, producing a momentary bilabial fricative (cf. **u**). To foreigners this sometimes sounds like a *b*. When the sound occurs short (usually in an unstressed position), the lip opening is not so narrow and the fricative element is absent. This sound is peculiar to the Scandinavian languages.

Examples : *bok* [bɔ:k] ' book ' ; *bro* [brɔ:] ' bridge ' ; *hon* [hɔn] ' she ' ; *ond* [ɔnd] ' angry,' ' bad.'

[ɵ]

20. This is one of the difficult sounds in Swedish. It only occurs short and is more advanced than the *u* in English *put*, i.e. the highest point of the tongue is further forward. It is a sound which is intermediate between the vowel in English *bird* and that in English *put* and should, if possible, be acquired by carefully imitating a Swedish speaker. During its articulation the muscles of the lips and tongue are slack.

Examples : *upp* [ɵp] ' up ' ; *kung* [kɵŋ] ' king.'

[ə]

21. This sound occurs only before *r* and can be long or short. The *r* has the effect of opening it, so that it sounds somewhat like the vowel in French *cœur*, but it is more retracted, being pronounced in rear of the central vowel

position. Perhaps the best way of acquiring this sound is to produce the vowel of English *up* and at the same time round the lips.

Examples: *föra* [ˈfɵˑːra] 'to lead'; *göra* [ˈjɵˑːra] 'to do'; *törst* [tɵşt] 'thirst.'

CONSONANTS
LABIAL

22. Swedish *p*, *b*, *m*, *f*, *v* are pronounced as in English; but the aspiration, or slight puff of breath resembling a weak *h*, which we hear after *p* at the beginning of a stressed syllable, is pronounced more vigorously in Swedish, e.g. *pisk* [**pisk**]. A good example of this aspirated *p* is heard in the Cockney pronunciation of an expression like: *the pig*!

23. Swedish *m* is pronounced voiceless, that is without any vibration of the vocal cords, in words of foreign origin ending in *-ism* or *-asm*. This *m* may be produced by trying to whisper the word *prism*; the lips are closed, and scarcely any sound is audible except the passage of the breath through the nostrils.

Examples: *mekanism* [**mɛkaˈnism̥**] 'mechanism'; *sarkasm* [**sarˈkasm̥**] 'sarcasm.'

This voiceless *m* also occurs in the word *rytm* [**rytm̥**] 'rhythm.'

DENTAL

24. The Swedish consonants *t*, *d*, *n*, *l*, *s* are pure dental sounds produced with the tip of the tongue against the upper teeth. The corresponding English sounds are alveolar, i.e. produced with the tongue touching the rim over the roots of the upper teeth.

25. To produce Swedish [**t**] the student should say the word *tea* with the tip of the tongue on the edge of the teeth, or even slightly protruded, and with aspiration as for Swedish [**p**]. The Swedish sound is more crisp and clear cut than the English; and in the initial position before a stressed vowel it is more vigorously aspirated.

Examples: *tid* [**tiːd**] 'time'; *vit* [**viːt**] 'white.'

26. Swedish [d] and [n] are like the English sounds, except for their more forward articulation which gives them a clearer quality.

Examples : *dag* [dɑ:g] ' day ' ; *nit* [ni:t] ' zeal.'

27. Swedish [l] in all positions is a clear front sound as in the English *leap* ; it is called ' clear ' because of the front vowel quality that runs through it. The ' dark ' sound heard in the English word *wool* does not occur in Swedish.

Examples : *lik* [li:k] ' like ' ; *ull* [əl] ' wool.'

28. The letter *s* has the voiceless [s] sound in all positions and never the voiced [z] sound of English *is, was*. In the few loan-words where *z* occurs it is always pronounced as a voiceless [s].

Examples : *sann* [san] ' true ' ; *is* [i:s] ' ice ' ; *zon* [so:n] ' zone.'

POST-ALVEOLAR

29. These sounds, as the heading implies, are produced behind the upper teeth-ridge. In the production of Southern English *r* the tip of the tongue is raised towards the back part of the teeth-ridge, the passage is narrowed, and slight friction is heard ; in the Northern English trilled *r* the tip of the tongue is raised to the teeth-ridge and so held that it vibrates up and down against the teeth-ridge as the breath-stream passes through the mouth. Both sounds are usually voiced. The Swedish *r* is post-alveolar and faintly trilled when it occurs between vowels and after a consonant ; in other positions a weak fricative *r* is heard.

Examples : *fira* ['fi`:ra] ' to celebrate ' ; *ivrig* ['i`:vrig] ' eager ' ; *skarp* [skarp].

30. When English *r* is immediately followed by the dental consonants *t, d, l, n, s*, it loses its sound value and is not pronounced (e.g. in *hurt, hard, girl, corn, curse*) ; but when the Swedish *r* is immediately followed by any of these consonants, an assimilation takes place and they become post-alveolar instead of dental in their articulation. In other words the *r* is amalgamated with the dental to form a single sound in which the *r* entirely loses its function as an

independent consonant. But it has a retracting influence on the dental consonant so that the latter is articulated, not against the inner edge of the upper teeth, but just behind the teeth-ridge. The student should first practise the pronunciation of a purely dental *t*, making sure that the tongue is against the upper teeth, and then gradually feel his way back with the tip of the tongue along the surface of the hard palate (the front portion of the roof of the mouth). It will be found that the limit of retraction is reached when the tongue comes to the so-called *cacuminal* position, i.e. the highest point of the palate. The position for Swedish *rt, rd, rl, rn* and *rs* is about midway between the purely dental and the cacuminal position. These sounds are known as *retroflex t, d,* etc. They are represented by the phonetic symbols : [ṭ], [ḍ], [ḷ], [ṇ], [ṣ].

The alternation between the dental and retroflex consonants may be illustrated by the following word pairs, which should be frequently practised :

Dental	*Retroflex*
fat [fɑ:t] ' dish '	*fart* [fɑ:ṭ] ' speed, pace '
mod [mo:d] ' courage '	*mord* [mo:ḍ] ' murder '
kal [kɑ:l] ' bald '	*Karl* [kɑ:ḷ] ' Charles '
kon [ko:n] ' cone '	*korn* [ko:ṇ] ' grain '
ros [ro:s] ' rose '	*till rors* [til ro:ṣ] 'at the helm '

31. The most difficult of the Swedish retroflex consonants is [ṣ]. The beginner should protrude and round the lips vigorously, form a groove down the middle of the tongue and then force out the breath so that a whistling sound is heard. This should gradually be reduced until only friction is heard. The Swedish sound is like the English *sh* sound, but is more vigorous and has a somewhat higher pitch. Particular attention should be paid to words like *mars, kors, hörs*.

It should be noted that initial *s* after a final *r* in the preceding word is pronounced with retroflex tongue position in rapid colloquial speech, e.g. *var för sig* [ˈvɑːr fə ˈṣɛj] ' separately '; *för sent* [fə ˈṣeːnt] ' too late,' *var så god* !

['vɑːʂo 'goːd].[1] Similarly, s after a retroflex t, d or n itself
becomes retroflex by attraction, when it belongs to the
same syllable ; but this change does not occur after a
retroflex l.

Examples :   kvarts [kvaʈʂ]   'quartz' ;   bordsbön
['boˈːɖʂbøːn] ' grace ' ;   barnslig ['baˈ ṉʂlig] 'childish.'

Since the retroflex [ʂ] is used by many educated Swedes
as the ordinary sh sound, the student is recommended to
follow this practice and use it throughout, e.g. in words like
mission [miˈʂoːn] 'mission' ;   sjuk [ʂuːk] 'ill' ;   sked
[ʂeːd] 'spoon' ;   skinn [ʂin] 'skin' ;   skjul [ʂuːl] 'shed' ;
stjärt [ʂæʈ] 'tail.'

PALATAL FRICATIVES

32. The voiceless palatal fricative [ç] is the sound heard
in the German ich ; it may be produced by whispering the
y in English yet, or by isolating the initial consonantal
sound in huge. The tongue is raised to the high front
position, closer to the palate than for [iː] and the breath is
forced through the narrow aperture so as to produce
audible friction. Many Swedish speakers form a very
short [t] in front of this sound ; but in this book it will not
be indicated in the phonetic transcriptions.

Examples : käpp [çɛp] 'stick' ;   kök [çøːk] 'kitchen' ;
kyrka ['çyˈrka]   'church' ;   tjänst [çɛnst]   'service' ;
tjuv [çuːv] 'thief.'

33. The corresponding voiced sound [j] is heard in
English yet ; but in Swedish it is accompanied by more
friction.

Examples : ja [jɑː] ' yes ' ;   gäst [jɛst] ' guest.'

It should be noted that k and g before all front vowels
(except long u) are always pronounced as fricatives.

VELAR CONSONANTS

34. Except before the front vowels, as mentioned above,
k at the beginning of a stressed syllable is pronounced as in

[1] This expression is used in offering something politely to a person
(cf. German bitte schön !) ; it has no exact equivalent in English.

English but with more aspiration, i.e. it is followed by a slight puff of breath.

Examples : *ko* [kɔ:] 'cow'; *klok* [klɔ:k] 'clever.'

Otherwise [k], [g] and [ŋ] are pronounced much the same as in English.

Examples : *länk* [lɛŋk] 'link'; *lag* [lɑ:g] 'law'; *sång* [sɔŋ] 'song.'

QUANTITY

35. In Swedish all stressed syllables are normally long and all unstressed syllables short. In the stressed syllable this length is expressed either in the vowel or in the consonant. If the vowel is short, it must be followed by a long consonant ; if the vowel is long, the following consonant is short. In the articulation of a long consonant, the speech organs get into position for the production of the consonant and hold that position longer than for the corresponding short consonant.

Long consonants occur in English, though much more rarely than in Swedish (cf. *black cat, mad dog, lamp-post, hat trick*). In such words the consonants are not pronounced double ; instead the first consonant becomes an ' incomplete plosive ' (speech organs in position, but no release and hence no plosive), while the second is pronounced as a normal plosive. This pronunciation is common in Italian (e.g. in *otto, vacca*), and the same thing is heard in Swedish. The student should compare Swedish *mamma* ['ma'mma], *pappa* ['pa'ppa] with the corresponding words in English. In such words English reduces the double consonants to a single one in the pronunciation ; and this is pronounced at the beginning of the second syllable.

When long voiced consonants occur between vowels in Swedish, e.g. in *bodde* (past tense of *bo* ' to dwell '), care should be taken to **keep the vocal cords vibrating** while the speech organs are held in position for the long consonant instead of starting the voicing when the release comes. This means producing voice without opening the mouth. In the case of long *b, d* or *g* the voicing is heard as a kind of buzz bottled up in the mouth; but in the articulation of long *l* or *r* the voiced sound can escape round the tongue, while in the articulation of long *m* or *n* it has a free outlet through the nose.

Swedish long consonants occur not only medially but also finally.[1]

Examples:

Long vowel	Short vowel
hat [hɑ:t] ' hate '	*hatt* [hat] ' hat '
lam [lɑ:m] ' lame '	*lamm* [lam] ' lamb '

Sometimes, when a word ends in *-m* or *-n*, there is no indication of the length of the consonant in the spelling; thus in *ram* ' frame ' it is short, but in *stam* ' stem ' it is long, and *man* pronounced with a short *n* means ' mane,' but with a long *n* means ' man.'

SPELLING AND SOUND VALUES

I. VOWELS

a

36. The Swedish letter *a* is pronounced:

(*a*) as long [ɑ:].

Examples: *dag* [dɑ:g] ' day '; *bad* [bɑ:d] ' bath.'

(*b*) as short [a].

Examples: *tack* [tak] ' thanks '; *hatt* [hat] ' hat ' *pappa* ['pa`ppa] ' pappa '; *Kina* ['çi`:na] ' China.'

Note.—Final *a* in Swedish is never pronounced as the murmur vowel [ə] heard in English words with final unstressed *a*, e.g. in ' China.'

e

37. This letter is pronounced:

(*a*) as long [e:].

Examples: *blek* [ble:k] ' pale '; *le* [le:] ' smile.'

[1] In this book final long consonants will not be indicated in the phonetic script since in the vast majority of cases they are evident from the spelling.

In the stressed prefix *er-* it represents [æ:r].

Examples : *erfara* ['æ:rfɑ`:ra] ' to learn ' ; *erövra* ['æ:rø`:vra] ' to conquer.'

(*b*) as short [ɛ].

Examples : *fest* [fɛst] 'festival ' ; *penna* ['pɛ`nna] ' pen.' When followed by *-r* this sound becomes the open [æ].

Examples : *berg* [bærj] ' mountain ' ; *verk* [værk] 'work.'

(*c*) as the murmur vowel [ə] in the prefixes *be-*, *ge-*, and in the unaccented final syllables ending in *-e*, *-el*, *-en*, *-er* as well as in the enclitic form of the definite article *-en*, *-et*.

Examples : *betala* [bə'tɑ`:la] ' to pay ' ; *gestalt* [jə'stalt] ' form ' ; *droppe* ['dro`ppə] ' drop ' ; *segel* ['se`:gəl] ' sail ' ; *tecken* ['tɛ`kkən] ' sign ' ; *finger* ['fi`ŋər] ' finger ' ; *hästen* ['hɛ`stən] ' the horse ' ; *huset* ['hu`:sət] ' the house.'

i

38. This letter is pronounced :

(*a*) as long [i:].

Examples : *bi* [bi:] ' bee ' ; *vit* [vi:t] ' white.'

(*b*) as short [i].

Examples : *vinst* [vinst] ' gain ' ; *bild* [bild] ' picture.'

o

39. This letter has three different sound values : [o], [o:] and [ɔ] ; the first can occur long or short, the second only long, the third only short.

(*a*) as long [o:].

Examples : *ko* [ko:] ' cow ' ; *sko* [sko:] ' shoe ' ; *bror* [bro:r] ' brother ' ; *jord* [jo:ḍ] ' earth.'

(*b*) as short [o].

Examples : *ost* [ost] ' cheese ' ; *onsdag* ['o`nsdɑ:g] ' Wednesday ' ; *orm* [ɔrm] ' snake ' ; *bonde* ['bo`ndə] ' farmer.'

(c) as long [o:].

Examples : *kol* [ko:l] ' coal ' ; *lov* [lo:v] ' permission '; *hov* [ho:v] ' court ' ; *son* [so:n] ' son.'

This pronunciation occurs in many words of foreign origin, e.g. *astronom* [astro'no:m] ' astronomer ' ; *filosof* [filo'so:f] ' philosopher ' ; *katalog* [kata'lo:g] ' catalogue.'

(d) as short [ɔ].

Examples : *som* [sɔm] ' as ' ; *socker* ['sɔ'kkər] ' sugar ' ; *boll* [bɔl] ' ball ' ; *sommar* ['sɔ'mmar] ' summer.'

u

40. This letter has two different sound values ; when it is long it represents [u:] and when short it represents [ə].

(a) as long [u:].

Examples : *bur* [b:ur] ' cage ' ; *djur* [ju:r] ' animal ' ; *hus* [hu:s] ' house ' ; *bjuda* ['bju`:da] ' to offer ' ; *sju* [ʂu:] ' seven ' ; *ut* [u:t] ' out.'

In the unstressed position the u is shortened, becomes more open and loses its friction.

Examples : *musik* [mu'si:k] ' music ' ; *butik* [bu'ti:k] ' shop '.

(b) as short [ə].

Examples : *ung* [əŋ] ' young ' ; *kund* [kənd] ' customer '; *bunden* ['bə`ndən] ' bound ' ; *under* ['ə`ndər] ' under.'

y

41. This letter is pronounced :

(a) as long [y:].

Examples : *yr* [y:r] ' giddy ' ; *vy* [vy:] ' view ' ; *syn* [sy:n] ' vision ' ; *fyra* ['fy`:ra] ' four ' ; *lyda* ['ly`:da] ' to obey.'

(b) as short [y].

Examples : *rygg* [ryg] ' back ' ; *lycka* ['ly`kka] ' fortune '; *syster* ['sy`stər] ' sister.'

å

42. This letter is pronounced :

(a) as long [o:].

Examples : *gå* [go:] ' go '; *får* [fo:r] ' sheep '; *måne* ['mo`:nǝ] ' moon.'

(b) as short [ɔ].

Examples : *gått* [gɔt] ' gone '; *sång* [sɔŋ] ' song '; *åtta* ['ɔ`tta] ' eight '; *hålla* ['hɔ`lla] ' to hold.'

ä

43. This letter represents two different sounds, according to whether it is followed by -r or not ; and each sound occurs both long and short :

(a) When followed by -r it represents [æ].

Examples (long) : *ära* ['æ`:ra] ' honour '; *lärd* [læ:ḍ] ' learned '; *järn* [jæ:ṇ] ' iron '; *värld* [væ:ḍ] ' world '; (short) : *bjärt* [bjæt] ' gaudy '; *hjärta* ['jæ`tta] ' heart '; *värka* ['væ`rka] ' to ache.'

(b) When not followed by -r it represents the closer [ɛ] sound.

Examples (long) : *fä* [fɛ:] ' beast '; *läsa* ['lɛ`:sa] ' to read '; *frän* [frɛ:n] ' rancid '; (short) : *bäst* [bɛst] ' best '; *säng* [sɛŋ] ' bed '; *sätta* ['sɛ`tta] ' to set.'

ö

44. This letter represents three different sounds : [ǝ], [ø:] and [œ] ; the first occurs long and short, the second long, and the third short.

(a) When followed by -r it represents [ǝ].

Examples (long) : *öra* ['ǝ`:ra] ' ear '; *mör* [mǝ:r] ' tender '; *örn* [ǝ:ṇ] ' eagle '; (short) : *först* [fǝst] ' first '; *mörk* [mǝrk] ' dark '; *törst* [tǝst] ' thirst.'

(b) When not followed by -r it represents :

(i) the long vowel [ø:].

Examples : *hö* [hø:] ' hay '; *bön* [bø:n] ' prayer '; *röd* [rø:d] ' red.'

(ii) the short vowel [œ].

Examples : *född* [fœd] ' born '; *höst* [hœst] ' autumn '; *mössa* ['mœ`ssa] ' cap.'

II. CONSONANTS

b

45. This is pronounced as in English, e.g. *baka* [ˈbɑˑˈka] 'to bake.'

46.   **c**

(*a*) Where it occurs in Germanic words, this letter is nearly always found in combination with *k*; the combined symbols are pronounced as a long [k].

Examples: *bock* [bɔk] 'buck'; *lucka* [ˈløˈkka] 'gap'.

In the word *och* 'and,' the *ch* is pronounced as if it were *ck* [ɔk]; the *ch* spelling is rare in Swedish words.

(*b*) Before the front vowels *e*, *i* and *y* in words of foreign origin *c* is pronounced as *s*.

Examples: *censur* [sɛnˈsuːr] 'censorship'; *citat* [siˈtɑːt] 'quotation'; *cyklon* [syˈkloːn] 'cyclone.'

(*c*) Initial *ch* in a number of loan words, mostly taken from the French, is pronounced as [ʂ].

Examples: *chef* [ʂeːf] 'chief, chef'; *chikan* [ʂiˈkɑːn] 'chicane'; *choklad* [ʂoˈklɑːd] 'chocolate.'

47.   **d**

(*a*) Swedish *d* represents a pure dental stop, except when preceded by *r*, when it becomes post-alveolar (see § 29).

(*b*) Before a genitival *s* a *d* is sometimes devoiced, i.e. pronounced like *t*.

Examples: *Guds nåd* [gøts noːd] 'the grace of God'; *godståg* [ˈgɔˈtstoːg] 'goods train'.

(*c*) In the combination *dj* at the beginning of a syllable the *d* is mute.

Examples: *djur* [juːr] 'animal'; *djärv* [jærv] 'bold'.

(*d*) In a few words *d* at the end of a syllable is assimilated to a following consonant.

Examples: *brådska* [ˈbrɔˈsska] 'haste'; *ledsen* [ˈlɛˈssən] 'sad'; *trädgård* [ˈtrɛˈggoːd] 'garden'; *gudskelov* [gøssəˈloːˈv] 'thank God.'

f

48. This is pronounced as in English, e.g. *far* [fɑ:r] ' father.'

g

49. This letter has several different sound values.

(*a*) Before a stressed back vowel or before a consonant it is pronounced as [g].

Examples : *gammal* [ˈgaˈmmal] ' old '; *god* [gʋ:d] ' good '; *gul* [gu:l] ' yellow '; *gås* [gɔ:s] ' goose '; *glad* [glɑ:d] ' glad '; *grop* [grʋ:p] ' pit.'

It is also pronounced as [g] at the end of a syllable after a vowel, and frequently before -*e* in an unstressed syllable.

Examples : *dag* [dɑ:g] ' day '; *seg* [se:g] ' tough '; *regel* [ˈreˈ:gəl] ' rule '; *sägen* [ˈsɛˈ:gən] ' legend '; *lager* [ˈlɑˈ:gər] ' layer '; *båge* [ˈbʋˈ:gə] ' bow, arc.' Exceptions to this rule are the words *Sverige* [ˈsvæˈrjə] ' Sweden,' *Norge* [ˈnɔˈrjə] ' Norway,' German loan words beginning with unstressed *ge-*, e.g. *gestalt* [jəˈstalt] and the verb *säga* ' to say,' which has the present tense *säger* [ˈsɛˈjər].

(*b*) Before a stressed front vowel, and, in a few words, after *l* or *r*, it is pronounced as [j].

Examples : *genast* [ˈjeˈ:nast] ' immediately '; *gikt* [jikt] ' gout '; *gök* [jø:k] ' cuckoo '; *bälg* [bɛlj] ' bellows '; *svalg* [svalj] ' throat '; *berg* [bærj] ' hill '; *korg* [kɔrj] ' basket.'

In words of foreign origin *g* is sometimes pronounced as [g] before a front vowel, whether stressed or unstressed.

Examples : *ginst* [ginst] ' broom (genista) '; *belgisk* [ˈbɛˈlgisk] ' Belgian ' (adj.).

(*c*) Before *s* and *t* it is devoiced and pronounced as [k].

Examples : *dagsnyheter* [ˈdaksnyˈ:he:tər] ' the day's news '; *skogsbrand* [ˈskʋˈksbrand] ' forest fire '; *högst* [hœkst] ' highest '; the past participles *bragt* [brakt] ' brought '; *lagt* [lakt] ' laid '; *sagt* [sakt] ' said.'

(*d*) In many loan words taken from the French it is pronounced as [ş] before *e* and *i*.

Examples : *gest* [şɛst] ' gesture ' ; *generös* [şɛnɛ'rø:s] ' generous ' ; *giraff* [şi'raf] ' giraffe.'

(*e*) The combined symbols *gn* represent the sounds [ŋn] when they belong to the stem of a word.

Examples : *ugn* [øŋn] ' oven ' ; *regn* [rɛŋn] ' rain '.

Contrast *vagnar* ['va`ŋnar] ' coaches ' with *lagning* ['la`:gniŋ] ' repair work,' where the *n* belongs to the suffix -*ning*.

(*f*) In the combined symbols *gj*, which only occur in a few words, the *g* is mute.

Examples : *gjorde, gjord, gjort* ['jo`:də, jo:d̦, jo:ț] ' did, done ' ; *gjuta* ['ju`:ta] ' to cast '.

(*g*) In the colloquial language *g* is assimilated to a preceding *r* in *morgon* ['mɔ`rrɔn] ' morning ' ; and it is mute in *jag* ' I', except in rhetorical speech.

h

50. In most positions this letter represents an aspirate, as in English ; but in the combination *hj* at the beginning of a word the *h* is mute.

Examples : *hjälp* [jɛlp] ' help ' ; *hjort* [jo:ț] ' stag ' ; *hjul* [ju:l] ' wheel.'

j

51. This letter represents a fricative [j] in all Germanic words ; but in loan words from the French it is pronounced [ş].

Examples : *ja* [ja:] ' yes ' ; *jakt* [jakt] ' hunt ' ; *jul* [ju:l] ' Christmas ' ; *jalusi* [şalu'si:] ' window blind ' ; *jasmin* [şas'mi:n] ' syringa ' ; *journal* [şo'na:l] ' journal.'

k

52. This letter has several different sound values.

(*a*) Before a back vowel or before or after a consonant, or at the end of a word it is pronounced [k].

Examples : *kal* [ka:l] ' bald ' ; *kort* [kɔț] ' card ' ; *kung* [køŋ] ' king ' ; *kål* [ko:l] ' cabbage ' ; *klar* [kla:r] ' clear ' ; *klocka* ['klɔ`kka] ' clock ' ; *bok* [bo:k] ' book.'

It is also pronounced as [k] before *e* and *i* in an unstressed syllable, and even in a stressed syllable in some loan words.

Examples: *bjälke* ['bjɛ'lkə] ' beam '; *turkisk* ['tø'rkisk] ' Turkish '; *mannekäng* [manɛ'kɛŋ] ' mannequin '; *kilo* ['ki'lo] ' kilo '; *keltisk* ['kɛ'ltisk] ' Celtic '; *anarki* [anar'ki:] ' anarchy '; *kex* [kɛks] ' biscuit ' (though [çɛks] is also heard).

(*b*) Before a stressed front vowel it is pronounced [ç].

Examples: *kedja* ['çe'':dja] ' chain '; *kil* [çi:l] ' wedge '; *kyla* ['çy'':la] ' chill '; *käpp* [çɛp] ' stick '; *köpa* ['çø'':pa] ' to buy.'

It also has this sound value initially before unstressed *e* and *i* in some loan words.

Examples: *kemi* [çɛ'mi:] ' chemistry '; *kerub* [çɛ'ru:b] ' cherub '; *kines* [çi'ne:s] ' Chinaman '; *kinin* [çi'ni:n] ' quinine.'

Note.—The initial combination *kj* is used in a few words; it is pronounced [ç].

Examples: *kjol* [ço:l] ' skirt '; and names like *Kjell* [çɛl].

1

53. This letter is mute in the initial combination *lj*.

Examples: *ljud* [ju:d] ' sound '; *ljung* [jøŋ] ' heather '; *ljus* [ju:s] ' light.' In two words it is mute in the combination *rl*, viz., *värld* [vɛː:ɖ] ' world '; *karl* [kɑ:r] ' fellow.'

m

54 This letter represents the voiced labial nasal in most positions, as in English; for its occurrence as a voiceless consonant see § 23.

n

55. For the sound represented by this letter see § 24. As in English, when it stands in the combination *nk* it represents the guttural nasal [ŋ]; and the same sound is represented by the combination *ng*.

Examples : *bänk* [bɛŋk] 'seat'; *blank* [blaŋk] 'shiny'; *kung* [køŋ] 'king'; *sång* [sɔŋ] 'song.'

Note.—n also has this sound value in some loan words of French origin when it stands before a consonant, e.g. *allians* [alliˈaŋs] 'alliance'; *kompliment* [kɔmpliˈmaŋ] 'compliment.' Other French loan words have been changed in spelling so as to conform more closely to the Swedish pronunciation, e.g. *kupong* [kuˈpɔŋ] 'coupon'; *poäng* [poɛŋ] 'point'; *evenemang* [ɛvɛnɛˈmaŋ] 'event.'

p

56. On the pronunciation of this letter see § 22.

q

57. This letter only occurs in names in the combination *qu* or *qv*, both pronounced [kv], e.g. *Lindquist* [ˈliˈndkvist], *Bergqvist* [ˈbæˈrjkvist].

r

58. On the pronunciation of this letter and its effect on a following *d, l, n, s, t*, see § 30.

s

59. On the pronunciation of this letter see § 28. In the group *-sion* the combination *si* is pronounced [ʂ].

Examples : *mission* [miˈʂoːn] 'mission'; *invasion* [invaˈʂoːn] 'invasion.'

The combinations *sch, sj, skj* and *stj* are pronounced [ʂ]. Examples : *schal* [ʂɑːl] 'shawl'; *schema* [ˈʂeˈːma] 'time-table'; *sjuk* [ʂuːk] 'ill'; *själ* [ʂɛːl] 'soul'; *skjul* [ʂuːl] 'shed'; *skjuta* [ˈʂuˈːta] 'to shoot'; *stjärna* [ˈʂæˈːɳa] 'star'; *stjärt* [ʂæʈ] 'tail.'

Initial *sc* in loan words is pronounced [s], e.g. *scen* [seːn] 'scene'; *scepter* [ˈsɛˈptər] 'sceptre'; but medially it is pronounced [ʂ], e.g. *opalescens* [ɔpaləˈʂɛns] 'opalescense'; *reminiscens* [rɛminiˈʂɛns] 'reminiscence.'

The combination *sk* represents two different sounds :

(*a*) Before a consonant, or a stressed back vowel or any unstressed vowel, it is pronounced [sk].

Examples : *skrapa* ['skrɑˋ:pa] ' to scrape ' ; *skald* [skald] ' poet ' ; *handske* ['haˋndskə] ' glove ' ; *slaskig* ['slaˋskig] ' splashy.' Two exceptions to this rule are the words *människa* ['mɛˋnniʂa] ' human being ' ; *marskalk* ['maˋʂalk] ' marshal.'

(*b*) Before a stressed front vowel it is pronounced [ʂ].

Examples : *skepp* [ʂɛp] ' ship ' ; *skina* ['ʂiˋ:na] ' to shine ' ; *skydd* [ʂyd] ' protection ' ; *skägg* [ʂɛg] ' beard ' ; *sköld* [ʂœld] ' shield.' Exceptions to this rule are the word *skiss* [skis] ' sketch ' and all words containing the front vowel [u], e.g. *skur* [sku:r] ' shower ' ; *skuta* ['skuˋ:ta] ' sloop.'

t

60. On the pronunciation of this letter see § 24. Abstract nouns in *-tion* borrowed from French and Latin sometimes have the suffix pronounced [ʂoːn] and sometimes [tʂoːn] ; the usage varies.

Examples : *station* [staˈʂoːn] ; *reaktion* [reakˈʂoːn] ; *nation* [natˈʂoːn] ; *variation* [variaˈʂon].

In some Latin and French loan words the combination *-ti-* before a vowel is pronounced [tsi], e.g. *initiativ* [initsiaˈtiːv] ' initiative.'

The combination *tj* is pronounced [ç], sometimes preceded by a slight [t].

Examples : *tjäna* ['çɛˋ:na] *or* ['tçɛˋ:na] ' to serve ' ; *tjog* [çoːg] *or* [tçoːg] ' score ' ; *tjuv* [çuːv] *or* [tçuːv] ' thief.'
A final *t* is silent in some French loan words, e.g. *dessert* [dɛˈsæːr] ' dessert ' ; *kuvert* [kuˈvæːr] ' envelope ' ; *konsert* [konˈsæːr] ' concert.'

In colloquial speech a medial *t* is sometimes mute in the combination *-st* when followed by *g* plus a front vowel ;

and the *s* fuses with the [j] sound to form [ʂʂ], e.g. *gästgivare* [ˈjɛˋʂʂiːvarə] 'innkeeper'; *östgöte* [ˈœˋʂʂøtə] 'man from (the province of) Östergötland.'

Occasionally a *t* is assimilated to a following *s*, e.g. *matsäck* [ˈmaˋsʂɛk] 'provision-bag, provisions (for a picnic).'

v

61. On the pronunciation of this letter see § 22.

Before an inflexional -*s*, and following a shortened vowel, the letter *v* is pronounced [f]; cf. *hav* [hɑːv] 'sea' and *havsluft* [ˈhaˋfsløft] 'sea air.'

w

62. This letter only occurs in loan words borrowed from the English and has the English sound value, e.g. *week-end* [ˈwiˈːkɛnd]; *whisky* [ˈwiˋski].

x

63. This letter is pronounced [ks].

Examples: *sex* [sɛks] 'six'; *yxa* [ˈyˋksa] 'axe'; *existens* [ɛksisˈtɛns] 'existence'; *xylograf* [ksyloˈgrɑːf] 'xylographer.' The combination -*xi* in words ending in -*xion* is pronounced [kʂ], e.g. *reflexion* [reflɛkˈʂoːn] 'reflection.'

z

64. This letter only occurs in words of foreign origin and is always pronounced [s], e.g. *zon* [soːn] 'zone.'; *zeppelinare* [sɛpɛˈliˈːnarə] 'zeppelin.'

SWEDISH ORTHOGRAPHY

65. Books printed before 1906 show certain features of spelling which were changed in the reforms introduced in that year. The chief of these are: initial *hv*, medial *fv* and final *f* have been replaced by *v*, in conformity with the pronunciation. Thus *hvad* ' what,' *lofva* ' to promise ' and *haf* ' sea ' are now spelt *vad, lova, hav*. Another reform is the substitution of *t* for *dt* in certain neuter adjectival forms, e.g. *händt* ' happened ' is now spelt *hänt* ; *godt* (neuter form of *god* ' good ') is now spelt *gott*.

STRESS

66. Swedish, like English, is characterized by dynamic stress or expiratory accent. This is of about the same strength as in English, so that there is a marked difference in force of articulation between stressed and unstressed syllables. There are three different degrees of stress :

(*a*) Full stress.

This normally falls on the first syllable of a word, e.g. *sovande* ['so`:vandə] ' sleeping ' ; *huset* ['hu´:sət] ' the house.' But in words of French or Latin origin the principal stress usually falls on some other syllable.

Examples : *adress* [a'drɛs] ' address ' ; *general* [jɛnə'rɑ:l] ' general ' ; *tragedi* [traşə'di:] ' tragedy ' ; *professor* [pro'fɛ`ssor] ' professor ' ; *professorer* [profə'so`:rer] ' professors ' ; *nation* [nat'şo:n] ' nation ' ; and all words ending in *-sion* or *-tion* from French or Latin, as well as all verbs ending in *-era*, e.g. *studera* [stu'de´:ra] ' to study.' Verbs beginning with the prefixes *be-* and *för-* have the principal stress on the second syllable, e.g. *befordra* [bə'fo´:dra] ' to forward ' ; *förlora* [fə'rlo´:ra] ' to lose.'

(*b*) Reduced main stress.

This falls on the first syllable of the second part of a compound word which has the full stress on the first part.

Examples : *matsal* ['mɑ`:tsɑ:l] ' dining hall ' ; *utkant* ['u`:tkant] ' outskirts ' ; *biskopssäte* ['biskɔps-sɛ`:tə] ' episcopal see ' ; *blågrön* ['blo´:grø:n] ' bluish green.'

Reduced main stress is also placed on many derivative suffixes, e.g. *-dom, -het, -lek, -skap, -bar, -fast, -sam*.

Examples : *kristendom* ['kri`st(ə)ndom] ' Christianity ' ; *godhet* ['go`:dhe:t] ' goodness ' ; *kärlek* ['çæ´:le:k] ' love ' ; *vänskap* ['vɛ`nskɑ:p] ' friendship ' ; *dyrbar* ['dy`r:bɑ:r]

'precious';   *trofast*   ['troˑ`ːfast]   'faithful';   *långsam*
['loˋŋsam]   'slow.'

(c) Weak stress.

This falls on the second syllable of disyllabic words, with
the double tone (Tone II), e.g. *blomma* ['bloˋmma] ' flower ';
falla ['faˋlla] ' to fall.'

LACK OF STRESS

67. Disyllabic words pronounced with the single tone
(Tone I) have the second syllable unstressed, e.g. *boken*
['boˑːkən] ' the book '; *handen* ['haˋndən] ' the hand ';
böcker ['bœˊkkər] ' books '; *händer* ['hɛˊndər] ' hands ';
also the present tense of the strong verbs, e.g. *faller* ['faˊllər]
' falls '; *binder* ['biˊndər] ' binds.' Some prefixes of Low
German or High German origin are always unstressed, e.g.
be-, ge- in *bereda* [bɛˊreˑːda] ' to prepare '; *gestalt* [jɛˈstalt]
' figure, form.' But the prefix *er-*, which is unstressed in
German, bears a stress in Swedish, e.g. *erövra* ['æːrøˋːvra]
' to conquer.' The prefix *för-* presents difficulties to the
learner. When it is borrowed from or modelled on the Low
German prefix *vor-* (cf. High German *ver-*), it is unstressed in
verbs, e.g. *förbjuda* [førˈbjuˊːda] ' to forbid '; *förbruka*
[førˈbruˊːka] ' to consume '; but when it represents the
old preposition (in many cases corresponding to English
fore-), it is stressed, e.g. *förord* ['føˋːroˑːd] ' foreword, preface '; *fördäck* ['føˋːdɛk] ' foredeck '; *förbereda* ['føˋːrbɛreˑːda]
' to prepare.'

INTONATION

68. Swedish, like Norwegian, not only has dynamic stress
(expiratory accent), it also makes considerable use of pitch
accent or differences in tones to distinguish between
different words and word forms. There are two tones, the
single and the double (also known as Tone I and Tone II),
and they are intimately connected with stress. They are
subject to a great many variations according to the position
of the word in the sentence and are best learnt by imitation,
since a good deal of ear training is required before the
student can recognize and analyse differences of tone.

THE SINGLE TONE

69. The single tone is a falling one. It is used with most monosyllabic nouns in isolation and in the same nouns when the post-positive definite article is added. Starting with a monosyllabic word, we may compare the Swedish *bok* with the English *book*; each has the same falling tone : ⟍

The definite form *boken* 'the book' may be compared with a disyllabic English word with one stress, like *father*. Both have a falling tone ; but whereas the English drops to a low tone on the first syllable and remains low on the second, the Swedish only drops slightly on the first syllable and then drops to a low tone. This may be represented by the following diagrams :

> English : *father* ⟍ .
>
> Swedish : *boken* ⎯ .

The single tone is the fundamental one. With few exceptions it is the only one found in monosyllabic words and it is also used in most words of foreign origin. In this book it will be indicated in the phonetic type by an acute accent placed immediately after the vowel on which the falling tone begins, e.g. [ˈboˊːkən]. The following are the main rules for the use of the single tone ; it is used :

(*a*) In monosyllabic words,[1] e.g. *hus* [huːs] 'house'; *lång* [lɔŋ] 'long' ; *kom* [kɔm] 'come.' In these words the tone falls continuously and may be represented diagrammatically by the intonation curve : ⟍

(*b*) In many disyllabic words ending in *-el*, *-en*, *-er* which were originally monosyllabic, e.g. *segel* [ˈseˊːgəl] 'sail' ; *vatten* [ˈvaˊtːən] 'water' ; *åker* [ˈoˊːkər] 'tilled field' ; *fager* [ˈfɑˊːgər] 'fair, beautiful.' The *-er* words include :

(i) many of the nouns having *-er* as their plural termination, with or without mutation of the root vowel,

---

[1] For this reason it will not be indicated in the phonetic transcriptions of monosyllabic words.

T.Y.S.—2*

e.g. *bönder* ['bœ'ndər] 'farmers'; *böcker* ['bœ'kkər] 'books'; *bröder* ['brø'ːdər] 'brothers'; *fäder* ['fɛ'ːdər] 'fathers'; *getter* ['jɛ'ttər] 'goats.'

(ii) All those verbs which have *-er* as their termination in the present tense, e.g. *bryter* ['bry'ːtər] 'break(s)'; *läser* ['lɛ'ːsər] 'read(s)'; *köper* ['çø'ːpər] 'buy(s).'

In all these words the tone falls as in *boken* and may be represented diagrammatically by :

(*c*) In the definite form, with the post-positive article, of all nouns falling into categories (*a*) and (*b*) above, e.g. ['hu'ːsət] 'the house'; *åkern* ['o'ːkən] 'the tilled field'; *bönderna* ['bœ'ndəna] 'the farmers'; *fäderna* ['fɛ'ːdəna] 'the fathers.'

(*d*) In comparative forms of adjectives and adverbs having the termination *-re*, e.g. *längre* ['lɛ'ŋrə] 'longer'; *större* ['stœ'rrə] 'larger'; *yngre* ['y'ŋrə] 'younger.' N.B.— Those with the termination *-are* have the double tone.

(*e*) In many names of countries, e.g. *England* ['ɛ'ŋland]; *Island* ['i'ːsland] 'Iceland'; *Norge* ['nɔ'rjə] 'Norway'; *America* [a'me'ːrika]. The corresponding adjectives in *-sk* also have the single tone, e.g. *engelsk* ['ɛ'ŋəlsk] 'English.'

(*f*) In most polysyllabic words of foreign origin which do not bear the chief stress on the first syllable, e.g. *student* [stu'dɛ'nt] 'student'; *parfym* [par'fy'ːm] 'perfume'; *finanser* [fi'na'ŋsər] 'finances'; *behandla* [bə'ha'ndla] 'to deal with, treat'; *förhöra* [før'hø'ːra] 'to interrogate, cross-examine'; *publicera* [pəbli'se'ːra] 'to publish'; *Linnæus* [li'nne'ːəs].

Note.—The simple verbs in *-a* always have the double tone, but the derivatives formed from them by the prefixes

be- or *för-* always have the single tone ; cf. *handla* [ˈhaˈndla]
' to deal, trade ' and *höra* [ˈhøˈːra] ' to hear,' with *behandla*
and *förhöra* above.

(*g*) In parts of speech which usually occur in an unstressed
position in the sentence, e.g. *efter* [ˈɛˈftər] ' after ' ; *eller*
[ˈɛˈllər] ' or ' ; *under* [ˈøˈndər] ' under.'

THE DOUBLE TONE

70. The double tone is only used with words of more than
one syllable[1]. In isolated words of two syllables having the
double tone, the pitch drops on each syllable, but the
second syllable begins on a higher pitch than the first. To
illustrate this we may compare the emphatic form of the
English word ' off-side ! ', as shouted on the football field,
with a Swedish exclamation like *utmärkt* ! [ˈuˈːtˈmæːrkt]
' splendid ! ' In the English word the pitch remains high
on the first syllable but drops on the second ; in the Swedish
word the drop occurs on each syllable, but the second starts
on a higher tone than the first, as explained above. The
two patterns may be illustrated by the following diagrams :

English :   *off-side* !

Swedish :   *utmärkt* !

The double tone is used in most native Swedish nouns
that have polysyllabic singular forms with the principal
stress on the first syllable, e.g. *flicka* [ˈfliˈkka]
' girl ' ; *bagare* [ˈbɑˈːgarə] ' baker.' Their definite singular
forms, formed by adding -*n*, also have the double tone.
So also do their plural forms, with or without the
addition of the definite article, e.g. *flickor* [ˈfliˈkkor]
' girls ' ; *flickorna* [ˈfliˈkkoṇa] ' the girls.' When, as in the
latter example, the word consists of three syllables, the
tones are distributed over the word according to the
pattern :

[1] There are a few monosyllabic words which are pronounced with
the double tone, but here they will be disregarded.

All disyllabic infinitives ending in *-a* have the double
tone, e.g. *kalla* [ˈkaˋlla] ' to call '; *stiga* [ˈstiˋ:ga] ' to rise ';
and the present, past and supine of verbs of the first weak
conjugation have the same tone, e.g. *kallar, kallade, kallat*.

In addition to the above, the following categories of
words are pronounced with the double tone :

(*a*) Most compound words, e.g. *luftpost* [ˈløˋftpost] ' air
mail '; *telegrafstation* [tɛlɛˈgraˋ:fstaˈsoːn] ' telegraph
station '; *postkontor* [ˈpoˋstkonˈtoːr] ' post-office.' This
includes many Swedish surnames of the type *Eriksson*
[ˈeˋ:rikˋson]; *Lindkvist* [ˈliˋndkvist]; *Berglund* [ˈbæˋrjlend]
Strindberg [ˈstriˋn(d)bærj]. Place-names show considerable
variations. Thus *Stockholm, Vaxholm* and *Kungsholm* have
almost level stress and the double tone, but *Gripsholm*
and *Djursholm* have stress on the second syllable and
the single tone. Similarly *Tranås, Bengtsfors* and *Varberg*
follow the first type, while *Borås, Alingsås, Västerås, Bofors,
Söderfors* and *Charlottenberg* follow the second.

(*b*) Abstract nouns formed with the suffixes *-dom, -else,
-het, -lek, -ning, -skap*, e.g. *barndom* [ˈbaˋndom] ' childhood';
liknelse [ˈliˋ:knelse] ' parable, simile '; *storhet* ˈstoˋ:rheːt]
' greatness '; *kärlek* [ˈçæˋ:rleːk] ' love '; *lösning* [ˈløˋ:sniŋ]
' solution '; *vänskap* [ˈvɛˋnskaːp] ' friendship '.

(*c*) Nomina agentis formed with the suffix *-are*, e.g.
bagare [ˈbɑˋ:gare] ' baker '; *domare* [ˈdoˋmare] ' judge.'
Similarly names of professions based on Latin words and
ending in *-or*, e.g. *doktor* [ˈdoˋktor] ' doctor '; *professor*
[proˈfɛˋssor] ' professor '; *revisor* [rɛˈviˋ:sor] ' auditor ';
but the plurals of these words, with change of stress, have
the single tone, e.g. *doktorer* [dokˈtoˊ:rer], etc.

(*d*) Nouns for females derived from nouns for males by
means of the suffixes *-essa, -inna, -ska*, e.g. *prinsessa*
[prinˈsɛˋssa] ' princess '; *lärarinna* [læ:raˈriˋnna] ' lady
teacher '; *studentska* [stuˈdɛˋntska] ' girl student.'

(*e*) Adjectives formed by means of the suffixes *-aktig,
-bar, -full, -ig, -lig, -lös, -sam, -vis*, e.g. *narraktig*

['na`rraktig] ' foolish, foppish ; ' *hållbar* ['ho`lbɑːr] ' tenable ' ; *nyckfull* ['ny`kføl] ' capricious ' ; *enig* ['eˑ:nig] ' agreed ' ; *härlig* ['hæ`ˑ:lig] ' glorious ' ; *fredlös* ['freˑ`dløːs] ' outlawed ' ; *långsam* ['lo`ŋsam] ' slow ' ; *korsvis* ['ko`ṣviːs] ' crosswise '.

(*f*) The comparative and superlative forms of adjectives having the terminations *-are, -ast,* e.g. *sannare* ['sa`nnarə] ' truer ' ; *sannast* ['sa`nnast] ' truest.' Similarly with the corresponding adverbs.

(*g*) Derivative verbs formed with adverbial prefixes, e.g. *anklaga* ['a`nklɑːga] ' to accuse ' ; *avgå* ['a`ːvgoː] ' to leave, depart ' ; *inta* ['i`ntɑː] ' to take in, occupy ' ; *medge* ['mɛ`ˑ:djeː] ' to concede, admit ' ; *motstå* ['moˑ`:tstoː] ' to resist ' ; *uppge* ['ø`pjeː] ' to abandon.'

HOMONYMS WITH DIFFERENT TONES

71. Like several other tone languages Swedish has a number of word pairs identical in form but different in meaning according to whether they are pronounced with the single or double tone.

Examples :

Single Tone	Double Tone
anden ['a`ndən] ' the duck '	*anden* ['a`ndən] ' the spirit '
tomten ['to`mtən] 'the building site '	*tomten* ['to`mtən] ' the goblin '

Many such homonyms arise because the definite form of a monosyllabic noun (with post-positive article *-en*) may be identical in spelling with the past participle of a strong verb.

Examples :

Single Tone	Compound Tone
biten ['biˑ`:tən] ' the bit, fragment '	*biten* ['biˑ:tən] ' bitten '
buren ['buˑ`:rən] ' the cage'	*buren* ['buˑ:rən] ' carried '
knuten ['knuˑ`:tən] ' the knot '	*knuten* ['knuˑ:tən] ' tied '
skuren ['skuˑ`:rən] ' the shower '	*skuren* ['skuˑ:rən] ' cut '

Similarly the definite form of a monosyllabic neuter noun (with post-positive article *-et*) may be identical in spelling with the neuter form of a past participle.

Examples :

Single Tone	Compound Tone
slaget ['slɑ´:gət] ' the bat- tle '	*slaget* ['slɑ`:gət] ' beaten '
fallet ['fa´l̪l̪ət] ' the case '	*fallet* ['fa`l̪l̪ət] ' fallen '

TONE VARIATIONS WITHIN THE SENTENCE

72. In connected speech unstressed words entirely give up their tone differences, while emphatic words show some modification of their basic tone pattern. As in English a rising tone is used in suspensive groups and a falling tone in conclusive groups. Thus when a word having the single tone occurs in the body of a sentence expressing a categorical statement and is emphatic, the tone pattern becomes ⟋ ·⃨ instead of ⟍ ,⃨ the latter occurring only at the end of the sentence. When a word with the double tone occurs in the body of such a sentence and is emphatic, the tone pattern becomes ⟍⟋ instead of ⟍⟍ ; and when it occurs at the end of the sentence, it is only the last syllable of the word that drops to the lowest tone, thus : ⟍⃨

Examples :

I. *Jag kom in i rummet och fann boken på bordet.*

II. *Jag kom hem från skolan och läste min läxa.*

In interrogative sentences the tone rises at the end.

Examples:

— —   .   .   ╱ ·

I.   *Låg boken på bordet ?*

_ · ╲ ╱ · ╲ ·

II.   *Läste flickan sin läxa ?*

COLLOQUIAL FORMS

73. In colloquial Swedish there are many divergences from the pronunciation represented by the written language. In some cases special forms are used, in others words are pronounced with sound values not heard in elevated speech (e.g. that of the pulpit). The following are the most important points ; they should be studied not only because the English student will hear them invariably used by Swedes, but also because he should adopt them in speaking Swedish so that his pronunciation may not appear stilted.

(*a*) Adjectives ending in *-ig* drop the *g*, e.g. *trevlig* ['tre`:vli], *trevligt* ['tre`:vlit][1], *trevliga* ['tre`:vlia] ' nice ' ; similarly with the adverb *trevligt*.

(*b*) The final *-o* is pronounced as a murmur vowel in the numerals *nio* ['ni`:ə] ' nine ' ; *tio* ['ti`:ə] ' ten ' ; and is dropped in the multiples of 10 from 30 to 90 inclusive, e.g. *trettio* ['trɛ`tti], *fyrtio* ['fœ`ti], etc.

(*c*) The final consonant is dropped in a number of short frequently used words, e.g. *dag* [dɑ:] ' day ' ; *god* [gɔ:] ' good ' ; *vad* [va] ' what ' ; *det* [dɛ] ' that ' ; *med* [me:] ' with ' ; *litet* ['li`:tə] ' (a) little ' ; *och* [ɔ] ' and.' The word *att* ' to ' before an infinitive is sometimes pronounced [ɔ].

(*d*) There are special colloquial forms of many pronouns, e.g. *jag* [jɑ:] ; *mig* [mɛj] ; *dig* [dɛj] ; *sig* [sɛj] (as against [mi:g, di:g, si:g] in the language of the pulpit) ; *de* and *dem* are pronounced [dɔm], e.g. *de såg mig* [dɔm so:(g) mɛj] 'they saw me' ; *jag såg dem* [jɑ: so:(g) dɔm] 'I saw them' ;

---

[1] Sometimes the *g* is pronounced as *k* before *t* : ['tre:`vlikt].

någonting ' something, anything ' is contracted and pronounced ['nɔntiŋ] ; the plural form *några* ' some, any ' has assimilation of *g* to *r* and is pronounced ['noːra] ; and the neut. sg. form *intet* ' nothing ' is pronounced as if it were written *inget* ['iŋət]. The spelling *inget* is also possible.

(*e*) In all verbs the old plural forms are replaced by the singular, so that in each tense there is one form only, irrespective of number or person.

Examples :   *vi lever* ' we live ' instead of *vi leva*.

   dom kan ' they can ' instead of *de kunna*.

   dom vann ' they won ' instead of *de vunno*.

(*f*) A few verbs have short colloquial forms in the infinitive and the present.

Examples :   *be, ber* instead of *bedja, beder* ' to request.'

   bli, blir instead of *bliva, bliver* ' to become.'

   ge, ger instead of *giva, giver* ' to give.'

   ta, tar instead of *taga, tager* ' to take.'

(*g*) The verbs *lägga* and *säga* (see § 49 *a*) have shortened colloquial forms in the past tense : *lade* [lɑː] ' laid,' and *sade* [sɑː] ' said ' ; *la* and *sa* are often used in the written language.

(*h*) The commonest auxiliary verbs have special colloquial forms :

jag är is pronounced as [jɑ(ː) eː]

de är is pronounced as [dɔm eː]

jag var is pronounced as [jɑ(ː) vɑ]

vi var is pronounced as [vi vɑ]

jag skall is pronounced as [jɑ(ː) skɑː]. and when unstressed as [ja ska]

vi skall is pronounced as [vi skɑː], and when unstressed as [vi ska].

Note.—The full forms [jɑːg], [æːr] and [vɑːr] are also frequently used in the colloquial.

PRONUNCIATION EXERCISE

Memorize the following text by the aid of the phonetic script ; then sing it to the music given below. It is one of the best known national songs of Sweden.

SVERIGE
'sværjə

Sverige,	Sverige,	Sverige,	fosterland,
'sværjə	'sværjə	'sværjə	'fostərland
Sweden	Sweden	Sweden	land of our birth

vår längtans bygd, vårt hem på jorden !
vo:r 'lɛntans bygd vo:t̨ hɛm po: 'jo:dən
abode of our longing, our home on earth !

Nu spela skällorna, där härar lysts av brand,
nu: 'spe:la 'ṣɛḷḷoṇa dæ:r 'hæ:rar ly:sts ɑ:v brand
Now the sleigh-bells play where armies (once) were lit by
fire (of battle).

och dåd blev saga, men med hand vid hand
ɔk do:d ble:v 'sɑ:ga mɛn me:d hand vi:d hand
and deeds became story, but with hand in hand

svär än ditt folk som förr de gamla trohetsorden.
svæ:r ɛn dit folk som før de: 'gamla 'tro:he:ts'o:dən
still swears thy people as then the age-old words of fealty.

Fall, julesnö,   och susa,   djupa mo !
fal 'julə'snø: ɔk 'su:sa 'ju:pa mo:
Fall, yuletide snow, and murmur, lowland heath !

Brinn, österstjärna, genom   junikvällen !
brin 'œstər'ṣæ:ṇa 'je:nom 'ju:ni'kvɛḷḷən
Burn, eastern star, through the June eve !

Sverige, moder !   Bliv vår   strid, vår   ro,
'sværjə 'mo:dər bli:v vo:r stri:d vo:r ro:
Sweden, mother ! Be (thou) our strife, our rest,

du land, där våra barn en gång få bo
du: land dæ:r 'vo:ra baṇ ɛn gɔŋ fo: bo:
thou land where (in which) our children one day shall dwell

och våra   fäder   sova   under kyrkohällen.
ɔk 'vo:ra 'fɛ:dər 'so:va 'əndər 'çyrko'hɛḷḷən
and (where) our fathers sleep beneath the churchyard
flagstone.

Sverige.

W. STENHAMMAR.

Sve - - ri - ge, Sve - - ri - ge, Sve - - ri - ge,

fos-terland, vår längtans bygd, vårt hem på jor-den.

Nu spe-la skäl-lor-na, där hä-rar lysts av brand, och

dåd blev saga, men med hand vid hand svär än ditt folk som

förr de gam-la trohets-or-den. Fall ju-le-snö, och

susa, dju-pa mo! Brinn ös-terstjärna ge-nom ju-nikväl-len!

Sverige, moder! Bliv vår strid, vår ro, du land, där vå-ra

barn en gång få bo och vå-ra fäder sova under kyrkohällen.

VERNER VON HEIDENSTAM.

Words and Music reproduced by kind permission of the publishers, Messrs.
Carl Gehrmans Musikförlag, (Abr. Hirschs Förlag) Stockholm.

ORTHOGRAPHICAL PECULIARITIES

USE OF CAPITAL LETTERS

74. In general, Swedish is more sparing in the use of capital letters than English. All names of countries are spelt with capital letters, but not nouns and adjectives denoting nationality, e.g. *Frankrike* 'France,' but *en fransman* ' a Frenchman,' *en fransk stad* ' a French town.' Similarly all place-names are spelt with capital letters but not compound nouns or derivatives containing a place-name, e.g. *Stockholm* but *en stockholmare* ' an inhabitant of Stockholm '; *Luleå* but *luleåkontraktet* ' the Lulea contract.' Names of months, days of the week and church festivals are spelt with small letters, e.g. *april, fredag* ' Friday,' *jul* ' Christmas,' *påsk* ' Easter.' In headings, titles of books, etc., consisting of more than one word, only the first is spelt with a capital, e.g. *Svensk språklära* ' Swedish Grammar ' (but : *Om svenska språket* ' On the Swedish Language '), *Röda rummet* ' The Red Room.' Titles used with names are written with small letters, e.g. *prins Carl, lord Linlithgow, sir John Simon, dr. Lagergren.*

REDUNDANT LETTERS

75. In Swedish names vowels are sometimes written double, e.g. *Bååth, Böök, Roos* ; but this does not affect the pronunciation. Similarly an *h* has no sound value in names like *Eldh, Thorsson, Phersson* (the latter a variant of Persson).

THREE CONSONANTS IN COMPOUNDS

76. When the first element in a compound ends in two consonants which are the same as the initial letter of the second element, one consonant is dropped, e.g. *äggula* ' egg yolk ' ; *nattåg* ' night train '. But the dropped consonant is restored in division : *ägg-gula, natt-tåg.*

FOREIGN WORDS

77. The Swedish vocabulary contains a number of French loan words which have been remodelled in spelling to conform to their pronunciation in Swedish, e.g. *balkong*

(<balcon) ; *ekipering* ' outfitters ' (<équiper) ; *konselj*
(< conseil) ; *kupong* (< coupon) ; *evenemang* (< événement);
mannekäng [**mannə'kɛŋ**] (<mannequin) ; *refräng* (< re-
frain) ; *poäng* (<point) ; *terräng* (<terrain) ; *depå*
(< dépôt) ; *byrå* (< bureau) ; *trikå* (< tricot) ; *revy*
(< revue) ; *polisonger* (< polissons) ; *plysch* ' plush '
(< peluche) ; *toalett* (< toilette) ; *karantän* (< quarantaine) ;
dansös (< danseuse) ; *frisör* (< friseur).

PUNCTUATION

78. The same punctuation marks are used in Swedish as
in English, but the rules for their use are stricter.

(a) The full stop is used at the end of an abbreviation
(e.g. *bibl.=biblisk* ' biblical ') ; but the colon is used as
an abbreviation sign within a word (e.g. *n:r=nummer*
' number ' ; *s:t=sankt* ' saint '). The full stop is not used
after ordinal numbers represented by figures, e.g.
Karl XII ; *den* 25 *januari*. But it is used to separate
groups of threes in numbers, where English uses a comma.

(b) The comma is used to separate dependent clauses
from main clauses. Note especially its use when a noun
clause follows the main clause, e.g. *Pojken sade, att han
skulle komma* ' The boy said that he would come.' Main
clauses connected by *och* are not separated by a comma
unless the subject of each is different, e.g. *Dagen var lång,
och natten var kall.* Swedish differs from English usage in
not placing a comma before and after adverbs used
parenthetically (such as *emellertid* ' however,' *alltså*
' therefore '). A comma is used to separate a noun from a
following apposition, but it is not used when the apposition precedes, cf. *Zola, den franske författaren* and *Den
franske författaren Zola.* Commas are used to mark off
decimals and sometimes the latter are printed in smaller
type, e.g. 1,₅.

(c) The colon is used in much the same way as in
English ; generally speaking, it points to what follows.

(d) The semicolon is used rather sparingly in Swedish ;
often a comma is used where English has a semicolon, e.g.
Att tänka fritt är stort, att tänka rätt är större ' To think

freely (be unfettered in one's thoughts) is great ; but to think rightly (justly) is greater.[1]

(e) The apostrophe serves to mark the genitive of a noun ending in *s*, e.g. *Borås' rådhus*. But in other genitives no apostrophe is used.

(f) The hyphen is used, as in some other Germanic languages, to represent the second part of a compound common to two or more nouns, e.g. *i med- och motgång* ' in prosperity as in adversity'; *land-, sjö- och luftstridskrafter* ' land, sea and air forces.'

It is also used in a number of compound names, e.g. *Anna-Greta, Karl-Henrik, Peterson-Berger, Dals-Ed.* In compound adjectives, when the first component is equal in importance to the second, a hyphen is used and the inflexional ending is only added to the second component, e.g. *etisk-pedagogiska institutet.*

(g) The exclamation mark is used rather more freely than in English. Thus after the words of address at the beginning of a letter, e.g. *Bäste Nils* ! ' Dear Nils,' and after words of caution in notices, e.g. *obs* ! ' N.B.'

ACCENT

79. The acute accent is used in some loan words and names to indicate stress, e.g. *armé* ' army,' *idé* ' idea,' *orkidé* ' orchid '; *Linné, Tegnér* [tɛŋ'neːr], *Wirsén* [vir'ʂeːn].

---

[1] Many other examples will be found in the Swedish rendering of the English exercises in this book ; see the key and compare with the original.

ABBREVIATIONS

80. The following are the most commonly used Swedish abbreviations :

bl. a.	= *bland annat*	inter alia
d:o	= *dito*	ditto
d. v. s.	= *det vill säga*	i.e.
d.y.	= *den yngre*	the Younger
d.ä.	= *den äldre*	the Elder
e.Kr.	= *efter Kristi födelse*	A.D.
e.m.	= *efter middagen*	p.m.
f.d.	= *före detta*	formerly, late
f.Kr.	= *före Kristi födelse*	B.C.
f.m.	= *före middagen*	a.m.
f.n.	= *för närvarande*	at present
f.ö.	= *för övrigt*	for the rest, moreover
i.st.f.	= *i stället för*	instead of
jfr	= *jämför*	cf.
kr.	= *krona (-or)*	crown(s)
m.a.o.	= *med andra ord*	in other words
m.fl.	= *med flera*	and several others
m.m.	= *med mera*	and many others
n:r, n:o	= *nummer, numro*	No.
näml.	= *nämligen*	namely (viz.)
obs.	= *observera*	N.B.
osv.	= *och så vidare*	and so on
s.k.	= *så kallad*	so called
ss.	= *såsom*	as
s:t	= *sankt*	St. (Saint)
t.ex.	= *till exempel*	e.g.
t.o.m.	= *till och med*	even

PART II
GRAMMAR

CHAPTER I

THE NOUN

81. In Swedish there were originally three genders, and, as in Modern German, gender was grammatical, not natural. But through the coalescence of the old masculines and feminines Modern Swedish has only two genders, the " common gender " and the " neuter gender."

When the definite article is used with a noun, its gender is sufficiently indicated ; but when a noun stands in isolation, its gender will be shown in this book by adding *c.* or *n.*

82.　　　　　　The Indefinite Article

Common	Neuter
en	*ett*

Examples :

en *häst* (a horse)	**ett** *hus* (a house)
en *sten* (a stone)	**ett** *djur* (an animal)

The Definite Article

83. Swedish, like the other Scandinavian languages, has a post-positive or enclitic definite article, i.e. the article is added as a termination to the noun with which it goes and is not placed in front of it as in English.

Singular

Common	Neuter
hästen (the horse)	*huset* (the house)
stenen (the stone)	*djuret* (the animal)

In the singular the definite article is :

　-en (or *-n*) for the common gender ;
　-et (or *-t*) for the neuter gender.

The reduced forms *-n* and *-t* are used when the noun ends in a vowel, e.g. *flickan* (the girl) ; *riket* (the realm) ; *kon* (the cow) ; and in a few other cases, which will be given below.

Plural

Common	Neuter
hästarna (the horses)	*husen* (the houses)
stenarna (the stones)	*djuren* (the animals)

All nouns of the common gender have the ending *-na* as the definite article in the plural ; and most neuter nouns have the ending *-en* (a few take *-a*[1]).

84. Remarks on the Definite Singular

(a) An *-e-* in an unstressed syllable is liable to be dropped before or after *l* or *r* in polysyllabic words. In nouns of the common gender, the *-e-* following the liquid drops when the definite article is added,[2] e.g. :

sadeln (the saddle)	*fjädern* (the feather)

but in neuter nouns the preceding *-e-* drops[3], e.g. :

Indefinite	Definite
ett tempel (a temple)	*templet* (the temple)
ett läger (a camp)	*lägret* (the camp)

(b) In nouns of either gender ending in unstressed *-en* the *-e-* preceding the *-n-* drops,[4] e.g. :

Indefinite	Definite
en sägen (a legend)	*sägnen* (the legend)
ett tecken (a sign)	*tecknet* (the sign)

(c) Nouns of Latin origin ending in *-or* drop the *-e-* of the definite article, e.g. :

Indefinite	Definite
en rektor (a headmaster)	*rektorn* (the headmaster)
en professor (a professor)	*professorn* (the professor)

[1] See § 90. [2] Except : *himmel*,[(II)] *himlen*, heaven. [3] Except : *papper*,[(II)] *papperet* paper. [4] Except : *siden*,[(II)] *sidenet*, silk.

Note : A small Roman numeral placed after a noun refers to the tone (see § 68).

(d) Some nouns take no terminal article :

(i) Abstract nouns derived from verbs and ending in *-an*, e.g. *anhållan* ' application ' ; *började* ' beginning.'

(ii) A number of words ending in *-en*, e.g. *borgen* ' guarantee, surety ' ; *botten*, ' bottom ' ; *fröken* ' Miss ' ; *orden* ' order ' ; and Latin words like *examen* ' examination ' ; *tentamen* ' preliminary examination.'

Note.—The article is also omitted when the noun is preceded by a determinative genitive, a possessive adjective or determinative pronoun, e.g. *husets namn* ' the name of the house ' ; *min vän* ' my friend ' ; *den professor, jag menar* ' the professor (that) I mean.'

(e) Latin words ending in *-eum, -ium* drop the *-um* before adding the terminal article *-et*, e.g. :

Indefinite	Definite
museum	*muse**et***
observatorium	*observatori**et***

85. Remarks on the Definite Plural

(a) In neuter nouns ending in unstressed *-el, -en, -er* the *-e-* is dropped when the definite article is added in the plural, e.g. :

Indefinite	Definite
segel (sails)	*seg**len*** (the sails)
tempel (temples)	*temp**len*** (the temples)
vatten (waters)	*vatt**nen*** (the waters)
tecken (signs)	*teck**nen*** (the signs)
läger (camps)	*läg**ren*** (the camps)
roder (rudders)	*rodr**en*** (the rudders)

(b) Some common nouns, which form their plurals by mutation (modification) of the root vowel, have an irregular terminal article :

		Indef. Plural	Definite Plural
man	man	*män*	*männen*[1]
gås [go:s]	goose	*gäss* [jɛs]	*gässen*
lus	louse	*löss*	*lössen*
mus	mouse	*möss*	*mössen*

[1] Note that this word has double *n* in the definite forms, both singular and plural : *mannen, männen.*

(c) The following neuter nouns have irregular plurals:

		Indef. Plural	Definite Plural
huvud	head	*huvuden*	*huvudena*
		(coll. *huven*)	(coll. *huvena*)
öga	eye	*ögon*	*ögonen*
			(coll. *ögona*)
öra	ear	*öron*	*öronen*
			(coll. *örona*)

(d) In literature and in formal style the older ending -*ne*[2] is found instead of -*na* in the definite plural of nouns denoting males, e.g. :

Indefinite	Definite
fiskare (fishermen)	*fiskarne* (now *fiskarna*)
knektar (soldiers)	*knektarne* (now *knektarna*)

Vocabulary

regel, c. ' rule '
meter, c. ' metre '
medel, n. ' means '
roder, n. ' rudder '
fågel, c. ' bird '
med ' with '
öken, c. ' desert '
vatten, n. ' water '

exempel, n. ' example '
finger, n. ' finger '
och ' and '
är ' is, are '
har ' has, have '
av ' of '
i ' in '
på ' on, in '

Exercise I
Translate :

(a) En häst är ett djur. Hästen och sadeln. Fågeln och fjädern. Huset och templet. Tecknet på himlen. Lägret är i öknen. Papperet och sidenet.

(b) The rudder in the water. The horse and the bird. The rule and the means. The temple and the camp. The bird in the desert. The finger ; the observatory ; the metre ; the example.

(c) Hästarna. Lössen. Männen med gässen. Fiskarna. Rodren. Knektarna är i lägren.

(d) The signs. The waters. The head. The men and the horses. The rudders and the sails. The eyes and the ears. The mice are in the house.

[2] This comes from the old nominative ending, whilst -*na* is from the old accusative, now generalized for all cases.

CHAPTER II

PLURAL OF NOUNS

86. The common nouns[1] *häst* and *sten* already given, have as their definite plural *hästarna, stenarna*. The plural ending of these nouns in the indefinite form is therefore *-ar*. But this is not the only possible ending in the plural; some nouns take *-or*, some *-er* and some *-n*. Other nouns, mostly neuter, such as the words *hus* and *djur* already quoted, have the same form for the indefinite, both singular and plural. According to the way in which they form the plural Swedish nouns fall into five declensions.

87.   First Declension

Plural ending *-or*

Singular :	Plural :
en flicka ' a girl '	*flickor* ' girls '
flickan ' the girl '	*flickorna* ' the girls '
en våg ' a wave '	*vågor* ' waves '
vågen ' the wave '	*vågorna* ' the waves '

This declension comprises :

(*a*) Common nouns of more than one syllable ending in *-a*, e.g. *prinsessa* ' princess '; *lärarinna* ' lady teacher '; *gata* ' street '; *fara* ' danger '; *karta* ' map.' In the plural they take the ending *-or*.

Exception.—The word *historia* ' story ' has plural *historier*.

(*b*) A few nouns ending in a consonant, e.g. *ros* ' rose '; *toffel* ' slipper.' These have as plural : *rosor, tofflor*.

---

[1] Wherever the expression " common nouns " is used in this book, it means nouns of the common or non-neuter gender, i.e. those that have *-n* or *-en* as the terminal definite article in the singular.

88.   Second Declension

Plural ending : *-ar*

Singular	Plural
en häst ' a horse '	*hästar* [II] ' horses '
hästen ' the horse '	*hästarna* ' the horses '
en krage ' a collar '	*kragar* ' collars '
kragen ' the collar '	*kragarna* ' the collars '
en fjäder ' a feather '	*fjädrar* ' feathers '
fjädern ' the feather '	*fjädrarna* ' the feathers '
en bro ' a bridge '	*broar* ' bridges '
bron ' the bridge '	*broarna* ' the bridges '

This declension comprises :

(*a*) A large number of common nouns of one syllable ending in a consonant.

(*b*) Most common nouns of more than one syllable ending in unstressed *-e*, *-el*, *-en* or *-er*. In the plural they drop the *-e* before the ending, e.g. *furste*, pl. *furstar* ' prince '; *bibel*, pl. *biblar* ' Bible '; *socken* ['soˈkkən], pl. *socknar* ' parish '; *seger*, pl. *segrar* ' victory.'

(*c*) Some monosyllabic nouns ending in a vowel, e.g. *by* ' village '; *fru* ' Mrs. or wife '; *sjö* ' lake '; *ö* ' island.'

(*d*) Common nouns ending in the suffixes *-dom*, *-ing*, *-ling*, *-ning*, e.g. *sjukdom* ' disease '; *inföding* ' native '; *yngling* ' youth '; *drottning* ' queen '.

Irregular plurals :

Singular	Plural
afton ' evening '	*aftnar*
morgon ' morning '	*morgnar* ['moˈ:ŋar]
sommar ' summer '	*somrar*
dotter ' daughter '	*döttrar*
moder ' mother '	*mödrar*

Note.—The words *föräldrar* [fərˈɛˈldrar] ' parents ' and *pengar* ' money,' occur in the plural only.

Third Declension

Plural ending : *-er*

Singular	Plural
en dam ' a lady '	*damer*[II] ' ladies '
damen ' the lady '	*damerna* ' the ladies '
en tand ' a tooth '	*tänder*[I] ' teeth '
tanden ' the tooth '	*tänderna* ' the teeth '
en student ' a student '	*studenter*[I] ' students '
studenten ' the student '	*studenterna* ' the students '
en fabel ' a fable '	*fabler*[I] ' fables '
fabeln ' the fable '	*fablerna* ' the fables '
en professor[1] ' a professor '	*professorer*[I] ' professors '
professorn ' the professor '	*professorerna* ' the professors '
ett bryggeri ' a brewery '	*bryggerier*[I] ' breweries '
bryggeriet ' the brewery '	*bryggerierna* ' the breweries '
ett jubileum ' a jubilee '	*jubileer*[I] ' jubilees '
jubileet ' the jubilee '	*jubileerna* ' the jubilees '

This declension comprises both common and neuter nouns. The principal categories are :

(*a*) Many monosyllabic nouns ending in a consonant, e.g. *bild* ' picture ' ; *färg* ' colour ' ; *klass* ' class ' ; *mängd* ' quantity ' ; *salt* ' salt.' All nouns of this type are pronounced with the double tone in the plural if the root vowel is not mutated.

---

[1] Note change of stress and tone in the plural : [proˈfɛˈssor], but [profəˈsoˈːrər].

(b) A few nouns which have mutation of the root-vowel in the plural (cf. Eng. *tooth—teeth*); the most important are:

Singular		Plural
hand	' hand '	*händer*
rand	' edge '	*ränder*
strand	' shore '	*stränder*
tand	' tooth '	*tänder*
natt	' night '	*nätter*
stad	' town '	*städer*
bok	' book '	*böcker*
fot	' foot '	*fötter*
rot	' root '	*rötter*
son	' son '	*söner* [II]
land (n.)	' country '	*länder*

Note.—With the exception of *söner* all the above nouns are pronounced with the single tone in the plural.

(c) The following nouns double the final consonant and shorten the root-vowel in the plural :

Singular		Plural
get [je:t]	' goat '	*getter* ['jɛ'ttər]
nöt [nø:t]	' nut '	*nötter* ['nœ'ttər]

(d) Loan words of the common gender having the stress on the last syllable, e.g. *armé* ' army ' ; *idé* ' idea ' ; *supé* ' dinner (party) ' ; *agent* [a'gɛnt] ' agent ' ; *diamant* ' diamond ' ; *advokat* ' lawyer ' ; *komedi* ' comedy ' ; *parfym* ' perfume ' ; *rekryt* ' recruit ' ; *uniform* ' uniform.'

(e) Loan words ending in -*or*, e.g. *assessor* ; *censor* ' examiner ' ; *doktor* ; *lektor* ' lecturer, senior master ' ; *professor* ; *rektor* ' headmaster ' ; *revisor* ' auditor.' In the singular these have the stress on the penultimate syllable and are pronounced with the double tone ; in the plural they have the stress on the -*or*- and are pronounced with the single tone.

(f) Neuter nouns formed with the suffix -*eri* and usually denoting a trade or the place where a trade is carried on, e.g. *färgeri* ' dye works ' ; *konditori* ' confectioner's (shop) ' ; *tryckeri* ' printing works ' ; *bokbinderi* ' book bindery ' ; *raffinaderi* ' sugar refinery.'

(*g*) A few loan words ending in unstressed -*el* or -*er*, e.g. *mirakel* ' miracle '; *tentakel* ' tentacle '; *regel* ' rule '; *fiber* ' fibre '; *neger* ' negro.' These drop the -*e* in the plural : *mirakler*, *tentakler*, *regler*, *fibrer*, *negrer*. But most loan words with these endings belong to the second declension.

(*h*) Neuter nouns borrowed from the Latin and ending in -*eum* and -*ium*. In the plural they drop the -*um*, e.g. *museum*, pl. *museer* ; *observatorium*, pl. *observatorier*.

(*i*) Common nouns formed with the suffixes -*arie* ['ɑ'ːriə] and *ie* [iə], e.g. *aktuarie* ' registrar '; *bibliotekarie* ' librarian '; *aktie* ' share '; *premie* ' premium.' In the plural they drop the -*e* before the -*e* of the ending : *aktuarier*, *bibliotekarier*, *aktier*, *premier*.

(*j*) Common nouns formed with the suffixes -*nad*, -*när*, -*het* and -*else*, e.g. *månad* ' month '; *byggnad* ' building '; *konstnär* ' artist '; *körsnär* ' furrier '; *enhet* ' unit '; *kvickhet* ' witticism '; *bakelse* ' pastry '; *händelse* ' event.' In the plural words ending in -*else* drop the final -*e* before the -*e* of the ending, e.g. *händelser*.

(*k*) A few common nouns ending in a vowel. In the plural they drop the -*e*- of the ending to avoid the hiatus of two vowels. The principal words in this category are :

Singular	Plural
hustru ['he'stru] ' wife '	*hustrur*
jungfru ['je'ŋfru] ' maid '	*jungfrur*
ko ' cow '	*kor*
klo ' claw '	*klor*
sko ' shoe '	*skor*
tå ' toe '	*tår*
bonde (II) ' farmer, peasant '	*bönder* (I)
fiende ' enemy '	*fiender*

(*l*) Some nouns of this declension occur in the plural only : *finanser* ' finances '; *grönsaker* ' vegetables '; *kalsonger* ' pants '; *specerier* ' groceries '; *viktualier* ' provisions.' But their singular forms are sometimes found in compounds, e.g. *finansminister* ' minister of finance '; *grönsaksaffär* ' greengrocer's shop '; *speceriaffär* ' grocer's shop '; *viktualiehandel* ' provision shop.'

90.   Fourth Declension

Plural ending : **-n**

ett dike 'a ditch'   **diken** 'ditches'
diket 'the ditch'   **dikena** 'the ditches'

ett bo 'a nest'   **bon** 'nests'
boet 'the nest'   **bona** [1] 'the nests'

This declension comprises a relatively small number of
nouns ; they are all neuter and end in a vowel. It should
be noted that the plural form of the definite article in this
declension is **-a**.

The following are the commonest words belonging to this
declension :

(a) *bälte* 'belt'; *lynne* 'disposition'; *lyte* 'blemish';
läte 'sound'; *märke* 'mark'; *näste* 'nest'; *nöje*
'pleasure'; *skede* 'phase, period'; *säte* 'seat'; *täcke*
'coverlet'; *yrke* 'occupation'; *äpple* 'apple'; *hjärta*
'heart'; *konto* 'account'; *motto* 'motto'; *piano* 'piano';
solo 'solo'; *foto* 'photograph'; *minne* 'memory.'

(b) *bi* 'bee'; *frö* 'seed'; *fä* 'beast'; *knä* 'knee';
spö 'rod'; *strå* 'straw.'

Two nouns in this declension have irregular plural forms :

Singular	Plural
ett öga 'an eye'	**ögon** 'eyes'
ögat 'the eye'	**ögonen** 'the eyes'
ett öra 'an ear'	**öron** 'ears'
örat 'the ear'	**öronen** 'the ears'

Proverb.—Väggarna ha öron ' (The) walls have ears.'

91.   Fifth Declension

Plural like singular :

ett bad 'a bath'   **bad** 'baths'
badet 'the bath'   **baden** 'the baths'

en domare 'a judge' **domare** 'judges'
domaren 'the judge' **domarna** 'the judges'

en resande ' a traveller '	**resande** ' travellers '
resanden ' the traveller '	**resandena** ' the travellers '

This declension includes the following categories :

(*a*) Most neuter nouns ending in a consonant (except those in *-um*, which have already been dealt with).

Examples : *barn* ' child '; *djur* ' animal '; *glas* ' glass '; *horn* ' horn '; *hus* ' house '; *ljus* ' light '; *namn* ' name '; *skåp* ' cupboard '; *träd* ' tree '; *tåg* ' train.'

(*b*) Common nouns ending in *-are* and usually denoting names of agents or instruments, e.g. *bagare* ' baker '; *bärare* ' porter '; *kypare* ' waiter '; *läkare* ' doctor '; *rökare* ' smoker '; *hammare* ' hammer '; *kokare* ' boiler '; *ångare* ' steamer.'

(*c*) A few present participles used as nouns, e.g. *studerande* ' student ' (of either sex); *främmande* ' stranger '; *ordförande* ' chairman '; and the legal terms *klagande, kärande, målsägande* (all meaning : plaintiff), *svarande* ' defendant.'

(*d*) Some nouns of nationality ending in *-er*, e.g. *australier* ' an Australian '; *belgier* ' a Belgian '; *indier* ' an Indian '; *rumänier* ' a Roumanian.'

(*e*) Some names of professions ending in *-er* and derived from words ending in *-ik*, e.g. *fysiker* 'physicist'; *matematiker* ' mathematician '; *musiker* ' musician.'

(*f*) The following nouns are irregular in the plural :

Singular	Plural
en man ' a man '	*män* ' men '
(*Note.*—*mannen* ' the man '	*männen* ' the men ').
en gås ' a goose '	*gäss* [jɛs] ' geese '
gåsen ' the goose '	*gässen* ' the geese '
en mus ' a mouse '	*möss* ' mice '
musen ' the mouse '	*mössen* ' the mice '
en fader ' a father '	*fäder* ' fathers '
fadern ' the father '	*fäderna* ' the fathers '
en broder ' a brother '	*bröder* ' brothers '
brodern ' the brother '	*bröderna* ' the brothers '

Remarks on the Declensions

92. As will be seen from the foregoing, there are a good many different ways of forming the plurals of nouns. Only a few rules can be given for the guidance of students ; thus disyllabic common nouns ending in unstressed *-a* always form their plural with the ending *-or*, and disyllabic common nouns ending in *-e* always form their plural with the ending *-ar* ; whilst all neuter nouns ending in a consonant have the same form in the plural as the singular. Apart from this the student must learn the plural form of each noun as he comes to it. It is best to note the definite form of the singular (since this will indicate the gender) and the indefinite form of the plural. These forms are usually given in dictionaries. Thus *häst-en—hästar ; park-en—parker.* In the word-lists contained in this book, the gender will be given as *c.* or *n.* and the number of the declension will be given in brackets. Thus *vers* c. (3) indicates that the forms are *versen—verser ; tak* n. (5) indicates that the forms are *taket—tak.*

Exercise 2

Give the definite plural forms of the following nouns : *pojken, flickan, mannen, hustrun, modern, dottern, sonen, bonden, läkaren, prinsessan, botanikern, studenten, lärarinnan resanden, negern, konstnären, professorn, agenten, barnet, djuret, hästen, kon, geten, biet, bron, diket, huset, sjön* [ʂœn], *träd.*

CHAPTER III

PERSONAL PRONOUNS—THE VERB *ha*—NUMERALS

93. The subject forms of the personal pronouns are as follows :

	Singular		Plural	
1st Person :	*jag* [jɑ:(g)]¹	' I '	*vi*	' we '
2nd Person :	*du, ni*	' thou, you '	*ni*	' you '
3rd Person :	*han*	' he '		
	hon	' she '	*de*	' they '
	den	' it '		
	det [dɛ]	' it '		

Remarks on the Personal Pronouns

94. In the Second Person *du* is only used between intimate friends and members of the family, like French *tu* and German *du* ; but its use is far more extensive than the corresponding forms in France and Germany, especially in student circles. The rules of etiquette require that the senior of two friends shall be the first to suggest that they *lägga bort titlarna* (" drop the titles ").

The word *ni* is the only other pronoun which it is possible to use in the second person. To some extent it corresponds to French *vous* and German *Sie*, but not entirely ; for in certain situations Swedes are reluctant to use it. When a Swede is introduced to a person, he makes a point of noting his title, if he has one, or profession (which can be used as a title) ; for it is considered more polite to use the definite form of the title (e.g. *professorn*) or the name (e.g. *Herr* [hæer] *Blanck*) with the third person of the verb than to use the direct form of address in the second person. This procedure often becomes very awkward, especially as the use of the third person of the pronoun (*han* or *hon*) referring to the person addressed is strictly taboo. In consequence efforts are being made to induce the Swedish public to adopt the use of *ni* more widely ; and it is certainly gaining ground.

¹ The final *g* is sometimes omitted in the spoken language.

It is always correct for an adult to use it in addressing young persons, strangers, servants, porters, etc. (except that a young child is always called *du*). The English student is recommended to rely on the word *ni*, as a foreigner cannot be expected to know all the niceties of Swedish etiquette. Further hints on how to address people will be given in a subsequent chapter.[1]

The pronoun **den** is used when referring to a noun of the common gender denoting an animal or an inanimate object ; **det** refers to a noun of the neuter gender denoting an animal or an inanimate object. When a neuter noun denotes a person, e.g. *stadsbud* [ˈstaˈsbuːd] ' town porter, district messenger,' the pronoun *han* is used in accordance with the natural gender. In the case of nouns like the neuter *barn* ' child,' *han* or *hon* would be used if the sex were known ; otherwise *det*.

95. The Verb ha(va)[2] to have.

The present tense of this verb is as follows :

jag har ' I have '	**den har** ' it has '
du har ' you have '	**det har** ' it has '
ni har ' you have '	**vi ha(r)** ' we have '
han har ' he has '	**ni ha(r)** ' you have '
hon har ' she has '	**de ha(r)** ' they have '

Note.—In the spoken language the verb ends in **-r** throughout ; in the written language (high style) the plural is **ha** (from the older **hava**). But the -r form is very usual in everyday prose and modern literature generally.

Imperative : **ha** ' have '

The interrogative is formed by transposing the subject and verb, e.g. **har jag? har du?** etc.

The negative is formed by the word **inte**[3] ' not ', e.g. :

jag har inte [ˈiˈntə] ' I have not '
har jag inte? ' have I not ? etc.'

[1] See Chapter XVIII.

[2] The shortened form *ha* has now almost entirely replaced the older *hava* ; but the latter is still heard in ceremonial and church style.

[3] In literary style *icke* is used.

96.   Numerals

1. *en* [ɛn], neuter *ett* [tɜ]   7. *sju* [ʂuː]
2. *två* [tvoː]   8. *åtta* [ˈɔˋtta]
3. *tre* [treː]   9. *nio* [ˈniˋːə][1]
4. *fyra* [ˈfyˋːra]   10. *tio* [ˈtiˋːə][1]
5. *fem* [fɛm]   11. *elva* [ˈɛˋlva]
6. *sex* [sɛks]   12. *tolv* [tɔlv]

---

[1]The pronunciations [ˈniˋːoː], [ˈtiˋːoː] are only heard in ceremonial or elevated style.

Vocabulary

klocka, c. (1) 'clock, watch'	*penna*[1], c. (1) ' pen, pencil'
rum [rɐm], n. (5) ' room '	*kopp*, c. (2) ' cup '
bord [boːɖ], n. (5) ' table '	*kaka*, c. (1) ' cake '
skåp, n. (5) ' cupboard '	*säng*, c. (2) ' bed '
stol, c. (2) ' chair '	*människa*, c. (1) ' human being '
matta, c. (1) ' carpet '	*sekel*, n. (5) ' century '
lampa, c. (1) ' lamp '	*tack* ' thanks '
kudde, c. (2) ' cushion '	*ja* ' yes '
fönster, n. (5) ' window '	*nej* ' no '

Exercise 3

Translate

(*a*) Har ni en klocka i rummet ? Hon har ett bord, ett skåp och två stolar. Har du en matta ? Han har fyra rum. Åtta hästar och nio kor. Nils[2] har en penna och en bok.

(*b*) They have a house. Have you twelve chairs and three tables ? Has the room two windows ? No, it has one window. The men[3] have six horses. The mother has two sons and one daughter.

(*c*) Bonden har tolv getter. Två skåp och en lampa. Seklet. Tre sekel. Huset har sju rum. I rummet är två sängar. Geten har horn. Människan har två ögon och två öron. Vi har fyra kuddar.

(*d*) You have three cushions and four chairs. Two centuries. Has he a pencil ? No. Have you a cup and two cakes ? Yes, thanks. Three beds. Four carpets. Eight chairs and five tables.

---

[1] When it means pencil the word *penna* is an ellipsis for *blyertspenna* ' lead pencil.'

[2] The name Nils is a contraction of Nikolaus.

[3] N.B. *männen*.

CHAPTER IV

PERSONAL PRONOUNS—THE VERB *vara*—NUMERALS

97. The personal pronouns used as objects and after prepositions are as follows :

	Singular	Plural
1st Person :	*mig* [mɛj[1]] ' me '	*oss* ' us '
2nd Person :	*dig* [dɛj[1]], *e(de)r* ' thee you '	*e(de) r* ' you '
3rd Person :	*honom* ['hɔ`nɔm] ' him '	
	henne ['hɛ`nnə] ' her '	*dem* ' them '
	den ' it '	
	det ' it '	

Further remarks on the Personal Pronouns

98. The object forms *den* and *det* above are used in the same way as the subject forms (see Chapter III). When a neuter noun denotes a person, the object form *honom* is used, in accordance with the natural gender. In the case of nouns like the neuter *barn* ' child ', *honom* or *henne* would be used if the sex were known ; otherwise *det*.

In the second person the shortened form *er* is the normal ; the full form *eder* is only used in formal style.

99. The Verb *vara* to be.

The present tense of this verb is as follows :

jag är ' I am '	*den är* ' it is '
du är ' you are '	*det är* ' it is '
ni är ' you are '	*vi är(o)* ' we are '
han är ' he is '	*ni är(o)* ' you are '
hon är ' she is '	*de är(o)* ' they are '

Note.—In the spoken language the verb is *är* throughout ; in the written language (high style) the plural is *äro*. But the shortened form is very usual in everyday prose and modern literature generally.

Imperative : *var* ' be '

[1] Only pronounced [mi:g] [di:g] in ceremonial or church style.

100.   Numerals

13. *tretton*   19. *nitton*

14. *fjorton* ['fjoˋ:ʈon]   20. *tjugo* ['çuˋ:go]

15. *femton*   21. *tjugoen* (*-ett*) [çu'goˋɛn, -'ɛt]

16. *sexton*   22. *tjugotvå* [çu'gəˋtvo:]

17. *sjutton* ['ʂeˋʈon]   23. *tjugotre*

18. *aderton* ['aˋ:ʈon]   30. *trettio* ['trɛˋtti]

Note.—*aderton* is only pronounced ['aˋ:dəʈon] in elevated style; *tjugo* is alternatively, but less frequently spelt *tjugu*; in colloquial speech the *-o-* in *tjugo, tjugotvå,* etc., is weakened to [ə].

Vocabulary

far[1], c. (5) ' father '   *trädgård* c. (2) ' garden '

mor[2], c. (2) ' mother '   *ljus*, n. (5) ' light '

kvinna, c. (1) ' woman '   *tallrik*, c. (2) ' plate '

golv, n. (5) ' floor '   *bröd*, n. (5) ' bread '

vägg, c. (2) ' wall '   *kniv*, c. (2) ' knife '

dörr, c. (2) ' door '   *gaffel*, c. (2) ' fork '

trappa, c. (1) ' staircase '   *sked* [ʂe:d], c. (2) ' spoon '

här ' here '   *där* ' there '   *var* ' where '

för ' for '   *på* ' on '   *mycket* ' much, very '

hur ' how '   *många* ' many '

Exercise 4

Translate

(*a*) Här är far. Där är far och mor. Var är kvinnan ? Var är trappan ? Är barnen i trädgården ? Hur många dörrar och fönster har huset ? Var är Nils ? Har bonden tolv getter och sex hästar ? Var är brödet ? Här är en tallrik för dig.

(*b*) The cushion is on the floor. The knives and forks and spoons are on the table. The house has four walls. Are you

---

[1] This is the contracted and more usual form of *fader* (see § 91*f*).

[2] This is the contracted and more usual form of *moder* (see § 88).

there, Nils ? Here is a light. Mother, where is the glass ?
Has the child a plate ? Have the children plates ? There is
the staircase. The carpet on the floor. The man on the
horse.

(c) Här är mattorna. Kopparna och glasen är i skåpet.
Barnen är i rummet. Var är glasen ? Trettio koppar. Har
du en kniv, en gaffel och en sked ? Huset har tjugoåtta
fönster och sexton dörrar. Hur många mattor är på golvet ?
Har ni mycket bröd ? Trettioåtta tallrikar. Far, har du en
penna ?

(d) Are the carpets on the floors ? Are the glasses in the
cupboard ? How many children are in the garden ? Six
glasses and seven cups for nine men and four women. Has
the house many doors and windows ? The lights in the
rooms. A house has four walls.

CHAPTER V

CASE OF NOUNS—POSSESSIVE ADJECTIVES AND PRONOUNS

101. In the older periods of the language Swedish nouns had an elaborate system of declensions, with special case endings for the nominative, accusative, genitive and dative, singular and plural. But as a result of an extensive process of simplification nearly all the old inflectional endings have disappeared. In Modern Swedish the nominative is also used as the objective case (both for the direct and indirect object); and the only special case form is the genitive, which is formed by adding -s to the nominative. This -s, which is not preceded by an apostrophe, is used with the definite and indefinite form of the noun, both singular and plural.

Examples:

Nominative	Genitive
en pojke ' a boy '	*en pojkes* ' of a boy '
pojken ' the boy '	*pojkens* ' of the boy '
pojkar ' boys '	*pojkars* ' of boys '
pojkarna ' the boys '	*pojkarnas* ' of the boys '

In English the possessive relationship can be expressed by the genitival -s or by the use of the preposition *of*, though the former is only possible when the possessor is a living being (cf. *the king's head, the head of the king*; *the leg of the table*). In Swedish the possessive relationship is usually expressed by the -s genitive, regardless of whether the possessor is a living being or an inanimate object. Thus ' the laws of the land ' must be translated as if it were ' the land's laws,' viz., *landets lagar*; and ' the King of Sweden ' is *Sveriges konung*[1]. For this reason the definite form of the dependent noun (cf. *the* laws, *the* King above) must be rendered by the indefinite form in Swedish.

[1] This is the older ceremonial form; the normal form is *kung*.

102. Remarks on the Genitive

(a) The genitive of a proper noun ending in -s has no additional -s; but in writing the genitive is indicated by adding an apostrophe, e.g. *Nils' penna* 'Nils' pencil.'

(b) The genitive of all other nouns ending in -s should be avoided in the indefinite form. Thus in translating 'Richmond is the name of a rose,' the genitive could be avoided by using a preposition: *Richmond är namnet på en ros*; and 'the scent of a rose' could be translated by *doften av en ros*.

(c) The construction with *av* 'of' usually indicates provenance or origin, e.g. *ringen är av guld* 'the ring is (made) of gold,'; *Hertiginnan av Gloucester* 'the Duchess of Gloucester.'

(d) In expressions like 'the University of London' Swedish sometimes uses a preposition, e.g. *universitetet i London*, sometimes an -s genitive, e.g. *Lunds universitet*, and sometimes uses the two nouns in apposition without any connecting link, e.g. *Uppsala universitet* (or *universtitetet i Uppsala*); cf. also *Stockholms stad* with *staden Göteborg* 'the city of Gothenburg.'

(e) Latin names ending in -us often take the Latin genitive ending, e.g. *Kristi födelse* 'the birth of Christ'; *Orphei Drängar* 'the Servants of Orpheus' (a male-voice choir).

103. Relics of old case endings

In Modern Swedish some old case endings have been preserved in a few words and set phrases.

Examples:

(a) The words *dager* 'light, daylight'; *slarver* 'little rascal' (beside *dag, slarv*) show relics of an old masculine singular nominative -er ending.

(b) The words *läroverk* 'school'; *veckodag* 'weekday'; *kyrkoherde* 'rector, vicar'; *ladugård* 'barn'; *varuhus* 'emporium'; *gatutrafik* 'street traffic' (cf. *lära, vecka, kyrka, lada, vara, gata*) and the phrase *till salu* 'for sale', show relics of old genitive singular endings of originally feminine nouns.

(c) The phrases *gammal i gårde* ' an old hand,' and *man ur huse* ' to a man, every man jack ' (cf. *gård, hus*) show relics of an old dative singular ending in originally masculine and neuter nouns.

(d) The old genitive plural ending *-a* is still used in expressions like *vikingatågen* ' the Viking expeditions,' *kungahuset* ' the Royal Family,' etc.

(e) The old dative plural ending *-om* is still used in the expressions *lagom*, adv. (=*med lag* ' with due order, moderation, neither too much nor too little '); *stundom*, adv. ' at times '; *i lönndom* ' in secret.'

104.   Possessive Adjectives

Singular		Plural
Common	Neuter	Both Genders
min [min]	*mitt*	*mina* ['mi`:na] ' my '
din	*ditt*	*dina* ' thy, your '
vår	*vårt*	*våra* ' our '
er	*ert*	*era* ' your '
Eder	*Edert*	*Edra* ' your '

105.   Remarks on the Possessive Adjectives

(a) The possessive adjectives agree with the following noun, as in French and German.

(b) The forms **er, ert, era** correspond to the personal pronoun **ni** and refer to one or several possessors.

(c) The fuller forms **Eder, Edert, Edra** are only used in formal style.

The possessive adjectives of the third person offer especial difficulty, as there are double forms with difference in meaning, like the Latin **eius** and **suus**. Note carefully the following points :

(a) When English ' his,' ' her,' ' its,' ' their ' do not refer back to the subject of the clause in which they occur, they are translated by the genitives of the personal pronouns *han, hon, den, det, de,* viz., **hans, hennes, dess, dess, deras.**

Examples :
Jag har hans bok ' I have his book.'
Han har hans bok ' He has his (another person's) book.'
(*b*) When the above English possessives are used reflexively, i.e. referring back to the subject of the clause in which they occur, the following forms are used in Swedish :

	Singular	Plural
Common	Neuter	Both Genders
sin	*sitt*	*sina*

These forms are used without regard to the gender or number of the subject ; and **they can only be used to qualify the object of a verb or preposition.**

Examples :
Han har sin bok ' He has his (own) book.'
Hon har sin bok ' She has her (own) book.'
De har sitt hus ' They have their (own) house.'
De har sina böcker ' They have their (own) books.'
Han gick till sitt rum 'He went to his room.'

Note the following :
If in the sentence *Studenten har professorns bok* ' The student has the professor's book,' we substitute pronouns for the persons, it becomes :
Han har hans bok ' He has his (the professor's) book.'

Note also :
Hennes (not *sin*) *far är här* ' Her father is here.'
Deras (not *sina*) *barn är på landet* ' Their children are in the country.'

106. Possessive Pronouns

In Swedish the possessive adjectives serve also as possessive pronouns, i.e. there are no special forms corresponding to the English ' mine,' ' yours,' ' hers,' etc.

Huset är mitt. ' The house is mine.'
Boken är hans. ' The book is his.'
Huset är inte vårt, det är deras. ' The house isn't ours, it's theirs.'
Era böcker är här, våra är där. ' Your books are here ; ours are there.'

Note.—The English construction ' a friend of mine '

cannot be rendered directly in Swedish ; it is expressed in other ways :

> *Han är en god vän till mig.* 'He is a friend of mine.'

> *En av mina vänner.* ' A friend of mine.'

Swedish, on the other hand, has a peculiar use of the possessive adjective which cannot be imitated in English, e.g. :

> *Din slyngel* ! 'You rascal ! '

> *Din fuling* ! ' You fright (ugly thing) ! '

Vocabulary

elev c. (3) ' pupil '	*vän, vännen* c. (3) ' friend '
skola, c. (1) ' school '	*föräldrar,* pl. ' parents '
i skolan ' at school '	*hemma* ' at home '
vem ' who '	*också* ' also, too '
detta ' this '	*nära* ' near '

Exercise 5

Translate

(a) My book is in the cupboard. His books are on the table. Who has her cup ? Nils, where are our forks ? Your room is near mine. Her house is near the school. The table is mine. No, it is hers. Are the spoons yours ? Is this your knife ? They are her friends.

(b) Skåpet är mitt. Nej, det är hennes. Är din vän i skolan (=at school) ? Min är hemma. Jag har min bok och hans också. Är knivarna era ? Nej, de är deras. Är dina föräldrar här ? Nej, de är hemma. Är hans kopp på bordet ? Ja, och hennes också.

(c) Nils is a friend of mine. Is he at home ? No, he is at school. Is the house yours ? No, it is his. She has her (own) book. Yes, and he has his. The professor has the students' books. He has theirs.

(d) Deras barn är hemma. Våra är här. Professorns barn är inte här ; de är på landet. Detta är en av mina elever. Är eleverna i skolan ? Nej, de är hemma. Deras barn är här ; var är era ? De är också här.

CHAPTER VI

ADJECTIVES

107. There are two declensions of the adjective : (*a*) the Indefinite Declension, used when the adjective is preceded by the indefinite article or used in isolation before a noun ; (*b*) the Definite Declension, used when the adjective is preceded by the *definite article of the adjective* or other determinant, such as a demonstrative or possessive. When in English a noun is preceded by the definite article and an adjective, Swedish uses two articles, one, a special form *den*, *det* or *de*, placed in front of the adjective, the other the usual terminal article added to the noun. The former is called the definite article of the adjective.

(*a*) Indefinite Declension

Singular		Plural
Common	Neuter	Both Genders
grön 'green'	**grönt**	**gröna**

Examples :

> *En grön färg* ' a green colour '
>
> *Ett grönt blad* ' a green leaf '
>
> *Gröna färger* ' green colours '

There are three forms in the indefinite declension : (i) the uninflected form, used in the singular of the common gender, e.g. *grön* ; (ii) the neuter singular form, which takes the ending *-t*, e.g. *grönt* ; (iii) the plural form for both genders, which takes the ending *-a*, e.g. *gröna*.

In Swedish, as in Latin and French, the predicative as well as the attributive adjective is inflected ; it takes the indefinite forms, e.g. :

> *Färgen är grön* ' The colour is green '
>
> *Bladet är grönt* ' The leaf is green '
>
> *Färgerna är gröna* ' The colours are green '

67

(b) Definite Declension

This has one form, singular and plural, for both genders ;
it has the ending -*a* and is thus the same as the plural of
the Indefinite Declension, e.g. :

 Den gröna färgen[1] ' The green colour '

 Det gröna bladet ' The green leaf '

 De gröna färgerna ' The green colours '

Note.—The definite form is usually preceded by the
Definite Article of the Adjective : *den, det, de,* as above,
although the noun takes the terminal definite article.

108. Remarks on the Indefinite Neuter Form of the Adjective

As has been shown above, the neuter singular form of the
adjective is usually formed by adding -*t*, e.g. *grön-grönt.*
This rule is subject to certain variations.

(*a*) Adjectives that end in a stressed vowel add double -*t*
in the neuter, with consequent shortening of the vowel, e.g. :

blå [blo:]	' blue '	neuter :	*blått* [blɔt]; pl.	*blåa*
grå	' grey '		*grått*	*gråa*
rå	' raw '		*rått*	*råa*
fri [fri:]	' free '		*fritt* [frit]	*fria*
ny [ny:]	' new '		*nytt* [nyt]	*nya*
slö [slø:]	' blunt, dull '		*slött* [slœt]	*slöa*

(*b*) Adjectives that end in unstressed -*en* substitute -*t* for
the -*n* in the neuter and drop the -*e* in the plural, e.g. :

egen	' own '	neuter :	*eget* ;	pl. *egna*
mogen	' ripe '		*moget*	*mogna*
sorgsen	' mournful '		*sorgset*	*sorgsna*
trogen	' faithful '		*troget*	*trogna*

In the plural forms of the above words the -*g*- is pronounced as a stop-consonant through the influence of the
singular forms ; hence ['eˈ:gna], etc. (See § 49.*e*).

Note the irregular plural of the following word :

 liten ' little, small ' neuter : *litet* ; pl. **små**

---

[1] With words denoting males the old masculine termination -*e* is
sometimes used instead of -*a*, e.g. *den gode mannen, den blinde* ' the
blind man ' ; but the tendency is to introduce the -*a* ending more
and more.

(c) Adjectives that end in -t preceded by a consonant remain unchanged in the neuter, e.g. :

brant 'steep'	neuter : *brant* ;	pl. *branta*
fast 'firm'	*fast*	*fasta*
halt 'lame'	*halt*	*halta*
svart 'black'	*svart*	*svarta*
tyst 'silent'	*tyst*	*tysta*

(d) Monosyllabic adjectives that end in -t preceded by a long vowel double the -t and consequently shorten the vowel in the neuter, e.g. :

blöt	'wet, soft'	neuter : *blött* ;	pl. *blöta*
het	'hot'	*hett*	*heta*
slät	'smooth'	*slätt*	*släta*
söt	'sweet'	*sött*	*söta*
vit	'white'	*vitt*	*vita*
våt	'wet'	*vått*	*våta*

(e) Adjectives that end in -tt in the uninflected form remain unchanged in the neuter, e.g. :

lätt	'light (weight)'	neuter : *lätt* ;	pl. *lätta*
glatt	'smooth, glossy'	*glatt*	*glatta*
matt	'faint, weak'	*matt*	*matta*
trött	'tired'	*trött*	*trötta*

(f) Adjectives that end in -d preceded by a consonant substitute -t for the -d in the neuter, e.g. :

blind	'blind'	neuter : *blint* ;	pl. *blinda*
hård	'hard'	*hårt*	*hårda*
mild	'mild'	*milt*	*milda*
ond	'evil'	*ont*	*onda*
rund	'round'	*runt*	*runda*
vild	'wild'	*vilt*	*vilda*

(g) Adjectives that end in -d preceded by a vowel substitute -tt for the -d and consequently shorten the vowel in the neuter, e.g. :

bred	'broad'	neuter : *brett* ;	pl. *breda*
god	'good'	*gott*	*goda*
glad	'glad'	*glatt*	*glada*
röd	'red'	*rött*	*röda*
vid	'wide'	*vitt*	*vida*

(*h*) Adjectives that end in -*nn* drop one -*n* and add -*t* in the neuter, e.g. :

grann	'showy'	neuter :	*grant* ; pl.	*granna*
sann	'true'		*sant*	*sanna*
tunn	'thin'		*tunt*	*tunna*

(*i*) The adjectives *lat* 'lazy'; *rädd* 'frightened'; *höger* 'right'; *vänster* 'left' are not used in the neuter.

(*j*) The adjective *stackars* is invariable because it goes back to the genitive form of a noun (*stafkarl* 'beggar'), e.g. *den stackars lilla flickan* ' the poor little girl '; *stackars du* ! ' (you) poor thing ! '; *stackars föräldrar* ! ' I pity his (etc.) poor parents !' The word always implies pity; ' poor ' in the sense of ' indigent ' is *fattig*.

Vocabulary

gata, c. (1) ' street '	*ord*, n. (5) ' word '
märke, n. (4) ' mark '	*vin*, n. (5) ' wine '
lång ' long '	*väder*, n. (5) ' weather '
kall ' cold '	*varm* ' warm '

Exercise 6

Translate

(*a*) A little dog. A little child. Little children. A new white house. A red house. A blue bird. A blue mark. A wild beast (*djur*). The leaf is green. The girl is pretty (*söt*). The wine is sweet. The horse is tired. The dogs are faithful. Grey eyes. Hard bread. A long street. Is it true ? True words.

(*b*) Ett runt bord. Många röda och vita hus. En vild häst. Rått och kallt väder. Varmt och milt väder. En liten flicka. Vi har rött och vitt vin. Vinet är gott. Äpplena är mogna. Ett fritt land. Granna färger. En bred och lång gata. Hur brett är bordet ? Två meter. Golvet är hårt och glatt. Jag är varm. Är du varm ? God jul (*Christmas*) och gott nytt år.

CHAPTER VII

ADJECTIVES (Continued)

109. There are a few irregularities to be noted in the formation of the plural and the definite declension of the adjective.

(a) Adjectives ending in unstressed *-el, -en, -er* drop the *-e-* in the plural and in the definite form, e.g. :

ädel ' noble '	pl. and def. form: *ädla*
trogen ' faithful '	*trogna*
vacker ' fine, beautiful '	*vackra*

Compare also :

gammal ' old '	*gamla*

(b) The adjective *liten* ' little,' has the definite form *lilla*, and the plural form *små*, e.g. :

Indefinite
{ *en liten råtta* ' a little mouse '[1]
  ett litet lamm ' a little lamb '
  små råttor (lamm) ' little mice (lambs) '

Definite
{ *den lilla råttan* ' the little mouse '
  det lilla lammet ' the little lamb '
  de små råttorna (lammen) ' the little mice (lambs) '

110.   Ordspråk   Proverbs

*Små smulor äro också   Small crumbs are bread, too.
bröd.   (i.e. half a loaf, etc.).*

*Vackra visor äro aldrig   Beautiful songs are never
långa.   long (i.e. all good
                                things soon come to an
                                end).*

*Den rike[2] har många   The rich man has many
vänner.   friends.*

---

[1] *råtta* is more usual than *mus* ; it also means ' rat.'
[2] Cf. page 68, footnote.

111.   Remarks on the Use of the Definite and Indefinite Declensions

(*a*) The indefinite form of the adjective is used :

(i) after the indefinite adjectives *mången*[1] ' many a ' ; *någon* ' some, any ' ; *varje* ' each, every ' ; and *ingen* ' no, not any,' e.g. :

Mången skicklig arbetare.	Many a skilled worker.
Någon ny tidning.	Some new newspaper.
Varje duktig elev.	Every proficient pupil.
Ingen dödlig människa.	No mortal man.

(ii) After *vilken* and *sådan* in exclamations, e.g. :

Vilken vacker dag !	What a fine day !
En sådan tokig karl [kɑ:r]!	What a mad (wild) fellow !

(*b*) The definite form of the adjective is used :

(i) After a genitival expression or a possessive adjective, e.g. :

Pojkens gamla kostym.	The boy's old suit.
Hans nya kostym.	His new suit.
Min nya adress.	My new address.

Exception.—The adjective *egen* own, is used in the indefinite form after a genitival expression or a possessive adjective, e.g. :

Familjens egen lilla villa.	The family's own little villa.
Vårt eget lilla hus.	Our own little house.

(ii) After personal pronouns in exclamations, e.g. :

Du saliga land !	Thou blessed country !
Ack, jag eländiga människa !	Oh, what a wretched man am I !

Note.—In *Jag fattig syndig människa* ' I (a) poor sinful man ' (in the General Confession), the indefinite form is used because the phrase is not an exclamation, but an apposition.

[1] This word is more usual in the plural : *många*.

(iii) After determinative or demonstrative adjectives, e.g. :

Det höga torn, som du ser i fjärran.	The high tower you (can) see in the distance.
Detta höga torn (det där höga tornet).	That high tower.

(iv) In forms of address, e.g. :

Kära du !	My dear !
Bästa Fru Olsson !	Dear Mrs. Olsson.

(v) When the adjective qualifies a following proper noun, e.g. :

Svarta Maria.	(The) Black Maria.
Hesa Fredrik.	Hoarse Frederick (nickname for the Swedish air-raid siren).

(vi) After the **indefinite** article when the adjective is an ordinal or its equivalent, e.g. :

en första början.	a first beginning.
ett andra pris.	a second prize.
en sista hälsning.	a last greeting.

(*c*) The definite article of the adjective is often omitted, usually for the sake of brevity :

(i) In topographical appellations, headings, etc., e.g. :

Svarta havet.	The Black Sea.
Norra ishavet.	The Arctic Ocean.
Södra Hamngatan.	South Harbour Street.
Svenska Dagbladet.	The Swedish Daily News.
Nordiska kompaniet.	The Nordic Company (largest emporium in Sweden, familiarly known as ' N.K. ' ['ɛ'ŋkoː]).

(ii) With a number of adjectives denoting order or quantity, e.g.:

första bandet.	volume I.
sista vagnen.	the last coach.
hela tiden.	the whole time.
halva stan (=*staden*).	half the town.

(*d*) Sometimes both the definite article of the adjective and the terminal article of the noun are omitted, e.g.: *samma dag* '(on) the same day'; *närslutna brev* 'the enclosed letter'; *nästa vecka* 'next week' (but note: *förra veckan* 'last week').

Comparison of Adjectives

112. Most Swedish adjectives form the comparative by adding *-are* and the superlative by adding *-ast* to the uninflected form of the positive.[1]

Examples:

Positive	Comparative	Superlative
rik 'rich'	*rikare* 'richer'	*rikast* 'richest'
dum 'stupid'	*dummare* 'more stupid'	*dummast* 'most stupid'
ny 'new'	*nyare* 'newer'	*nyast* 'newest'

113. **Irregularities**

(*a*) Adjectives ending in unstressed *-el*, *-en*, *-er* drop the *-e* of this ending in the comparative and superlative, e.g.:

ädel 'noble'	*ädlare*	*ädlast*
trogen 'faithful'	*trognare*	*trognast*
säker 'sure, certain'	*säkrare*	*säkrast*

(*b*) Adjectives ending in unstressed *-a* drop the *-a* in the comparative and superlative, e.g.:

ringa 'humble'	*ringare*	*ringast*

[1] On the tones see § 70 (*f*).

(c) Some adjectives take the endings *-re* and *-st* in the comparative and superlative,[1] with mutation of the root vowel (*o* > *ö*, *u* > *y*, *å* > *ä*), e.g. :

grov ' coarse '	*grövre*	*grövst*
hög ' high, tall '	*högre*	*högst* [hœkst]
stor ' big, great '	*större*	*störst*
ung ' young '	*yngre*	*yngst*
tung ' heavy '	*tyngre*	*tyngst*
lång ' long '	*längre*	*längst*
trång 'narrow, confined'	*trängre*	*trängst*
låg ' low '	*lägre*	*lägst* [lɛ:kst]

There are also two defective adjectives in this category :

få ' few '	*färre*	—
—	*smärre* ' minor '	—

(d) The following adjectives form their comparative and superlative from an entirely different stem :

god (or *bra*[2]) ' good '	*bättre*	*bäst* (def. form : *bästa*)
dålig ' bad '	*sämre*	*sämst* (def. form: *sämsta*)
ond ' bad, evil '	*värre*	*värst* (def. form : *värsta*)
gammal ' old '	*äldre*	*äldst* (def. form : *äldsta*)
liten ' little '	*mindre*	*minst* (def. form : *minsta*)
många, pl. ' many '	*flera* (or *fler*)	de *flesta*
mycken ' much '	*mera* (or *mer*)	*mest* (def. form : *mesta*)

Note.—The adjective *god* has *godare*, *godast* when it applies to food, i.e. with the meaning ' tasty.'

The adjective *mycken* is mainly used in the neut. sing. form (with substantival force), no matter what the gender or number of the following noun may be, e.g.: *mycket* ['my`kkə] *fisk* ' much (a lot of) fish.'

(e) Some adjectives form their comparative and superlative by using *mera* ' more,' and *mest* ' most,' instead of

---

[1] On the tones see § 69 (d).

[2] The adjective *bra* is indeclinable ; it is also used as an adverb = well.

endings ; chief of these are : those that end in *-ad* and *-isk*, and all present and past participles used as adjectives, e.g. :

högsinnad ' high-minded '	*mer(a) högsinnad*	*mest högsinnad*
kritisk ' critical '	*mer(a) kritisk*	*mest kritisk*
närande ' nourishing '	*mer(a) närande*	*mest närande*

(*f*) Some adjectives have comparative and superlative forms with no corresponding form in the positive, e.g. :

bakre ' rear '	*bakerst* ' rearmost '
bortre ' further '	*borterst* ' furthermost '
främre ' front '	*främst* ' foremost '
inre ' inner '	*innerst* ' innermost '
nedre ' lower '	*nederst* ' lowest '
yttre ' outer '	*ytterst* ' outermost '
övre ' upper '	*överst* ' uppermost '

114. Note the following expressions of comparison :

*Han är **lika** lång **som** jag.*	He is as tall as I.
*Han är inte **så** lång **som** jag.*	He is not as tall as I.
*Han är längre **än** jag.*	He is taller than I.
***Ju** längre **dess** bättre.*	The longer the better.

The comparative is sometimes used in Swedish where *rather+positive* is used in English, e.g. *en längre promenad* ' a rather long walk ' ; *ett större företag* ' a rather big undertaking.' In the same way Swedish uses *bättre* ironically to convey a sense of disparagement where English uses ' glorified,' e.g. :

Han kallar det ett hotell, men det är egentligen bara ett slags bättre pensionat.	He calls it an hotel ; but it is really only a sort of glorified boarding-house.

Vocabulary

Ryssland ' Russia '
Sverige ['svæ'rjə] ' Sweden '
Danmark ' Denmark '
Finland ' Finland '
Island ' Iceland '
Norge ['nɔ'rjə] ' Norway '
engelsk ' English '
svensk ' Swedish '
Göteborg [jøtə'bɔrj] ' Gothenburg '
Vänern ' (Lake) Väner '

bly, n. (4) ' lead '
guld, n. (5) ' gold '
järn, n. (5) ' iron '
hamn, c. (2) ' port, harbour '
klimat [kli'mɑ:t], n. (5) ' climate '
luft, c. ' air '
sommar, c. (2) ' summer '
vinter, c. (2) ' winter '
precis [prə'si:s] ' exactly '

kall ' cold '	*mörk* ' dark '	*ren* ' pure '
torr ' dry '	*ännu* ' still '	*som* ' like, as '
men ' but '	*emellertid* ' however '	

Exercise 7

Translate

(*a*) Sverige är ett stort land ; men det är inte så stort som Ryssland. Staden Göteborg är mindre än Stockholm ; men Göteborgs hamn är större än Stockholms (*that of St.*). Sverige har ett kallt klimat ; vintertemperaturen är mycket lägre i Sverige än i England. Det engelska klimatet är emellertid inte så torrt som det svenska ; luften är klarare och renare i Sverige. Sverige har många stora sjöar : störst är Vänern.

Note.—All the names of countries, towns and islands in the following exercise are neuter.

(*b*) Russia is much larger than Sweden. Norway[1] is exactly as large as Finland. The days are longer in summer (*på sommaren*) than in winter. Gold is heavier than iron ; but lead is heaviest. Iceland is smaller than Norway ; but Denmark is still smaller. The winter is darker in Sweden. Sweden has many islands ; (the) largest is Gotland. Gotland is larger than Öland. Malmö is not so big as Gothenburg.

[1] i.e. including Spitzbergen.

CHAPTER VIII
ADJECTIVES (Continued)
Declension of the Comparative and Superlative
I. The Comparative

115. The comparative form of the adjective is indeclinable.

Examples :

Indefinite Declension

en grönare färg	a greener colour
ett grönare blad	a greener leaf
grönare färger	greener colours

Definite Declension

den grönare färgen	the greener colour
det grönare bladet	the greener leaf
de grönare färgerna	the greener colours

II. The Superlative
Indefinite Declension

116. The indefinite form of the superlative (which can only be used predicatively) ends in *-ast* (or *-st*) irrespective of gender or number, e.g. :

färgen är grönast	the colour is greenest
bladet är grönast	the leaf is greenest
färgerna är grönast	the colours are greenest

Definite Declension

117. According as the superlative ends in *-ast* or *-st* so the termination is differentiated in the definite form ; the former takes -e and the latter takes -a irrespective of gender or number, e.g. :

den grönaste färgen	the greenest colour
det grönaste bladet	the greenest leaf
de grönaste färgerna	the greenest colours
den största sjön	the largest lake
det största landet	the largest country
de största sjöarna	the largest lakes

118. When used **predicatively** (i.e. in the predicate of a sentence) the superlative may usually be declined according to the definite or indefinite declension, e.g. :

Min dotter är yngst.	My daughter is youngest.
Min dotter är den yngsta.	My daughter is the youngest (one).

But when the comparison refers to different parts of the same thing, the indefinite form must be used, e.g. :

Här är dimman tätast.	Here the fog is thickest.

When the superlative is followed by a qualifying clause or phrase, the definite form must be used, e.g. :

Att gå på bio är det roligaste, jag vet.	Going to the pictures is the jolliest (thing) I know (of).
Den sjön är den största i Sverige.	That lake is the largest in Sweden.

The word *som* is sometimes placed before a superlative used predicatively :

Då denna författare är som bäst.	When this author is at his best.

119. When used **attributively** (i.e. qualifying a noun) the superlative is declined according to the definite declension and is usually preceded by the definite article of the adjective (*den, det, de*), e.g. : *den varmaste dagen* ' the hottest day ' ; *det högsta trädet* ' the highest tree ' ; *de djupaste sjöarna* ' the deepest lakes.'

The definite article is, however, omitted in a number of set phrases, e.g. :

I bästa (värsta) fall.	At best (the worst).
Efter bästa förmåga.	To the best of one's ability.
Med största nöje.	With the greatest of pleasure.
Med varmaste hälsningar.	With warmest greetings.

120. **Ordspråk**	**Proverbs**
Borta (är) bra; men hemma (är) bäst.	Away is good, but at home is best (i.e. East or west, home's best).
Bättre sent än aldrig.	Better late than never.
Blodet är tjockare än vattnet.	Blood is thicker than water.
I det lugnaste vattnet gå de största fiskarna.	The biggest fish move in the calmest water (i.e. Still waters run deep).

Genitive of Adjectives

121. The adjective takes a genitival -*s* ending in the following cases :

(*a*) When it follows the noun it qualifies, e.g. :

Karl den stores liv.	The life of Charles the Great.

(*b*) When it is used as a noun, e.g. :

De gamlas tröst.	The consolation of the aged.
Den enes död den andres bröd.	One man's death, the other's bread (i.e. One man's meat is another man's poison).

Relics of old case-endings

122. As with the noun, so also with the adjective some old case-endings have been preserved in a few set phrases.

Examples :

(*a*) The phrases *på ljusan dag* 'in broad daylight'; *i rättan tid* ' at the right time ' ; *i ljusan låga* ' all ablaze,' show relics of an old masculine singular accusative -*an* ending.

(*b*) The phrases *håll till godo* ! ' you can keep this for yourself, help yourself ' ; *i godo* ' amicably ' ; *i allo* ' in all respects ' ; *till fullo* ' in full, fully,' show relics of an old neuter singular dative ending of the indefinite declension.

(c) The proverb *Lyckan står dem djärvom bi* 'Fortune favours the brave,' and the expression *Det är icke allom givet* ' it is not everybody's lot,' illustrate the old dative plural ending.

(d) The phrase *i sinom tid* ' duly, in due season,' shows an old masculine singular dative ending of the possessive adjective.

123. The past tenses of *ha* and *vara* are as follows :

(a) *jag, du, ni, han* **hade**   I, etc., had

     vi, ni, de **hade**   we, etc., had

(b) *jag, du, ni, han* **var**   I, etc., was

     vi, ni, de **voro**   we, etc., were

Note.—In the spoken language the form **var** is used throughout ; in the written language the plural was formerly **voro,** but nowadays **var** is used in literature generally.

124.   Numerals

fyrtio [ˈføˈʈi]	.. 40	*åttio* [ˈɔˈʈʈi] ..	..	80
femtio [ˈfɛˋmti]	.. 50	*nittio* [ˈniˋʈʈi] ..	..	90
sextio [ˈsɛˋksti]	.. 60	*(ett) hundra* [ˈhøˈndra]		100
sjuttio [ˈsøˋʈʈi]	.. 70	*(ett) hundraen (-ett)*	..	101
fyrtioen (-ett)	.. 41	*(ett) hundraåttiofem*	..	185
sjuttiosju [ˈsøˈʈʈiˋsu]..	.. 77	*fem hundra* ..	..	500
	tusen ..	..	1,000	

The words *hundra* and *tusen* are treated as neuter nouns (*ett hundra, ett tusen*) ; but the article is often omitted and they are rarely followed by *och,* whereas ' a hundred ' and 'a thousand' are followed by 'and'in English. Long numerals may be written as one continuous word or as separate words, except that numerals consisting of two digits are always written as one word. Thus 1467 is written either as *ett tusen fyra hundra sextiosju* or as *etttusenfyrahundrasextiosju.* If it represents a date, the first two figures are written as *fjortonhundra.*

125. Write in full, and pronounce: 17, 18, 22, 43, 57, 65, 78, 40, 50, 88, 179, 589, 972.

126.   The Names of the Months

(*Månadernas namn*)

januari [janu'ɑ′ːri]	*juli* ['ju′ːli]
februari [fɛbru'ɑ′ːri]	*augusti* [au'ge′sti]
mars [maʂ]	*september* [sɛp'tɛ′mbər]
april [a'pril]	*oktober* [ɔk'to′bər]
maj [maj]	*november* [nɔ'vɛ′mbər]
juni ['ju′ːni]	*december* [də'sɛ′mbər]

Vocabulary

berg, n. (5) ' mountain '
bror[1], c. (5) ' brother '
cykel, c. (2) ' bicycle '
papper, n. (5) ' paper '
paraply, n. (5) ' umbrella '
syster, c. (2) ' sister '
sida, c. (1) ' side, page '
stad[2], c. (3) ' town '
kött, n. (5) ' meat '
ägg, n. (5) ' egg '
år, n. (5) ' year '
månad, c. (3) ' month '
vecka, c. (1) ' week '
dag, c. (2) ' day '

dygn, n. (5) ' a day and night '
timme[3], c. (2) ' hour '
minut, c. (3) ' minute '
sekund, c. (3) ' second '
på våren ' in spring '
värld [væːɖ], c. (2) 'world'
mycket mera ' much more'
många fler ' many more '
fattig ' poor '
ful ' ugly '
tjock ' thick'
tunn ' thin '
dyr ' dear '

Exercise 8
Translate

(*a*) Min bror är äldre än min syster. Min far är den äldsta mannen i vår stad. Bröd är närande. Kött är mera närande. Ägg är mest närande. Mount Everest är det högsta berget i världen. Den största svenska sjön är Vänern. England har många fler städer än Sverige. Hur många

---

[1] This is the contracted and more usual form of *broder* (see § 91*f*).
[2] The definite singular *staden* is often contracted to *stan*.
[3] The singular *timma* also occurs ; plural always *timmar*.

sidor är det (=*are there*) i hans bok ? Tvåhundratjugofem.
Ett år har trehundrasextiofem dagar.   En månad är fyra
veckor. En vecka är sju dagar. Ett dygn är en dag och en
natt. Ett dygn är tjugofyra timmar. En timme är sextio
minuter.   En minut är sextio sekunder.

(*b*) I have a larger house than you. My book is newer
than yours. Your bicycle is dearer than mine. The leaves
are greenest in spring. What an ugly house ! It is the
ugliest house in the town. Storgatan is the longest street in
our town. Her book is thicker than his. His has 200 pages,
but hers has more than 300. Yes, but the paper is much
thinner. He had much more paper than I. The more
money (pl.) you have, the better. My eldest brother is as
tall (=*lång*) as my father. My mother was poorer than her
sister. Here is the newest umbrella in the house. Few
people (=*människor*) ; fewer children.

CHAPTER IX

THE VERB—AUXILIARIES

127. In most Swedish verbs the infinitive ends in *-a*,
e.g. : *kalla* ' to call ' ; *binda* ' to bind ' ; but a few, which
are monosyllabic and end in a vowel, have no final *-a*, e.g. :
bo ' to dwell ' ; *sy* ' to sew.'

Sometimes the infinitive is preceded by *att*, which corresponds to the English ' to.' As in English, it is omitted after
auxiliary verbs, e.g. :

Jag skall skriva snart.   I shall write soon.

Contrast :
Jag lovar att skicka ett   I promise to send a telegram.
telegram.

128. The present tense of nearly all Swedish verbs ends
in *-r*, e.g. : *jag, du, ni, han, hon, den, det, vi, ni, de*
     kallar ' call,' *binder* ' bind,' *bor* ' live,' *syr* ' sew'.

The principal exceptions are :
(*a*) the auxiliary verbs, e.g. :
          jag ' etc.', *skall, vill, kan, måste.*

(*b*) Passive forms and deponent verbs (see § 192), which
have the termination *-s*, e.g. :
     jag räddas ' I am saved '.   *jag hoppas* ' I hope '.

129. Swedish has no progressive or continuous form.
Thus *jag kallar* can be translated ' I call ' or ' I am calling,
according to the context. If it is necessary to emphasize the
continuous nature of an action, this is done by using a
periphrase with *jag håller på att* ' I am engaged in, keep on.'
Thus ' I am calling ' is either expressed by the simple verb
jag kallar or, more emphatically, by *jag håller på att kalla.*

130. Swedish has no equivalent of the English periphrastic constructions with ' do ' which are used in the
interrogative and negative forms of verbs :

Sjunger du ?   Do you sing ?
Sjunger Herr Petersson ?   Do you sing, Mr. Petersson ?
Nej, jag sjunger inte.   No, I don't sing.

Simple and Compound Tenses

131. In Swedish, as in English, some tenses can be expressed by a single word, e.g. : *jag går* ' I go '; others have to be built up by a combination of some part of the verb with an auxiliary. Thus to form the future tense English makes use of the auxiliary verbs ' shall ' and ' will ' together with the infinitive of the verb ; similarly Swedish forms the future by using the auxiliary *skall* :

Jag skall gå ' I shall go.'

The Supine and Past Participle

132. Another compound tense is the Perfect. In English this is formed by using the past participle of the verb together with the auxiliary verb ' have ' (and never with the verb ' to be,' as in French and German : *je suis venu, ich bin gekommen*).

Swedish, like English, always forms the perfect tense with the auxiliary ' to have '; but it combines it with a **special form of the past participle,** called the **Supine,** which is only used for this purpose. The past participle proper is only used as an adjective.

In the English ' I have fallen ' the past participle fulfils a verbal function ; in ' a fallen king ' it is adjectival. Swedish has separate forms :

*Jag har fall**it**.*   (Supine)

*En fall**en** kung.* (Past Participle)

Compare also :

*Vi har älska**t** vår kung.*　　We have loved our king.

*En älska**d** kung.*　　A beloved king.

The termination of the Supine is the principal distinguishing feature in the four Conjugations of Swedish verbs.

Auxiliary Verbs

133. The present and past forms of the verbs *ha* and *vara* have already been given; the following are the complete forms of these verbs:

(a) *att ha* 'to have'

Present	Past
Sing. *jag* etc. **har** 'I have'	*jag* etc. **hade** 'I had'
Plur. *vi* etc. **har** (*ha*[1])	*vi* etc. **hade**

Present Perfect	Past Perfect
jag **har haft** 'I have had'	*jag* **hade haft** 'I had had'

Future	Future in the Past[2]
Sing. *jag* **skall ha** 'I shall have'	*jag* **skulle ha** 'I should have'
Plur. *vi* **skall** (*skola*) **ha** 'we shall have'	*vi* **skulle ha** 'we should have'

Imperative	Present Participle	Supine	Past Participle
ha 'have'	**havande** 'having'	**haft** 'had'	**havd** 'had'

(b) *att vara* 'to be'.

Present	Past
Sing. *jag* **är** 'I am'	*jag* **var** 'I was'
Plur. *vi* **är** (*äro*) 'we are'	*vi* **var** (*voro*) 'we were'

Present Perfect	Past Perfect
jag **har varit** 'I have been'	*jag* **hade varit** 'I had been'

Future	Future in the Past
jag **skall vara** 'I shall be'	*jag* **skulle vara** 'I should be'

Imperative	Present Participle	Supine
var 'be'	**varande** 'being'	**varit** 'been'

[1] Forms given in brackets are those used in the written language (high style); but the singular forms of all verbs are now commonly used for the plural in good everyday prose, and always in the spoken language (see § 73 e). Students should always use the colloquial forms but note the bracketed forms, as they will encounter them in reading.

[2] This is equivalent to the Conditional Mood.

Subjunctive

Present	Past
jag **vare** ' I be '	*jag* **vore** ' I were '
vi **vare** ' we be '	*vi* **vore** ' we were '

Other Auxiliary Verbs

Present	Past
(c) *jag* **skall** ' I shall '	*jag* **skulle** ' I should '
vi **skall** (*skola*) ' we shall '	*vi* **skulle** ' we should '

Infinitive	Supine
att skola ' to be obliged '	**skolat**

Present	Past
(d) *jag* **vill** ' I will, want to '	*jag* **ville** ' I would '
vi **vill** (*vilja*) ' we will '	*vi* **ville** ' we would '

Infinitive	Supine
att vilja ' to be willing, want '	**velat**

Present	Past
(e) *jag* **kan** ' I can '	*jag* **kunde** ' I could '
vi **kan** (*kunna*) ' we can '	*vi* **kunde** ' we could '

Infinitive	Supine
att kunna ' to be able '	**kunnat**

Present	Past
(f) *jag* **måste** ' I must '	*jag* **måste** ' I had to '
vi **måste** ' we must '	*vi* **måste** ' we had to '

Present	Past
(g) *jag* **må** ' I may '	*jag* **måtte** ' I might '
vi **må** ' we may '	*vi* **måtte** ' we might '

Note.—Where parts of the above verbs are omitted, this is an indication that they are not used.

The Verb *att bli (bliva)*

134. This verb corresponds closely in usage and meaning to the German *werden*. It functions partly as an auxiliary verb, partly as an independent verb used with nouns and adjectives with the meaning ' to become '.

Present	Past
jag **blir** ' I become '	*jag* **blev** ' I became '
vi **blir** (*bliva, bli*) ' we become '	*vi* **blev** (*blevo*) ' we became '

Present Perfect	Past Perfect
jag **har blivit** ' I have become '	*jag* **hade blivit** ' I had become '

Future	Future in the Past
jag **skall bli** ' I shall become '	*jag* **skulle bli** ' I should become '

Imperative	Present Participle	Supine
bli (*bliv*) ' become '	**blivande** ' becoming '[1]	**blivit**

Examples of **bli** with the meaning ' become ' :

Han blir gammal.	He is becoming (i.e. growing) old.
Han blev soldat.	He became a soldier.
Det blev ingenting av.	Nothing came of it (it didn't come off).

By a slight change of meaning, **bli** has also developed the sense of ' is going to happen ' or transition from one state to another, e.g.:

Det blir snart jul.	It will soon be Christmas.
Det skall bli skönt att sitta vid brasan.	It will be nice to sit by the fire.

As an auxiliary **bli** is used with the past participle of verbs to form their Passive Voice, e.g.:

Han blev sårad i kriget.	He was wounded in the war.
Jag tror att han blir vald.	I think he will be elected.

---

[1] *blivande* is used as a pure adjective with the meaning ' intended, future, expectant,' e.g. *min blivande svärson* ' my future son-in-law,' *blivande mödrar* ' expectant mothers'.

It is especially important to distinguish between the use of *vara* and *bli* with adjectives ; the former denotes a **state,** the latter **change of state.** Compare :

Han var kär i henne.	He was in love with her.
Han blev kär i henne.	He fell in love with her.

Nouns Denoting Kinship

135. The Swedish vocabulary possesses a considerable number of words expressing family relationships (*släktskap*), different words being used according to whether the person referred to is a relative (*släkting*) on the father's side (*på fädernet*) or the mother's side (*på mödernet*). Thus the grandparents on the male side (*farföräldrar*) are called *farfar* ' father's father ' and *farmor* ' father's mother,' whilst the *morföräldrar* consist of *morfar* and *mormor*. Similarly an uncle is either *farbror* ' father's brother ' or *morbror* ' mother's brother,' and an aunt is either *faster* or *moster*. A nephew is either *brorson* or *systerson*, and a niece is either *brorsdotter* or *systerdotter*. On the other hand there is only one word for cousin, viz. *kusin* (male or female). A collective word for ' brothers and sisters ' is *syskon* (neut. pl.). For ' grandchildren ' (*barnbarn*) there are the words *sonson, dotterson, sondotter* and *dotterdotter*.

If a man is married (*gift*), his parents-in-law (*svärföräldrar*) are called *svärfar* and *svärmor*, and he is their *svärson* or *måg* ; his brother-in-law is called *svåger* and his sister-in-law is called *svägerska*.

Beside the words *faster* and *moster* for ' aunt ' there is also the word *tant*. This does not indicate kinship but is used by young people as an affectionate form of address for a lady with whom they are on familiar terms. The corresponding masculine form is *farbror* ; but this can also denote true kinship (see above). Children when addressed by, or addressing strangers, sometimes use the word *farbror* or *tant* (in the third person), this having a more friendly ring than *min herre* or *damen*, used by adults.

Vocabulary

brev, n. (5) ' letter '	*rock*, c. (2) ' coat '
knapp, c. (2) ' button '	*sjuk* ' sick, ill '
vad ' what ? '	*sjukhus*, n. (5) ' hospital '
var ' where ? '	*till* ' to '
Fru ' Mrs. '	*Fröken* ' Miss '

Exercise 9

Translate

(*a*) Fru Afzelius är en gammal god vän till oss. Jag kallar henne " tant." Moster Greta har många syskon ; hon bor här i stan.[1] Jag måste skriva ett brev till mormor ; hon är sjuk. Min syster skall sy i en knapp i min nya rock. Deras föräldrar är inte hemma. Jag måste vara hemma snart. Fröken Norén är hennes faster ; hon bor i det stora huset på landet. Farfar har fallit i (=*on*) trappan ; han är mycket sjuk. Min svåger blev sårad i kriget ; han blev opererad på (=*at*) sjukhuset. Min kusin Ingrid är i skolan nu ; men hon skall bli lärarinna en dag. Vad vill ni ha ? Jag vill ha sex bra svenska böcker. Taken på husen i vår stad är röda.

(*b*) I shall write a letter to my sister-in-law soon. Karl has become (a) grandfather. Does your sister live in London ? Do your brothers and sisters live in London too ? No, they live in the country. What does he want (=*vill han ha*) ? Where can I send a telegram ? The hospital has one hundred and ninety-three beds. February is a cold month. It is winter ; it is very cold. The summer is much warmer in Sweden. I cannot go[2] to the town now ; I haven't time. But I shall go soon. The year 1945. Twelve small Swedish towns. Do you sing, Miss Andersson ? No, not much.

---

[1] See page 82, footnote 2.
[2] Here ' go ' is equivalent to ' walk ' ; use *gå*.

CHAPTER X

CONJUGATION OF VERBS

136. So far we have only dealt with auxiliary verbs—those used to help other verbs form their various tenses and moods. Swedish verbs with full meaning, i.e. those that can stand independently and make sense, are classified as Strong or Weak according to the way in which their past tense is formed. If the root vowel is changed but no consonantal (dental) ending added, the verb is strong, e.g. :

Infinitive	Past Tense
springa	*sprang*

like the English ' spring, sprang.' If on the other hand the past tense is formed by adding *-ade*, *-te* or *-dde* to the root, the verb is weak, e.g. :

> *kalla* ' to call ' *kallade*
>
> *köpa* ' to buy ' *köpte*
>
> *bo* ' to dwell ' *bodde*

In English practically all weak verbs form their past tense by adding *-ed* (e.g. call—called) ; but as the Swedish weak verbs have a greater variety of endings, it is necessary to subdivide them. They constitute the first three conjugations, distinguished according to the ending of the past tense as given above ; the fourth conjugation comprises the strong verbs.

The vast majority of Swedish verbs belong to the First Conjugation. It includes all verbs of foreign origin ending in *-era*, e.g. *reagera* ' to react '; *korrigera* ' to correct '; *studera* ' to study '; *telegrafera* ' to telegraph.'[1] Apart from this ending there is no means of telling from the infinitive of a verb which conjugation it belongs to ; parts of verbs have to be learnt individually, like the plural forms of nouns. But if the student can recognise a cognate German or English verb which is strong, the chances are

[1] See § 66.*a* on stress.

that the Swedish verb is strong too, i.e. it belongs to the Fourth Conjugation.[1] Thus compare:

German	Swedish
binden—band—gebunden	*binda—band—bunden*
schreiben—schrieb—geschrieben	*skriva—skrev—skriven*
scheren—schor—geschoren	*skära—skar—skuren*
fahren—fuhr—gefahren	*fara—for—faren*

English	Swedish
ride—rode—ridden	*rida—red—riden*
take—took—taken	*ta(ga)—tog—tagen*

In this book the conjugation of verbs will be indicated where necessary by a small Roman figure, thus: *köpa*[II]. Lists of verbs will be a regular feature of several of the ensuing chapters. They should be carefully memorized and constantly revised.

First Conjugation

137. Past tense ends in **-ade**.

Supine ends in **-at.**

Example:

Present	Past
jag kallar[2] ' I call '	*jag kallade* ' I called '
Present Perfect	Past Perfect
jag har kallat ' I have called '	*jag hade kallat* ' I had called '
Future	Future in the Past
jag skall kalla ' I shall call '	*jag skulle kalla* ' I should call '

Imperative	.. ..	**kalla** ' call '
Infinitive	.. ..	**att kalla** ' to call '
Present Participle	..	**kallande** ' calling '
Supine ..	.. ..	(*jag har*) **kallat** ' called '
Past Participle	..	**kallad** ' called '

[1] This must not be regarded as an invariable rule, however.
[2] Since the verb has the same form for all persons, singular and plural, only the first person singular is given. In elevated literary style the present plural occasionally has the form of the infinitive, i.e. drops the *-r* termination, but this usage is on the wane.

Note.—Negative and interrogative forms are constructed as shown in § 130, i.e. *jag kallar inte*[1] ' I do not call '; *kallar jag* ? ' do I call (am I calling) ? ' ; *kallade jag inte* ? ' did I not call ? ' etc.

138. The following verbs belong to the First Conjugation:

bada ' bath(e) '	*rädda* ' save '
borsta ['bɔ`ʂʈa] ' brush '	*skaffa* ' obtain '
cykla ' cycle '	*skicka* ' send '
fråga ' ask (question) '	*stanna* (trans. and intrans.)
hoppa ' jump '	' stay, stop '
jaga ' chase, hunt '	*tala* ' speak, talk '
kasta ' throw, cast '	*telegrafera* ' telegraph '
klara ' manage '	*titta* ' look, peep '
kosta ['kɔ`sta] ' cost '	*tvätta* ' wash '
kämpa ' fight '	*vakna* ' awake '
laga ' prepare (food), mend '	*våga* ' dare, venture '
plocka ' pluck, pick '	*vänta* ' await, expect '
plåga ' bother, pester, torture '	*älska* ' love '
	önska ' wish '

139.   Ordinal Numbers

(den, det) första ['fœ`ʂʈa]	1 : *sta*	' first '
andra	2 : *dra*	' second '
tredje ['tre`:dje]	3 : *dje*	' third '
fjärde ['fjæ`:de]	4 : *de*	' fourth '
femte	5 : *te*	' fifth '
sjätte ['ʂɛ`tte]	6 : *te*	' sixth '
sjunde ['ʂø`nde]	7 : *de*	' seventh '
åttonde ['ɔ`ttonde]	8 : *de*	' eighth '
nionde	9 : *de*	' ninth '
tionde	10 : *de*	' tenth '
elfte	11 : *te*	' eleventh '
tolfte	12 : *te*	' twelfth '
trettonde	13 : *de*	' thirteenth '
adertonde	18 : *de*	' eighteenth '
tjugonde	20 : *de*	' twentieth '

[1] *icke* in literature.

tjugoförsta	21 : *sta*	' twenty-first '
tjugonionde	29 : *de*	' twenty-ninth '
trettionde	30 : *de*	' thirtieth '
trettioförsta	31 : *sta*	' thirty-first '

The ordinal numerals are declined like adjectives in the definite declension, but always end in -*e*, except *första* and *andra*. In writing dates the endings of the numeral are not written, nor is any abbreviation mark placed after it, e.g. : *den 6 juli* (which is read as : *den sjätte juli*). In other contexts the abbreviation is written, e.g. : 5:*te sidan* ' fifth page ' ; 3:*dje deklinationen* ' third declension.'

Note the following expressions :

För det första, andra, tredje	Firstly, secondly, thirdly
Först och främst	First and foremost
Först nu	Not until now
Till sist	Lastly

140.   The Days of the Week
                                (Veckodagarna)

söndag ['sø'nda:g]	*onsdag* ['o'nsda:g]
måndag ['mɔ'nda:g]	*torsdag* ['to'sda:g]
tisdag ['ti'sda:g]	*fredag* ['fre':da:g]

                    lördag ['lø':da:g]

Note.—When the names of the days of the week occur in an unemphatic position, the final *g* is not pronounced and the *a* is shortened, e.g. ['sø'nda].

| *sön- och helgdagar* | Sundays and public holidays |
| *vardagar* | weekdays |

                The Reflexive Pronoun : *Sig*

141. Special attention should be paid to the reflexive pronoun *sig*, as it has no equivalent in English (but cf. German *sich*, French *se*). It always refers back to the subject of the clause in which it occurs and is only used when the subject is in the third person (singular or plural). Thus it usually corresponds to the English ' himself, herself, itself, themselves.' In the first and second persons the

ordinary object forms of the personal pronoun (*mig, dig, er; oss, er*) serve as reflexive pronouns.

Jag tvättar mig.	I wash myself.
Du tvättar dig.	You wash yourself.
Ni tvättar er.	You wash yourself.
Han tvättar sig.	He washes himself.
Hon tvättar sig.	She washes herself.
Barnet tvättar sig.	The child washes itself.
Vi tvättar oss.	We wash ourselves.
Ni tvättar er.	You wash yourselves.
De tvättar sig.	They wash themselves.

Infinitive : *att tvätta sig* ' to wash oneself.'

Vocabulary

varför ' why '
kontor, n. (5) ' office '
hjälte ['jɛˋltə], c. (2) 'hero'
fosterland, n. (5) ' father-
land '
soldat, c. (3) ' soldier '
lat [lɑːt] ' lazy '
liv, n. (5) ' life '
årstid, c. (3) ' season '
födelse, c. (3) ' birth '
jul, c. (2) ' Christmas '
julafton, c. (2) ' Christmas
Eve '

kaffe ['kaˋffə], n.
' coffee '
kilo ['kiˊːlo], n. (4)
' kilogram '
mat, c. ' food '
svamp[1], c. ' mushrooms '
tåg, n. (5) ' train '
i går ' yesterday '
i dag ' to-day '
i kväll ' this evening '
i morgon ['mɔˋrrɔn] ' to-
morrow '
från ' from '

Exercise 10 Translate

(*a*) Hon stannade här. Vi skall stanna här en vecka. Min syster cyklar till kontoret. Soldaterna kämpade som hjältar för fosterlandet. Jag kallade honom ' Broder.' Han blev sjuk i går. Titta, där är din far ! Har du tittat i boken ? En vecka är sju dagar. Veckans första dag är söndag. Hur många timmar är ett dygn ? Min födelsedag är den 24 december. Den 24 december är julafton. April är årets fjärde månad. Hur många dagar har februari ? Skall vi plocka svamp i dag ? Vill du skaffa mig ett kilo kaffe. Fråga honom, hur mycket det kostar.[2] Hur mycket kostar kaffet ? Det kostar fyra kronor kilot (*per kilo*).

(*b*) Stay here. The train does not stop here. You must stay at home. Why ? I am not ill. The little girl called me ' Uncle.' To-morrow is my birthday. Why is your brother so lazy ? He is not lazy, he is ill. Winter is the cold season. How many months has a year ? How many days has January ? The third day of the week is Tuesday. Do not bother me now ! Have you been picking mushrooms ? The boy was throwing stones. We bathed in the lake. I woke up (awakened). Will you brush my coat ? I am washing my (=the) hands. The soldier saved the man's life. I wish to send a telegram ; how much does it cost to telegraph to London ? I am expecting a letter from my cousin. Gustaf VI Adolf is the King of Sweden.

[1] This is a singular form with collective meaning.
[2] Note use of comma to mark off a subordinate clause and cf. § 78 (b).

CHAPTER XI

VERBS—SECOND CONJUGATION

142. Nearly all verbs of the Second Conjugation have a front vowel (*e, i, y, ä, ö*) in the root. They are divided into two classes according to whether the root ends in a voiced or voiceless consonant. (Voiced consonants are : *d, j, l, m, n, r, v* ; voiceless are : *k, p, s, t*). The first class forms its past tense by adding *-de*, the second class by adding *-te* ; but in both classes the supine ends in *-t*.

(a) First Class

143. Past tense ends in *-de*.
Supine ends in *-t*.

Example :

Present	Past
jag böjer ' I bend '	*jag böjde* ' I bent '
Present Perfect	Past Perfect
jag har böjt ' I have bent '	*jag hade böjt* ' I had bent '
Future	Future in the Past
jag skall böja ' I shall bend '	*jag skulle böja* 'I should bend '

Imperative	.. ..	*böj* ' bend '
Infinitive	.. ..	*att böja* ' to bend '
Present Participle	..	*böjande* ' bending '
Supine	.. ..	(*jag har*) *böjt* ' bent '
Past Participle	..	*böjd* ' bent '

Note.—(*a*) When the root ends in *-r*, it absorbs the *-er* ending in the present forms, e.g. : *hör* ' hear ' ; *kör* ' drive'; *lär* ' teach[1] ' ; *rör* ' move ' (instead of *hörer, körer, lärer, rörer*).

Note.—(*b*) There are a few exceptions to the rule that verbs of the Second Conjugation have a front vowel in the root; such are: *befalla* 'command'; *blåsa* 'blow'; *gnaga* 'gnaw'; *åka* 'drive, ride' (intrans.).

[1] *lära* to teach ; *lära sig* (reflexive) to learn.

(c) When the root has a long vowel followed by -d, the Past, Supine and Past Participle have the short vowel and double consonant, e.g. :

Infinitive	Past	Supine	Past Participle
leda ' lead '	ledde	lett	ledd

and similarly lyda ' obey ' ; råda (tr.) ' advise ' (intr.) ' hold sway ' ; sveda ' scorch.'

(d) When the root ends in -nd, the -d is dropped before the -d or -t of the past forms, e.g. :

Infinitive	Past	Supine	Past Participle
sända ' send '	sände	sänt	sänd
vända ' turn '	vände	vänt	vänd

(e) When the root ends in -mm or -nn, the double consonant is simplified in the past forms, e.g. :

Infinitive	Past	Supine	Past Participle
glömma ' forget '	glömde	glömt	glömd
gömma ' hide '	gömde	gömt	gömd
klämma ' squeeze '	klämde	klämt	klämd
känna[1] ' know, feel '	kände	känt	känd[2]
bränna (tr.) ' burn '	brände	bränt	bränd
spänna ' stretch '	spände	spänt	spänd

(f) When the root ends in -ll, the double consonant is retained throughout, e.g. :

Infinitive	Past	Supine	Past Participle
hälla ' pour '	hällde	hällt	hälld
ställa ' put '	ställde	ställt	ställd

(g) The following verb is irregular :

Infinitive	Past	Supine	Past Participle
leva ' live '	levde	levat	—

[1] att känna sig (reflexive) to feel (intransitive).
[2] känd can mean ' known ' or 'well known.'

(b) Second Class

144. Past tense ends in **-te**.
Supine and Past participle end in **-t**.

Present	Past
jag köper ' I buy '	*jag köpte* ' I bought '
Present Perfect	Past Perfect
jag har köpt ' I have bought '	*jag hade köpt* ' I had bought '
Future	Future in the Past
jag skall köpa ' I shall buy '	*jag skulle köpa* 'I should buy '

Imperative	.. ..	*köp* ' buy '
Infinitive	.. ..	*att köpa* ' to buy '
Present Participle	..	*köpande* ' buying '
Supine	.. ..	*(jag har) köpt* ' bought '
Past Participle	..	*köpt* ' bought '

Note.—(a) When the root has a long vowel followed by -*t*, the Past, Supine and Past Participle have the short vowel and double -*t*, e.g. :

Infinitive	Past	Supine	Past Participle
blöta ' soak '	*blötte*	*blött*	*blött*
byta ' change '	*bytte*	*bytt*	*bytt*
mäta ' measure '	*mätte*	*mätt*	*mätt*
möta ' meet '	*mötte*	*mött*	*mött*
sköta ' look after '	*skötte*	*skött*	*skött*
stöta 'bump, offend'	*stötte*	*stött*	*stött*

(b) The following verb has the shortened vowel in the Past Tense, but is irregular in the Supine :

Infinitive	Past	Supine	Past Participle
heta ' be called '	*hette*	*hetat*	—

Vad heter ni ? (or : *Hur var namnet ?*)	What is your name ?
Jag heter Johansson (or : *Mitt namn är Johansson.*)	My name is Johansson.
Vad heter hon i sig själv ?	What was her maiden name?

145. The following verbs are regular and are conjugated like *köpa* :

hjälpa ' help '	*smeka* ' caress '
klippa ' cut (hair, etc.) ' [1]	*söka* ' seek '
leka ' play '	*trycka* ' press, print '
läsa ' read '	*tycka* ' think, be of
resa ' travel '	opinion '
räcka (intr.) ' suffice ; (tr.)	*täcka* ' cover '
' hand, pass "	*tänka* ' think, imagine '
röka (tr.) ' smoke '	*väcka* ' wake, rouse '
släppa ' let go, release '	

The difference in meaning between *tycka* and *tänka* may be illustrated by the following examples :

Jag tycker jag ser honom i fjärran.	I think I can see him in the distance.
Säg vad du själv tycker.	Tell us your own opinion.
Tänk på ett tal.	Think of a number.
När tänker ni resa ?	When are you (thinking of) leaving ?

Note the following idioms :

Jag tycker om henne (with stress on *om*).	I like her.
Jag tycker riktigt synd om henne (with stress on *synd*).	I feel really sorry for her.
Tänk bara !	Fancy that! (Well I never!)

Irregular Verbs of the Second Conjugation

145. Some verbs of the Second Conjugation have a *-j*-suffix in the Infinitive (and hence usually in the Present)—but drop it in the Past forms ; this causes modification or mutation of the root vowel in the Infinitive and Present as against the unmutated vowel in the Past. Such verbs may be compared with verbs like *sell—sold—sold* in English.

Examples :

Infinitive	Present	Past	Supine	Past Part.
glädja ' gladden '	*gläder*	*gladde*	*glatt*	—
skilja ' separate '	*skiljer*	*skilde*	*skilt*	*skild*
smörja ' smear '	*smörjer*	*smorde* ['smoː:də]	*smort*	*smord*

[1] Note : *att klippa sig* (reflexive) ' to get one's hair cut '; cf. § 141.

Infinitive	Present	Past	Supine	Past Part.
sälja ' sell '	*säljer*	*sålde*	**sålt**	*såld*
		[ˈsɔˈldə]		
välja ' choose '	*väljer*	*valde*	*valt*	*vald*
		[ˈvaˈːldə]	[vaːlt]	[vaːld]

147. In some verbs the *-j-* has disappeared, but the vowel change remains. The following examples should be noted :

Infinitive	Present	Past	Supine	Past Part.
böra ' ought to '	**bör**	*borde*	*bort*	—
göra ' do, make '	**gör**	*gjorde*	*gjort*	*gjord*
[ˈjœˈːra]	[jœːr]	[ˈjoˈːdə]		
lägga[2] ' lay '	*lägger*	*lade*[1]	*lagt* [lakt] *lagd*	
säga[3] ' say '	*säger*	*sade*[1]	*sagt* [sakt]*sagd*	
sätta[4] ' set '	*sätter*	*satte*	*satt*	*satt*

Word-Order

148. The normal word-order in Swedish is : subject—verb—object, as in English. But when the sentence opens with a word which is not the subject—a construction which is very usual in Swedish—the subject is at once placed after the verb. This is known as " inverted word-order." It occurs in all the Germanic languages, but is now comparatively rare in English (cf. Hardly *had I* gone . . . ; Brothers and sisters *have I* none, etc.). The sentence may begin with an adverb or an adverbial phrase, e.g. :

Nu **skall vi** *resa.* Now we are going to leave.

Om somrarna **bor vi** *på landet.* In the summer(s) we live in the country.

The inversion also occurs when a principal clause is preceded by a subordinate clause, e.g. :

När jag kom hem, **rökte jag** *en cigarr.* When I got home, I smoked a cigar.

' *Vad har du köpt ?* ' **frågade han.** ' What have you bought ? ' he asked.

---

[1] See § 73.*g.*
[2] *att lägga sig* (reflexive) ' to lie down, go to bed '.
[3] See § 49.*a.*
[4] *att sätta sig* (reflexive) ' to sit down '.

The sentence may begin with the object to bring emphasis on the word, e.g. :

Ägg **har vi** *inte*.	We have no eggs.
Det **skall jag** *göra*.	I'll do so (that).

The Use of *det*

149. The word *det*, besides referring to a word of the neuter gender ' it,' can also represent several other English words, while sometimes it has no exact equivalent in English.

(a) *Det* = it, that.

Vad var **det** ? **Det** *var ett flyglarm*.	What was that ? It was an air-raid warning.
Hur mycket blir **det** *tillsammans* ? **Det** *blir kr.* 8 (= *åtta kronor*).	How much will that be altogether ? It comes to 8 crowns.
Hurudant väder är **det** *i dag* ? **Det** *är mycket kallt*.	What sort of weather is it to-day ? It is very cold.
Det *var skönt att vara hemma igen*.	It was (is) nice to be home again.
Det *var jag, som gjorde det*.	It was I who did it.

Note.—*Det* is usually omitted in a sentence beginning with *här* or *där* followed by the verb *vara* and an adjective, e.g. : *Här är kallt* (instead of : *Här är det kallt*) ' It is cold here '; *Där var vackert* ' It was beautiful there.' This construction is occasionally found when the adverb does not occur in the initial position, e.g. : *Skönt och ensligt var där* (Viktor Rydberg) ' It was beautiful and solitary there.'

(b) **Det** = there (provisional subject).

Det *var en gång en vacker prinsessa*.	Once upon a time there was a beautiful princess.
Det *står en man därute*.	There is a man standing outside.

(c) **Det** = he, she *or* they.

Vem är den gamla damen i hörnet ? **Det** *är min mor*.	Who is the old lady in the corner ? She is my mother.
Vilka är de långa herrarna i frack ? **Det** *är svenskar*.	Who are the tall gentlemen in evening dress ? They are Swedes.

(d) **Det** = so.

Jag är mycket trött. **Det** *är jag också.*	I am very tired. So am I.
Tycker du om äpplen ? *Ja.* **Det** *gör jag också.*	Do you like apples ? Yes. So do I.
Är mamma hemma ? *Ja, jag tror* **det**.	Is mama (at) home ? Yes, I think so.
Sade han **det** ?	Did he say so ?

(e) **Det** with no exact equivalent in English.

Skall vi gå på teatern ? *Ja,* **det** *gör vi* !	Shall we go to the theatre ? Yes, let's !
Har du begärt notan ? *Ja,* **det** *har jag.*	Have you asked for the bill ? Yes, I have.
Talar ni engelska ? *Nej,* **det** *gör jag tyvärr inte.*	Do you speak English ? No, unfortunately I don't.
Hälsa så mycket till Karin[1]. *Tack,* **det** *skall jag göra.*	Give my kind regards to Karin. I will.
Vad sade han ? **Det** *vet jag inte.*	What did he say ? I don't know.

Expressions of Thanks

150. The usual word for 'thanks' is *tack*, or, more emphatic, *tack så mycket* [ˈmyˈkkə] 'thank you very much.' Very profuse thanks are expressed by inserting the adverb *rysligt* [ˈryˈːslit] 'awfully' before *mycket* in the above phrase, or by using the expression *tusen tack* 'a thousand thanks'. Occasionally the form *tackar* is used; it is an ellipsis of *jag tackar* 'I thank (you).' A more intimate phrase, used between friends, is *Tack ska' du ha*[2] ! literally '(My) thanks shall you have !' There are two expressions for 'Yes, please,' viz., *Ja tack* in answer to a question in the positive, e.g. *Vill ni ha en kopp té ?* ' Will you have a cup of tea ?' and *Jo, tack* when the question is put in the negative, e.g. *Vill ni inte ha en kopp té till ?* ' Won't you have another cup of tea ?' This corresponds to the use of

---

[1] This name is a contraction of *Katarina*.

[2] *ska'* = *skall* ; on the inverted word-order, see § 148.

oui and *si* in French. The opposite is *Nej, tack* ' no thank you.' The word *tack* is often preceded by the neuter form of the indefinite article and the adjective in written expressions like *Ett varmt* (or *hjärtligt*) *tack för all gästfrihet* ' Cordial (hearty) thanks for all (your) hospitality.'

The Swedes have a reputation for politeness ; and there are a number of polite phrases for expressing thanks which are invariably used in certain situations. Thus at the end of a meal it is usual for the guests on rising from the table to bow to the hostess and say *tack för maten* ; literally, ' thanks for the food.' To this she will usually answer, *tack, tack* ! which implies ' Don't mention it ' or ' It is for *me* to thank *you*.' The latter meaning is also conveyed by the phrase *tack själv* ' thank *you* ' (or : ' the same to you ').

If anyone has spent a pleasant time with a friend (e.g. enjoyed his hospitality), it is usual on parting to say *Adjö* [a'jø:], *och tack för i dag*[1] (*i kväll*) ' Good-bye, and thank you for a pleasant day (evening).' If they meet again on the following day, the greeting would be *God dag, och tack* (*så mycket*) *för i går* (or : *i går kväll*) ' Good day, and thanks (very much) for yesterday (evening).' To which the reply would be *Å, för all del* ' Oh, don't mention it ' or *Tack, tack*. If on the other hand they do not meet until several days after the occasion, the greeting becomes *Tack för sist* (or *senast*) literally ' Thanks for last, i.e. ' I'm very much indebted to you for, e.g. the jolly evening last week ' or ' Much obliged for your recent hospitality.' If no meeting takes place, it is considered polite to write and express one's *tack för sist*. The following phrases should also be noted :

Tack för sällskapet. *Tack för gott sällskap.*	Thanks for your (good) company.
Tack för trevlig samvaro. *Tack för den här tiden.*	Thank you for the pleasant time we have spent together.

[1] This may even be heard on the wireless. When the Swedish Broadcasting Company (*Sveriges Radio*) closes down at the end of the day's programme, the announcer (*hallåmannen*) may sometimes be heard to say *Så får vi önska våra lyssnare God natt, god natt, och tacka för i dag*. " And now it remains for us to wish our listeners ' Good night,' and thank you for to-day."

Tack för hjälpen.	Thanks for your help.
Tack för lånet.	Thanks for the loan.
Tack för skjutsen ['ṣө'ssən].	Thanks for the ride (giving me a lift).
Tack för uppmärksamheten.	Thanks for your attention (i.e. listening so attentively to my lecture).
Tack för titten. (*titt* = look, peep)	Thank you for looking me up. (I'm glad you called).
Tack för visiten.	Thank you for calling.
Tack för att du kom.	Thank you for coming.
Tack för att du var så snäll mot mig.	Thank you for being so kind (all your kindness) to me.
Tack, snälla du (ni).	Thank you ; it's really kind of you.
Tack, kära du !	Thank you, my dear.
Tack i alla fall.	Thank you all the same.
Tack för det år, som gått.	Thank you for the past year (said on December 31st).
Tack för allt.	Thanks for everything (e.g. for everything that you have done to make my stay enjoyable. Also said at the graveside by friends or colleagues of the deceased, meaning : Our thanks for all that you have meant to us during your life).

Note that in some of these expressions the Swedish uses a noun in the definite form where English uses a possessive adjective with the noun, e.g. *hjälpen* = your help.

Vocabulary

bil, c. (2) 'automobile, motor-car'
biljett, c. (3) 'ticket'
blomma, c. (1) 'flower'
cigarrett, c. (3) 'cigarette'
från 'from'

förlåt [fo'lo:t] 'pardon (me)'
gräs, n. (5) 'grass'
krig, n. (5) 'war'
köld, c. 'cold'
lärare, c. (5) 'teacher'

modern [mo'dæːn̩] 'modern'	*utland*, n. (5) ' foreign coun-
målare, c. (5) ' painter '	tries (collectively) '
näsduk, c. (2) ' handker-	*till utlandet* ' abroad '
chief '	*varandra* ' each other '
pipa, c. (1) ' pipe '	*väckarklocka*, c. (1) ' alarm
plats, c. (3) ' place, appoint-	clock '
ment '	*bara* ' only '
program, n. (5) 'programme'	*bra* ' good, well '
radio, c. ' radio, wireless '	*efter* ' after '
språk, n. (5) ' language '	*om* ' about '
spårvagn, c. (2) ' tramcar '	*väl* ' well '
sätt, n. (5) ' way, manner '	

Exercise 11

Translate :

(a) Jag kände kölden. Kan du höra mig ? Ja, jag hör dig bra. Jag läste många böcker om Sverige. Hon köpte boken i stan men glömde den i spårvagnen. Nils kör bilen bra. Min bror söker en plats som lärare. Han har läst moderna[1] språk. Vi bytte tåg i Hallsberg. Tågen mötte varandra[1] där. Jag har köpt biljetterna för teatern i kväll. Tack ska' du ha ! Vill du ha en cigarrett ? Nej, tack ; jag röker bara pipa. Studenterna reste till utlandet. Jag tänker resa till Sverige efter kriget. Det skall jag också göra. Jag hör radioprogrammen från Sverige. Det är ett bra sätt att lära sig språket. När vill du bli väckt ? Precis kl. 7. Jag måste klippa mig snart.

(b) I knew the man very well (= *mycket väl*). I met father yesterday. He had bought (some) flowers for (= *åt*) mother. (I beg) pardon, what did you say ? I haven't said so. I feel the cold, I must go to bed. I laid the book on the table. Who has hidden my pen ? I like reading (= to read). Yesterday I read about Anders Zorn [soːn]. He was a well-known painter. The book is printed in Lund. What have you been doing ? I have only been smoking a cigarette. To-day I forgot my handkerchief, but I bought a new (one). I chose a large (one). I have cut (= clipped) the grass. He set the alarm-clock for exactly 7 (o'clock).

[1] Met each other, i.e. passed each other in opposite directions. Some Swedish railways are single line (*enspårig*) and trains can only pass at stations ; such trains are called *mötestÃ¥g*.

CHAPTER XII
VERBS—THIRD CONJUGATION

151. There are not many verbs in this class; they are characterised by the fact that the infinitive is monosyllabic and ends in a vowel, but not the *-a* which is found in most verbs.

152. Past tense ends in *-dde*.

Supine ends in *-tt*.

Examples:

Present	Past
jag bor ' I dwell, live '	*jag bodde* ' I dwelt '

Present Perfect	Past Perfect
jag har bott ' I have dwelt '	*jag hade bott* ' I had dwelt '

Future	Future in the Past
jag skall bo ' I shall dwell '	*jag skulle bo* ' I should dwell '

Imperative	.. ..	*bo* ' dwell '
Infinitive	.. ..	*att bo* ' to dwell '
Present Participle	..	*boende* ' dwelling'
Supine ..	.. ..	(*jag har*) *bott* ' dwelt '
Past Participle	..	*bodd*

153. The following verbs are regular and are conjugated like *bo* :

glo ' stare, glare at (*på*) '	*sy* ' sew '
gro ' germinate, sprout '	*klå* ' scratch, beat '
ro ' row '	*må* ' be, feel, thrive '
tro ' believe, think '	*rå* [1] ' hold sway, prevail '
fly ' flee '	*så* ' sow '
bry ' bother, puzzle '	*spå* ' tell fortunes, foretell '
gry ' dawn '	*två* 'wash[2] '
	strö ' strew, sprinkle '

[1] This is a shortened form of *råda*.

[2] *tvätta* ' to wash ' is more usual; *två* is generally figurative, e.g. *Pilatus sade* : ' *Jag tvår mina händer.* '

Examples :

Varför glor du så på mig ?	Why are you glaring at me like that ?
Jag tror[1] det.	I think so.
Det tror jag inte.	I don't think so.
Tror ni på andar ?	Do you believe in ghosts ?
Jag trodde honom.	I believed him.
Bry dig inte om honom.	Don't bother (yourself) about him.
Dagen grydde.	The day dawned (broke).
Jag skall sy en ny kostym.	I'm going to have a new suit made.
Hur mår du ? Tack, bra.	How are you ? Quite well, thank you.
Jag mår illa.	I feel sick (queer).
Må så gott !	(Goodbye), keep well !

154.　　Ordspråk　　　　　　　**Proverb**

Människan spår, men Gud rår.　　Man proposes, God disposes.

Demonstrative Adjectives and Pronouns

155. No distinction is made between demonstrative adjectives and pronouns ; the forms are :

Common	Neuter	Plural
den ' that '	**det** ' that '	**de** ' those '
denna(-e) ' this '	**detta** ' this '	**dessa** ' these '
den där ' that '	**det där** ' that '	**de där** ' those '
den här ' this '	**det här** ' this '	**de här** ' these '

Remarks on the Demonstratives

156. (*a*) *Den, det, de* are identical in form with the Definite Article of the Adjective. Thus in *den gamle mannen* ' the old man,' *den* is used as Article ; when it is used as Demonstrative it is more strongly stressed, e.g. *Är **den** gamle mannen din far ?* ' Is **that** old man your father ? '

(*b*) *Denna, detta, dessa* are more usual in written Swedish than in the colloquial language. When referring to a masculine noun *denne* is often used instead of *denna*. As a

---

[1] Cf. use of *glauben* in German.

pronoun it can be inflected in the genitive and takes the ending -s, e.g. *Läraren såg på pojken* ; *det var dennes fel, att olyckan hade hänt.* ' The teacher looked at the boy ; it was his (the latter's) fault that the accident had happened.' The genitive *dennes*, abbreviated to *ds.*, is used in business letters for ' inst.', e.g. *Som svar å eder skrivelse av den 5 ds.* ' In reply to your letter (favour) of the 5th inst.'

(c) *Den här, den där*, etc., are the forms generally used in colloquial Swedish. Though ' this here man ' sounds vulgar in English, *den här mannen* is perfectly good Swedish.

Note.—When **denna, detta, dessa** are used as demonstrative adjectives, the noun following does not take the terminal definite article (except in the colloquial) ; with the other demonstratives the article is required.

Examples :

Den vägen är kortare.	That road is shorter.
Den narren !	What a fool he is !
På det sättet (viset) . . .	In this (that) way . . .
Det barnet tycker jag om.	I like that child.
De breven skall jag stoppa i brevlådan.	I will put those letters in the letter-box (post those letters).
Denna biljett(en) gäller tre dagar.	This ticket is available for three days.
Detta kan inte vara sant.	This cannot be true.
Dessa skor är inte mina.	These shoes are not mine.
Den här boken är min ; den där är din.	This book is mine ; that one is yours.
Det här går inte an.	This won't do.
De här äpplena är billigare än de där.	These apples are cheaper than those.

(d) The Demonstrative Pronouns are often used with substantival force in Swedish where English uses ' this one ' or ' that one ' ; thus the word ' one ' is not translated.

Jag tycker inte om den här ; jag vill ha den där.	I don't like this one ; I want that one.

(e) Where English uses ' this ' (that, these, those) as the subject of the verb ' to be ' with a following noun (singular or plural) in the predicate, Swedish invariably uses **det här, det där** (or : **detta**), i.e. the neuter singular form, irrespective of what follows. (Cf. French **ce** *sont mes amis*, German **das** *sind meine Freunde*).

Får jag lov att presentera : *det här är min bror* (*mina bröder*).	Permit me to introduce (you) : this is my brother (these are my brothers).

(f) Where English uses a demonstrative (or determinative) pronoun before a noun in the genitive (' that of . . . '), Swedish uses a plain genitive.

Månens ljus är blekare än solens.	The light of the moon is paler than that of the sun.

The Numerals in Dates

157. In reading dates the same method is employed in Swedish as in English ; the thousands are not read separately from the hundreds, e.g. 1945 is read as *nittonhundra-fyrtiofem*.

Hur gammal är ni ?	How old are you ?
Jag är 25 (tjugofem).	I am 25.
När är ni född ?	When were you born ?
Jag är född den 17 (sjuttonde) juli 1920 (nittonhundra-tjugo).	I was born on July 17th, 1920.
Kriget började [år[1]] 1939 (nittonhundratrettionio).	The war began in (the year) 1939.
London den 12 (tolfte) april 1940 (nittonhundrafyrtio).	London, 12th April, 1940.

Practice reading aloud the following dates in Swedish : 1000, 1066, 1215, 1688, 1745, 1815, 1870, 1900, 1914.

158. The word for ' century ' is *sekel* (n.5) ; but this word is not used in combination with numerals. Instead of saying ' the 20th century,' Swedish uses the equivalent of

[1] This may be omitted ; note that in any case no preposition is required.

'the nineteen-hundreds,' viz.: **1900-talet** (*nittonhundra-talet*).

Heidenstam är nittiotalets banbrytare.	Heidenstam is the pioneer of the nineties.
Seklets sista decennium.	The last decade of the century.
Sekelskiftet.	The turn of the century.
Dickens levde på **1800-talet.**	Dickens lived in the **19**th century.

Vocabulary

bio[1], c. ' cinema '
butik, c. (3) ' shop'
båt, c. (2) ' boat '
fiska[1] ' fish '
fånge, c. (2) ' prisoner '
födelse, c. ' birth '
gräns, c. (3) ' frontier, bor-
    der '
hel ' whole ' (§ 111 c. ii.)
hos ' with, at (the house of) '
hund, c. (2) ' dog '
häkta[1] ' arrest '

hända[11] ' happen '
ingenting ' nothing '
jaså 'oh, indeed ! is that so!'
kläder, pl. ' clothes '
naturligtvis ' of course,
    naturally '
regn, n. (5) ' rain '
svar, n. (5) ' answer '
säd, c. ' grain '
stund, c. (3) ' while '
tid, c. (3) ' time '
tobak, c. ' tobacco '

Exercise 12
Translate :

(a) Är detta hans båt ? Ja, jag tror det. Det svaret tycker jag om. Du kan ro och jag skall fiska ; och när du har rott en stund, kan vi byta. Ja, det skall vi göra. Min syster ville inte gå på bio ; för det första var hon mycket trött, och för det andra brydde hon sig inte om det. Jag har varit hos mina föräldrar en tid. Jaså, hur mådde de ? Tack, inte så värst (= *not so very, not particularly*) bra. De har varit sjuka. När dagen grydde, flydde fångarna. Bönderna som bodde nära gränsen, hjälpte dem. De sydde deras kläder. Det rådde kallt väder hela tiden. Bonden spådde regnväder. Den här fången blev häktad.

(b) This apple is mine ; that one is yours. Is this your pen ? These are my books. Are you reading this book ? Yes, of course. Do not read that book. It is no good (*inte bra*). That dog is ugly. Is that dog yours ? No, it is hers. The little (one) is mine. Father buys his tobacco in this shop. Is this tobacco his ? No, it is mine. Is this the way to Uppsala ? Is this the train to Stockholm ? Is that tall gentleman your teacher ? No, he's my father. What are you doing in this room ? Nothing. Don't stay here. It is cold in here (*Här är kallt*). The prisoners fled to Sweden. The farmer has sowed his grain. When does the grain germinate ; in the winter ? No, of course not. I didn't believe what he said.[2] An accident has happened near the house.

[1] Short for *biografteater*.   [2] See § 78 (*b*) on punctuation.

CHAPTER XIII
IRREGULAR VERBS

159. A number of old strong verbs have retained their strong forms with change of root vowel in the past tense (some of them also in the past participle), but in other respects they are conjugated like weak verbs of the Third Conjugation ; they may therefore be classed as " mixed".

Infinitive	Present	Past		Supine	Past Part.
		Singular	Plural		
be(dja)[1] 'request, pray'	*ber* [**be:r**]	*bad*	*bådo*	*bett*	*bedd*
dö ' die '	*dör*	*dog* [do:g]	*dogo*	*dött*	—
få ' get '	*får*	*fick*	*fingo*	*fått*	—
gå ' go, walk '	*går*	*gick* [jik]	*gingo*	*gått*	*gången*
le 'smile'	*ler* [le:r]	*log* [lo:g]	*logo*	*lett*	—
se ' see '	*ser* [se:r]	*såg*	*sågo*	*sett*	*sedd*
slå 'strike'	*slår*	*slog* [slo:g]	*slogo*	*slagit*	*slagen*
stå 'stand'	*står*	*stod*	*stodo*	*stått*	—

Note.—The disyllabic Past Plural forms only occur in literature. In the spoken language the monosyllabic Singular forms are used throughout the Past.

160. Examples :

Jag bad om ett glas vatten.   I asked for a glass of water.

Jag ber om ursäkt [**u`:'sɛkt**]   I beg (your) pardon.

Note.—An infinitive dependent on *be* is used without *att* :

Han bad mig stiga in.   He asked me to come in.

Hans far dog i influensa.   His father died of influenza.

---

[1] The full form is almost entirely restricted to Church usage, e.g. *Låtom oss bedja* ' let us pray.'

113

The verb *få* is used (*a*) in the sense ' get, receive '; (*b*) as an auxiliary with the sense ' be obliged to,' ' be permitted to,' ' have an opportunity to.'

Jag fick ett brev från honom.	I received a letter from him.
När får du din lön ?	When do you get your salary ?
Han får bra betalt.	He is well paid.
Du får lov att gå nu.	You can get (=have) permission to go (=may go) now ; or : You will have to go now.
Kan jag få gå nu ?	May I go now ?
Får jag lov att presentera . . .	May I (be permitted to) introduce . . .
Får jag be om namnet ?	May I ask your name ?
Kan jag få ett glas mjölk ?	Can I get (=may I have) a glass of milk ?
Skall vi gå ut och gå ?	Shall we go for a walk ?
Vi gick **på** *bio (teatern).*	We went to the pictures (theatre).
Vi gick **till** *stationen (posten).*	We went to the station (post-office).
Jag går **upp** *kl. (klockan) 7.*	I get up at 7 o'clock.

Note.—*gå* never means ' travel,' which is *resa.*

Solen går upp kl. 7.	The sun rises at 7 o'clock.
Vad står på ?	What's the matter ?
Klockan har slagit 10.	The clock has struck 10.
Han slog mig i ansiktet.	He struck me in the face.

Fractions

161. Most of the fractions are formed by adding *-del* ' part ' to the ordinal numerals, e.g. : $\frac{1}{3}$ *en tredjedel* ; $\frac{2}{3}$ *två tredjedelar* ; $\frac{3}{5}$ *tre femtedelar*, etc. If the ordinal ends in *-de*, this is dropped before *-del* (except in *fjärdedel* fourth and *sjundedel* seventh) ; thus $\frac{1}{8}$ *en åttondel* ; $\frac{1}{9}$ *en niondel*).

Special forms to be noted are : ½ *en halv* ; 1½ *en och en halv* or *halvannan.* When *halv* is treated as an adjective, it agrees with the following noun in gender, e.g. *en halv mil*[1] ' half a mile ' ; *ett halvt kilo*[2] ' half a kilo ' ; *en och en halv* (or *halvannan*) *mil* ' a mile and a half ' ; *ett och ett halvt* (or *halvannat*) *kilo* ' a kilo and a half.' Beside the word *fjärdedel* there is *en kvart*, which in isolation means ' a quarter of an hour.' As a measure it is used in the genitive, e.g. *en och tre kvarts* [**kvaʈʂ**] *liter*, 1¾ litres ; *två och ett kvarts kilo*, 2¼ kilos. So also are the other fractions except *halv.*

Note the following expressions :

Fem och ett halvt år.	Five years and a half.
Två och en femtedels kilo-meter.	Two and a fifth kilometres.
Ett dussin ['**de'ssin**] ; *tre dussin knappar.*	A dozen ; three dozen buttons.
Ett tjog [**ço:g**] ; *tre tjog kräftor.*	A score ; three score of crayfish.
Dussintals flaskor (buteljer).	Dozens of bottles.

Like *dussintals* are : *tjogtals, hundratals, tusentals.* The noun corresponding to *halv* is *hälft* (c.) ; cf. *halva vägen* and *hälften av vägen* ' half (the) way ' ; the former is more usual. The adverb is *halvvägs.*

162.   Time by the Clock

Vad är klockan ?		⎫	What time is it ?
Hur mycket är klockan ?		⎭	
Klockan är . . .			It is . . . o'clock.
ett	..	1.00	one
tio över ett	..	1.10	ten past one
en kvart över ett		1.15	a quarter past one
fem i halv två		1.25	twenty-five past one
halv två	..	1.30	half past one
fem över halv två		1.35	twenty-five to two
en kvart i två	..	1.45	a quarter to two
tio i två	..	1.50	ten to two
precis [**prə'si:s**] *två*	..	2.00	exactly two o'clock

[1] A Swedish mile is equal to six English miles.
[2] When *kilo* is used alone, it always stands for *kilogram* (n.). Otherwise the full form has to be used, e.g. *kilometer* (c.) kilometre, *kilovatt* (c.) kilo**watt.**

Officially the 24 hour system is now used ; thus when the time signal is given on the wireless, the announcer says *Nu skall vi höra, vad klockan är* ' Now we'll hear what the time is ' ; and the recorded voice of *Fröken Ur* (Miss Clock) replies *Nitton, elva och tio* = 19 hours 11 minutes and 10 seconds.

Note the following expressions :

Hur(u) dags [hur'daks] *är ni hemma ?*	When (i.e. at what time) will you be home ?
Vi är hemma strax före (efter) tre.	We shall be home just before (after) three.
Vid tre-tiden.	At about 3 o'clock.
Vi är hemma (vid) tédags.	We shall be home at (about) tea-time.
Nu är det kaffedags (sängdags).	Now it is time for coffee (bed).
Hon kom kl. 3 på pricken.	She arrived on the stroke of three.
För *en kvart* **sedan.**	A quarter of an hour ago.
Om en kvart.	In a quarter of an hour.
För en timme sedan.	An hour ago.
Om en timme (en timmes tid).	In an hour (an hour's time).
Om fem minuter.	In five minutes (time).

A Railway Time-table

Km.	Statens järnvägar	St. 9 1, 2
0	fr. Stockholm C	14.30
2	fr. Stockholm S	|
133	t. Katrineholm	16.23
133	fr. Katrineholm	16.26
312	t. Skövde	18.57
312	fr. Skövde	19.00
456	t. Göteborg C........	21.05

Statens järnvägar 'The State Railways; St. = *Snälltåg*
'Express Train'; C = *Central*; S = *Södra* 'South';
fr. = *från* 'from (departs)'; t. = *till* 'to (arrives).'

Relative Pronouns

164. The commonest relative pronoun and practically
the only one used in conversation is *som*; it is invariable
and may be used for both genders, singular and plural. It
can serve

(*a*) as the subject of a sentence, e.g. :

Jag har en bror, **som** *talar* I have a brother who speaks
tyska. German.

Ljuset **som** *lyser där borta,* The light that is shining
är en trafiksignal. over there is a traffic sign.

(*b*) as the object of a sentence, e.g. :

Jag lämnade tillbaka pen- I returned the money (that)
garna, **som** *jag hade lånat.* I had borrowed.

As object it is often omitted, though not to the same
extent as in English. Thus in the last example it would be
possible to say : *Jag lämnade tillbaka pengarna, jag hade
lånat.*

165. *Som* cannot be used in the genitive; this has to be
replaced by *vars* (both genders) or *vilkens, vilkets, vilkas*;
but the genitives are avoided in conversation. Thus, instead
of saying *Här är mannen, vars namn jag har glömt* ' Here is
the man whose name I have forgotten,' it would be more
usual to substitute a prepositional expression and say
Här är mannen, som jag har glömt namnet på ' Here is the
man that I have forgotten the name of.'

166. *Som* cannot be used with a preceding preposition;
this is placed at the end of the relative clause. Thus ' He is
a man on whom I can rely ' is translated *Han är en man,
som jag kan lita på.*

167. The relatives *vilken, vilket, vilka* are more usual in
written Swedish than in the colloquial; but the neuter

form *vilket* must be used when referring back to a whole clause or a noun standing in the predicate, e.g. :

Han har klarat sin examen, ***vilket*** *gläder mig.*	He has passed his examination, which I am glad to hear.
Han vill bli läkare, ***vilket*** *hans far också var.*	He intends to be a doctor, which (as) his father was too.

168.   The pronoun *vad*, which is invariable, is sometimes used as a relative pronoun. It usually comprises both the relative and its correlate (i.e. = that which).

Vad *du gör, gör ordentligt.* [ɔ'dɛ'ntli(k)t]	What you do, do properly.
Efter ***vad*** *jag har hört . . .*	According to what I have heard . . .
Hör nu, ***vad*** *jag säger.*	Listen to what I (have to) say.

Vad is generally used as the relative when the antecedent is *allt* (cf. German *alles, was*), e.g. :

Hörde du ***allt,*** *vad han sade ?*	Did you hear everything he said ?

Vocabulary

bank, c. (3) ' bank '
brygga, c. (1) ' jetty '
död ' dead '
film, c. (3) ' film '
kypare ['çy`:parə], c. (5) ' waiter '
lunch [lʊnʂ], c. (3) ' lunch '
lunginflammation, c. ' pneumonia '
låna⁽¹⁾ ' borrow, lend '
lämna⁽¹⁾ *tillbaka* ' hand back, return '

lön, c. (3) ' salary, reward '
mena⁽¹⁾ ' mean '
mera än ' more than '
person [pæ'ʂoˈ:n], c.(3) ' person '
regn [rɛŋn], n. (5) ' rain '
smör, n. (5) ' butter '
vara⁽¹⁾ ' last '
då ' then '
på sista tiden ' lately '
på gatan ' in the street '

Exercise 13

Translate

(a) Jag skall be att få[1] ett kvarts kilo smör. Kan jag få (*get = have*) ett tjog ägg ? Nej, då[2] ; så många ägg kan vi inte sälja. Får jag be om saltet ? Ja, då ; var så god[3] ! Tack så mycket. När får vi lunch? Vid ett-tiden. Hur mycket är klockan nu? Klockan är snart tolv. Jaså; då måste vi gå. Ja, jag skall be kyparen om notan. Kan jag få notan ? Hur mycket blir det (*does it come to*) ? Den person, du tänker på, är inte den jag menar. Vad sade hon, när hon fick se (*caught sight of*) honom ? Hur mycket är två tredjedelar av tre femtedelar ? Det är två femtedelar. Har du fått din lön ? Ja, och nu måste jag gå på banken. Har du sett den nya filmen ? Nej, jag har inte gått på bio på sista tiden. Jag såg honom på gatan för en halv timme sedan. Det stod dussintals flaskor (buteljer) på golvet.

(b) The film lasted an hour and a half. Here is a book you must read. Where did you get it ? I must return the book (that) I borrowed. The rain lasted two and a half days. I saw everything he did. I stood in the street (for) more than half an hour. My brother stood on the jetty and saw me on the boat. When do you get up ? I get up at half past seven. And when do you go to bed[4] ? At about eleven. My old teacher is dead. He died of pneumonia. How old was he ? He was sixty. Is this the train that goes to Uppsala ? Yes. When does it start (= go) ? In half an hour's time. And when are we in Uppsala ? Just after five. Is that the man you mean ? I saw him in the street a quarter of an hour ago. It is a quarter past two now. May I have (= Can I get) another cup of coffee ? The man you mean lives $5\frac{3}{4}$ kilometres from the town. We had to walk half the way, which made me very tired.

[1] Note this phrase ; it is a polite way of saying ' Please may I have. . . .'

[2] In *ja, då* (do) and *nej, då* the word *då* merely strengthens the affirmation or negation ; it cannot be translated.

[3] See § 31.   [4] See page 101, footnote 2.

CHAPTER XIV

STRONG VERBS—PARTICIPLES

169. The Fourth Conjugation comprises the Strong Verbs. With a few exceptions they all have disyllabic infinitives ending in -*a*; they form the Past Tense by a change of root vowel; the Supine ends in -*it* and the Past Participle in -*en* (cf. English *chosen, written*, etc.). As they fall into various classes according to the change of vowel in the Past Tense, only the first class will be given in this chapter. The remainder will be given in several of the ensuing chapters; they should be carefully memorized and constantly revised.

170. Class I. Vowel change: (long) *i—e—i*

Present	Past
jag skriver ' I write '	*jag skrev* ' I wrote '
vi skriva[1] ' we write '	*vi skrevo*[1] ' we wrote '

Present Perfect	Past Perfect
jag har skrivit ' I have written '	*jag hade skrivit* ' I had written '

Future	Future in the Past
jag skall skriva ' I shall write '	*jag skulle skriva* 'I should write '

Imperative	.. ..	*skriv* ' write '
Infinitive	.. ..	*att skriva* ' to write '
Present Participle	..	*skrivande* ' writing '
Supine ..	.. ..	(*jag har*) *skrivit* ' written '
Past Participle	..	*skriven* ' written '

171. Other strong verbs of this class are :

bita ' bite '	*rida* ' ride '
bli(va) ' become[2] '	*sprida* ' spread ' (tr.)
gripa ' grasp '	*skrika* ' cry, bawl '
lida ' suffer '	*stiga* ' rise '

[1] These forms are rarely used nowadays, even in poetry : in collo-quial usage and everyday written prose the singular forms of the verb are used for the plural. In subsequent chapters the plural forms will only be given when they are formed irregularly.

[2] See § 134.

Inflection of Participles

I.—The Present Participle

172. The Present Participle ends in **-ande**, except in the Third Conjugation, where it ends in **-ende**. When used as an adjective it is indeclinable.

Examples :

En väntande bil.	A waiting car.
Ett spännande ögonblick	An exciting moment.
Den flyende soldaten.	The fleeing soldier.
Den fallande snön.	The falling snow.

173. When used as a noun, the Present Participle takes the **-s** ending in the genitive, e.g. :

En ropandes röst i öknen.   The voice of one crying in the wilderness.

2.—The Past Participle

174. A. Indefinite Declension.

(a) Past Participles ending in **-ad** (1st Conjugation).

The neuter singular is formed by changing the final **-d** into **-t**, and the plural is formed by adding **-e** to the uninflected singular, e.g. :

En älskad vän.	A beloved friend.
Ett älskat barn.	A beloved child.
Älskade vänner.	Beloved friends.

(b) Past Participles ending in **-d** (2nd Conjugation).

The neuter singular is formed by changing the final **-d** into **-t**, and the plural is formed by adding **-a** to the uninflected singular, e.g. :

En spänd situation.	A tense situation.
Ett spänt rep.	A stretched rope.
Spända förhållanden.	Strained relations.

(c) Past Participles ending in **-t** (2nd Conjugation).

The uninflected singular form remains unchanged in the neuter, while the plural is formed by adding **-a**, e.g. :

En tryckt bok.	A printed book.
Ett tryckt plakat.	A printed placard.
Tryckta bokstäver.	Printed letters.

(d) Past Participles ending in -*dd* (3rd Conjugation).

The neuter singular is formed by changing the -*dd* into -*tt*, and the plural is formed by adding -*a* to the uninflected singular, e.g. :

En sydd sula.	A sewn sole.
Ett sytt täcke.	A sewn coverlet.
Sydda lakan.	Sewn sheets.

(e) Past Participles ending in -*en* (4th Conjugation).

The neuter singular is formed by changing the final -*n* into -*t*, while the plural is formed by dropping the -*e* before the -*n*[1] and adding -*a*, e.g. :

En fallen kung.	A fallen king.
Ett fallet blad.	A fallen leaf.
Fallna änglar.	Fallen angels.

175. B. Definite Declension.

The definite forms of the Past Participles are the same as the plural forms of the indefinite declension, viz. :

(a) Past Participles of the 1st Conjugation, which end in -*ad*, add -*e* in the definite declension, e.g. :

Den älskade vännen, det älskade barnet, de älskade vännerna.

(b) All other Past Participles add -*a* in the definite declension, e.g. :

Den spända situationen, det spända repet, de spända förhållandena ; den tryckta boken, det tryckta plakatet, de tryckta bokstäverna ; den sydda sulan, det sydda täcket, de sydda lakanen ; den fallna[2] *kungen, det fallna bladet, de fallna änglarna.*

176. C. Genitive.

All Past Participles used as nouns take -*s* in the genitive, e.g. :

Den älskades död.	The death of the beloved one.
De fallnas ära.	The honour of the fallen.

[1] Cf. adjectives ending in unstressed -*en*, § 109.*a*.
[2] or *den fallne kungen* (cf. p. 68, footnote 1).

Determinative Adjective and Pronouns

177. The forms **den, det, de** serve not only as Demonstrative Adjectives and Pronouns (see § 155), but also as Determinatives referring to a following relative clause or a phrase.

Den *som vinner tid, vinner allt.*	He who gains time gains everything.
Det *som är sällsynt, är dyrt.*	That which is rare is costly.
De *som inte vill arbeta, måste svälta.*	Those who will not work must starve.
Den *man, ni ser på, är inte* **den** *jag menar.*	The man you are looking at is not the one I mean.
Det *hus, som du ser i fjärran, är mitt hem.*	The house you (can) see in the distance is my home.
Jag har **den** *äran att gratulera*[1].	Allow me to congratulate you !
Jag har **det** *stora nöjet att presentera. . . .*	I have great pleasure in introducing. . . .
De *personer, som inte vill stanna, får gå nu.*	Those persons who do not wish to stay, may go now.

Note.—When nouns in the plural are preceded by the Determinative Adjective, they do not take the terminal definite article (cf. *de personer som* above) ; but in the singular they fluctuate (e.g. *den man* or *den mann***en**, du ser **på**).

Determinative Adjectives and Pronouns are always stressed.

The Passive Voice

178. As already stated in § 134, the Passive Voice is formed by using the auxiliary verb **bli** with the Past Participle, e.g. *Han blev sårad* ' He was wounded.' This is the usual way of forming the Passive in the colloquial language.

But side by side with this, Swedish has another form, which is one of the characteristic features of the Scandinavian languages : the passive sense may be indicated by

[1] This expression is the usual one for ' Many Happy Returns of the Day ' and for congratulations of any kind.

adding -*s* to all the active forms of the verb. This -*s* is a relic of the old reflexive pronoun *sik* (Modern Swedish *sig*), which properly belongs to the third person only. From a reflexive expression like *han kallar sig Olaf* ' he calls himself Olaf,' there arises by the enclitic use of the reflexive pronoun, weakened to -*s*, the expression *han kallas Olaf* (with loss of the verbal ending -*r*). This, by an easy transition of meaning, acquires the sense ' he is called Olaf.' The -*s* then becomes generalized for all persons of the verb, singular and plural, and is even extended to the Infinitive and Supine. The following are the Passive forms of the Four Conjugations.

179.   First Conjugation

Present	Past
jag kallas ' I am called '	*jag kallades* ' I was called '

Present Perfect	Past Perfect
jag har kallats 'I have been called '	*jag hade kallats* ' I had been called '

Future	Future in the Past
jag skall kallas ' I shall be called '	*jag skulle kallas* ' I should be called '

Infinitive .. .. **att kallas** ' to be called '

Supine .. .. **kallats** ' been called '

Second, Third and Fourth Conjugations

180. In the Second and Fourth Conjugations, in which the Active Form often ends in -*er*, the -*e* is generally dropped before the -*s* in the colloquial.[1]

Infinitive	Present	Past	Supine
II. *att höras* ' to be heard '	*hör(e)s*	*hördes*	*hörts*
att sökas ' to be sought '	*sök(e)s*	*söktes*	*sökts*
III. *att tros* ' to be believed '	*tros*	*troddes*	*trotts*
IV. *att skrivas* ' to be written '	*skriv(e)s*	*skrevs*	*skrivits*

[1] The full forms with -*e*- are now rarely used.

Note.—An English passive infinitive after the verbs 'to be,' 'to remain,' 'to leave,' corresponds to an **active infinitive** in Swedish (cf. the similar use of the English active infinitive in expressions like 'this house to let, land to feu,' etc.).

Examples :

*Det var ingenting annat **att vänta**.*	Nothing else was to be expected.
*Orsaken är **att söka** i högkonjunkturen.*	The cause is to be looked for in the favourable market conditions.
*Hans uppträdande lämnade mycket **att önska**.*	His behaviour left much to be desired.

Remarks on the Use of the s-Forms

181. The Passive formed by combining *bli* with the Past Participle is far more frequently used than the *s*-form, and they are not always interchangeable. As a rule the compound form refers to a single action or event, while the *s*-form, although it may also refer to a single action, often implies customary or repeated actions or processes. Thus it is often seen in public notices and advertisements, e.g. :

Kyrkan hålles öppen kl. 10—12.	The church is (kept) open from 10 a.m. to noon.
Biblioteket öppnas kl. 10.	The library opens at 10.
Butiken stänges kl. 6.	This shop closes at 6.0.
Té serveras inte på rummen.	Tea is not served in the (hotel) rooms.
Klockor repareras.	Clocks repaired.
Att hämtas[1].	To be called for.

[1] Literally 'to be fetched.' The verb *hämta* originally meant *hem ta* 'to home take,' i.e. 'take home,' but it now has the generalized meaning 'fetch, recover, regain.'

The WANTED advertisement columns of Swedish newspapers are usually headed ÖNSKAS HYRA 'wanted to hire' or ÖNSKAS KÖPA 'wanted to purchase'; a typical FOR SALE advertisement reads as follows :

Till salu[1].

SOFFA

säljes billigt.[2] Besked[3] kan lämnas[4] kl. 10—11 fm. pr. tel. 15 75 49.

The -*s* forms are very frequently used in descriptions of processes, e.g. recipes. The following is a typical Swedish recipe :

Recept för inkokning av blandad svamp.

Blandad svamp[5] || salt

Olika sorter svamp rensas och skäras i lagom[6] stora, jämna bitar samt[7] sköljas, om så behövs. Till varje liter rensad svamp tages ungefär 1 tsk. (=tesked) salt. Svamp och salt nedlägges i en kastrull. Denna sättes över elden och svampen förvälles i sitt eget spad under omröring. Då den kännes mjuk, uppslås den i ett porslinskärl och får stå på kallt ställe till följande dag. Svampen öses då på lämpligt stora burkar tillsammans med sitt spad. Intet vatten hälles på. Burkarna tillslutas och steriliseras vid 100° C. under 2 tim. (=timmar). De avkylas så hastigt som möjligt och förvaras på svalt ställe.

Translation

Recipe for preserving (by boiling) of assorted mushrooms.

Assorted mushrooms : salt.

Various kinds of mushrooms are cleaned and cut into moderately large pieces of equal size and rinsed, if necessary. To each litre of cleaned mushrooms is taken (i.e. add) about 1 teaspoonful of salt. The mushrooms and salt are put (down) into a saucepan. This is placed over the fire and the

---

[1] § 103 (*b*).
[2] cheaply.   [3] particulars.
[4] From *lämna* to furnish, supply, deliver.
[5] See page 96, footnote 1.   [6] See § 103 (*e*).   [7] = och.

mushrooms are stewed in their own juice (accompanied by) stirring. When they feel soft, they are poured off into a porcelain vessel and allowed to stand in a cool place till the following day. The mushrooms together with the liquor are then poured into conveniently large jars. No water is poured on (added). The jars are sealed and sterilized at 100°C. (i.e. boiling point) for 2 hours. They are cooled as quickly as possible and preserved (kept) in a cool place.

Note.—In English recipes directions are usually given in the imperative ; in Swedish the process is described in the passive.

Some *s*-forms used both in writing and conversation have no strictly passive meaning and cannot therefore be replaced by the compound form with **bli**. The following examples should be noted :

höras to be audible.

Orden hörs tydligt.	The words are clearly audible.

kännas ' to be perceptible (felt).'

Det känns i öronen.	You can feel it in your ears.
Hur känns det ?	{ How do you feel ? { What does it feel like ?
Känns det ?	Can you feel anything ?

märkas ' to be noticeable.'

Det märks inte.	Nobody will notice it.
Det märks, när han har varit här.	You can tell when he has been here.

behövas ' to be necessary.'

Kan jag hjälpa dig med kappan ? Nej tack, det behövs [be'hœfs] *inte.*	Can I help you with your overcoat ? No thanks, it's not necessary (there's no need to).

synas ' to be apparent.'

Det syns på dig att du är sjuk.	Anyone can tell by the look of you that you are ill.

tyckas ' to seem (i.e. one would think).'

Det tycks vara sant.	It seems (would seem) to be true.

Vocabulary

duka⁽¹⁾ ' lay (the table) '
hota⁽¹⁾ ' threaten '
kalla⁽¹⁾ ' call '
koka⁽¹⁾ or ⁽¹¹⁾ ' boil, cook '
lasta⁽¹⁾ ' load '
placera⁽¹⁾ [pla'se':ra] 'place'
raka⁽¹⁾ ' shave '
rinna⁽ᴵⱽ⁾ ' run '
rädda⁽¹⁾ ' rescue '
rusa⁽¹⁾ ' dash, rush '
skala⁽¹⁾ ' peel, shell '
skälla⁽¹¹⁾ ' bark '
stava⁽¹⁾ ' spell '
steka⁽¹¹⁾ ' roast, fry '
titta⁽¹⁾ ' peep, look '
tuta⁽¹⁾ ' hoot '
vaka⁽¹⁾ ' keep watch '
vandra⁽¹⁾ ' walk, wander '
önska⁽¹⁾ ' wish '
arbete, n. (4) ' work '

egendom, c. (2) ' estate, property '
flygburen ' air-borne '
förbi (adv.) ' past '
genom ['je'ːnɔm] ' through '
handelsresande, c. (5) ' commercial traveller '
krigare, c. (5) ' warrior '
kyckling, c. (2) ' chicken '
löv, n. (5) ' leaf '
mark, c. ' ground, soil '
potatis, c. (2) [pɔ'taːˈtis] ' potato(es) '
redan ['re'ːdan] 'already '
tom [tɔm] ' empty '
trupper, pl. 'troops'
tvärs över ' across '
väska, c. (1) ' handbag '
då och då ' now and then '

Exercise 14

Translate

(a) Fallande snö. En sydd väska. Ett sytt arbete.[1] En köpt egendom. Ett groende sädeskorn. Löskokta (=soft boiled) ägg. Ett skrikande barn. En lastad vagn. Den handelsresandens namn. Alla rum har rinnande varmt och kallt vatten. Den sårade (wounded) soldat(en), jag talade om, är död. Min älskade mor. Hästen är redan såld. Hur skrives detta ? Ordet ' kom ! ' kallas imperativ. Bordet dukades av (=by) husets döttrar. Prinsessan räddas av hjälten. När placeras subjektet efter predikatet ? De barn, vi talade om, är sjuka. Dina ord hördes av oss alla. Rakas eller klippas ? (Shave or haircut ?). God jul och gott nytt år önskas av Familjen Tamm.

[1] When used with the indefinite article arbete can mean ' a piece of work '; here ' a piece of needlework.'

(b) Jag tittar ut genom fönstret. Kvällen (*evening*) är nära, och den stigande månen skiner över sjön. De fallna löven täcker marken. Det är höst, och gatan är nästan (*nearly*) tom. Bara en vakande poliskonstapel går fram och tillbaka (*to and fro*). Då och då hörs en tutande bil, som rusar förbi. Från det hus, jag ser tvärs över gatan, hörs en skällande hund.

(c) Exciting stories.[1] A dying warrior. The threatening storm. Air-borne troops. The names of the fallen. The money (*pl.*) I received (= *fick*) for the houses sold.[2] Peeled potatoes. Roast chicken. A falling tree. How is this word spelt ? The castle you (can) see in the distance is owned by (= *äges av*) the king. He is no longer (= *inte längre*) the man he was. I am tired. Yes, you look it. Nobody noticed that the king was there. It is the (*omit Article*) same person I saw yesterday.

---

[1] See § 87.
[2] The participle precedes the noun in Swedish.

CHAPTER XV

ADVERBS—DEPONENT VERBS

182. Many Adverbs are formed direct from Adjectives by adding *-t*; thus the Adverb is identical with the neuter form of the corresponding Adjective (see the rules given in § 108).

Examples :

*Det var **vackert** sagt.*	That was nicely spoken (i.e. a kind thing to say).
*Han talade **fritt**.*	He spoke freely.
*Hon suckade **sorgset**.*	She sighed sadly.
*Barnet sover **sött**.*	The child is sleeping sweetly.
*Han reste **runt**.*	He travelled around.
*En **vilt** främmande människa.*	A wildly strange person (i.e. a complete, utter stranger).
*Han satt **troget** vid arbetet.*	He sat faithfully (devotedly) at his work.
*Han levde **måttligt** ['mɔ`tlit]*[1]	He lived moderately (i.e. temperately).

Note.—The adjective *bra* is invariable (see page 75, footnote 2) ; hence the corresponding adverb is *bra*, e.g. *Han talade bra* ' He spoke well.'

183. Present Participles and Past Participles may be used as Adverbs ; the former are invariable, the latter take a *-t* ending, corresponding to the neuter form of the adjective.

Examples :

*En **strålande** vacker kvinna*	A radiantly beautiful woman.
*Jag är **rasande** hungrig.*	I am furiously (i.e. ravenously) hungry.
*Detta är **avgjort** bättre.*	That is decidedly better.

[1] Adverbs ending in *-igt* sometimes drop the *-g* in pronunciation; see § 73 (1). But the pronunciation [-**ikt**] is also heard.

In the colloquial language the adverbial past participles *förbannat* and *förbaskat*, both meaning ' cursedly, deucedly ' are frequently used in situations where English has 'damned,' e.g. : *Han kommer alltid så förbaskat sent* ' He's always so damned late.' They are mainly used by men.[2] On the other hand the adverbs *hemskt*, literally 'uncannily', and *bedårande* or *förtjusande*, literally ' enchantingly ', are frequently used as intensives by ladies; the nearest equivalent in English is the use of ' awfully ' or ' frightfully.'

Examples :

' *Var du på balen i går kväll ?* '	'Were you at the dance yesterday evening ? '
' *Ja, då* ; *det var* **hemskt** *roligt, tyckte jag.*'	'Yes, I was ; I thought it was awfully nice.'
' *Hon har en* **bedårande** *söt liten flicka* (*ett* **förtjusande** *trevligt hem*) '.	'She has an awfully (lit. charmingly) pretty little girl (nice home).'

More general is the use of *väldigt*, literally 'powerfully', and *förfärligt* ' awfully ' as intensives instead of *mycket* ' very.'

Comparison of Adverbs

184. Adverbs derived from Adjectives form their degrees of comparison in exactly the same way as the Adjectives.

sent ' late '	*senare*	*senast*
tidigt ' early '	*tidigare*	*tidigast*
kärleksfullt ' lovingly '	*kärleksfullare*	*kärleksfullast*
högt ' high(ly) '	*högre*	*högst* [hœkst]

Note.—tala högt ' to speak aloud '; *högst* **intressant** ' extremely interesting.'

When the Superlative is used to express a high degree, it is preceded by *på det* (cf. German *aufs*) :

Jag gratulerar er på det **I** congratulate you most *hjärtligaste.*	cordially.

[2] It is not suggested that students should use such expressions ; they are given here in order to present an accurate record of Swedish usage.

This is known as the Elative or Absolute use of the Superlative.

Sometimes the Superlative of an Adverb is preceded by *som*, which adds the sense ' as possible ' :

Jag vill bara **som hastigast** *ge några exempel.*	I will just very quickly (as quickly as possible) give some examples.

This construction, which is contracted from a subordinate clause of comparison, dates from Old Norse times.

185. Some Adverbs not derived from Adjectives also have degrees of comparison :

fort ' quickly '	*fortare*	*fortast*
gärna ' willingly '	**hellre** ' rather'	**helst** 'preferably'
illa ' badly '	*värre*	*värst*[1]
nära ' near '	*närmare*	*närmast*
ofta ' often '	*oftare*	*oftast*
väl, bra ' well '	*bättre*	*bäst*

On the tone variations, see §§ 69 (*d*) and 70 (*f*).

Adverbs with Double Forms

186. Some Adverbs of Place have two forms, one used with a Verb of Motion (indicating **Direction**) and the other used with a Verb indicating **Rest**. Compare the following examples :

Jag bilade **hem**.	I motored home.
Jag är sällan **hemma**.	I am seldom at home.
Han gick **in**.	He went in.
Han är **inne**.	He is in.
Han gick **ut**.	He went out.
Han är **ute**.	He is out.
Han har rest **bort**.	He has gone away.
Han är **borta**.	He is away.
Kom **hit** !	Come here (*lit.* hither) !
Han är **här**.	He is here.

[1] See page 137, footnote 3.

Han gick **dit.**	He went there (*lit.* thither).
Han är där.	He is there.
Vart *går du* ?	Where (*lit.* whither) are you going ?
Var *är du* ?	Where are you ?
Han går **upp** *tidigt.*	He gets up early.
Han är ofta sent **uppe.**	He is often up late.
Vi kom **fram** *kl. 7.*	We arrived at 7 o'clock.
Kom **fram** !	Step forward !
Är vi **framme** ?	Are we there (i.e. have we arrived at our destination) ?
Jag kan inte få **ned** (**ner**) *en bit.*	I can't get anything down (swallow a morsel of food).
Han är mycket **nere.**	He is very down(-hearted).

Note.—**ned** and **ner** are interchangeable; but **nere** is the only form used to denote rest.

Alphabetical List of Adverbs frequently used in Everyday Speech

aldrig ' never '
alldeles ['a`ldələs] ' entirely '
alltför ' (far) too '
alltid ['a`lti:d] ' always '
alltjämt ' constantly '
alltså ['a`ltso:] ' so, consequently '
annars ['a`nnaṣ] ' otherwise '
antagligen ' presumably '
bara [ba`:ra] ' only '
dessutom ' besides '
dock ' however, nevertheless '
då ' then, at that moment '
då och då ' now and then '

därför ['dæ`:rfor] ' therefore '
efteråt ['ɛ`fterɔ:t] ' afterwards '
egentligen [ɛ`jɛ`ntligən] ' actually '
ej ' not '
emellertid [ɛ`mɛ`llərṭi:d] ' however '
en aning ' slightly '
endast ' only '
en smula ' a trifle '
fort ' quickly '
fortfarande ' still '
för ' too '
förmodligen ' presumably '

förr;   *förut* [ˈfœˈruːt] 'before'

för resten 'by the way, moreover'

först [fœʂt] 'not until, only, first'

förstås[1] [fəˈʂtos] 'of course'

ganska 'rather, quite'

genast [ˈjeˈːnast] 'at once'

här om dagen (kvällen) 'the other day (evening)'

högst 'extremely'

i alla fall 'anyway, all the same'

ibland [iˈblan(d)] 'sometimes'

i fjol [fjoːl] 'last year'

i dag 'to-day'

i afton, i kväll 'this evening'

i går 'yesterday'

i morgon [ˈmoˈrrɔn] 'to-morrow'

i våras 'in the (past) spring'

igen [iˈjɛn] 'again'

i somras 'in the (past) summer'

i höstas 'in the (past) autumn'

i vintras 'in the (past) winter'

i morse [ˈmoˈʂʂə] 'early this morning'

i synnerhet 'in particular'

i sär 'apart'

i tu 'in pieces'

i väg 'off'

ingalunda 'by no means'

inte 'not'

inte alls 'not at all'

ja 'yes'

jo 'yes' (after a question in the negative)

just 'just, exactly'

kanske [ˈkaˈnʂə];   *kanhända* [kanˈhɛˈnda] 'perhaps'

knappast 'hardly, scarcely'

litet [ˈliˈːtə] 'a little'

långt, 'far, a good way'

länge 'a long time'

med detsamma [dɛˈsaˈmma] 'at once'

mestadels 'for the most part'

mindre 'less, not very'

mycket [ˈmyˈkkə] 'very'

möjligen;   *möjligtvis* 'possibly'

naturligtvis 'of course'

nu 'now'

nu för tiden 'nowadays'

nyss 'recently'

någorlunda 'in some degree'

något 'somewhat'

när 'when'

när som helst 'at any time'

nästan 'almost'

också 'also'

ofta 'often'

omedelbart 'immediately'

om igen 'over again'

ordentligt [ɔˈdɛˈntli(k)t] 'properly'

plötsligt 'suddenly'

precis 'exactly'

på måfå 'at random'

---

[1] This is really the passive form of the verb *förstå* 'understand'; it may be compared with the German *das versteht sich von selbst*.

på sista tiden, på sistone
 ' lately '
redan ['re`:dan] ' already '
sannolikt ' probably '
sedan ' then (after that),
 afterward '
sist ' last '
slutligen ' finally '
snart ' soon '
stundom ' sometimes '
synnerligen ' particularly '
så ' so, thus '
således (i) ' consequently ';
 (ii) ' thus '
sålunda ' thus, in this manner '
sällan ' seldom, rarely '
sönder ' in pieces '
tillfälligt(vis) ' casually '
till sist ' finally '
till slut ' in conclusion '

tvärtom ' on the contrary '
tämligen ' rather, fairly '
undan ' away '
under tiden ' meanwhile '
utomordentligt ['u:tɔmɔ-
 'dɛ'ntli(k)t] ' extraordina-
 rily '
vanligen, vanligtvis
 ' usually '
varför ' why '
varifrån ' from where,
 whence '
verkligen ' really '
visst ' certainly '
ytterst ' utterly, extremely '
ånyo [o'ny`:ɔ] ' afresh,
 anew '
ännu ['ɛ`nnu] ' yet, still '
äntligen ' at last '
överallt [øvə'ralt] ' every-
 where '

187.   The difference between *då* and *sedan* is important.
Both may be translated by ' then '; but the former is used
when ' then ' means ' at that moment ' or ' in that case,'
and the latter when it means ' after that,' ' subsequently,'
i.e. in a sequence of actions.

*Just då gick dörren upp, och
 en man steg in i rummet.
 Då reste jag mig hastigt.*

Just then the door opened
 and a man came into the
 room. Then I jumped up.

*Vad skall du göra, om han
 hotar dig? Då skriker
 jag.*

What will you do if he
 threatens you? Then (in
 that case) I shall scream.

Först tar jag litet mjöl.

First I take a little flour.

*Sedan blandar jag det med
 ett ägg. Sedan späder jag
 med litet mjölk. Sedan gör
 jag pannkakor.*

Then I mix it with an egg.
 Then I thin it with a
 little milk. Then I make
 pancakes.

Word-Order—Adverbs

188. The inverted word-order, used when a sentence begins with an Adverb or Adverbial Phrase, has already been dealt with (cf. § 148). When the Adverb does not stand at the head of the sentence, its position varies as follows :

(a) In Principal Clauses the Adverb **follows** the Verb, e.g. :

*Spring **aldrig** efter spår-vagnar.*	Never run after trams.
*Han kommer **strax** tillbaka.*	He will soon be back.

If the Verb is in a Compound Tense, the Adverb comes immediately after the Auxiliary Verb, e.g. :

*Jag har **ofta** sett honom här.*	I have often seen him here.

(b) In Subordinate Clauses certain Adverbs **precede** the Verb (or the Auxiliary Verb in a Compound Tense), viz. :

aldrig, alltid, antagligen, bara, egentligen, ej, förmodligen, inte, möjligen, ofta, snart, strax, sällan and a few others.

Examples :

*Det var synd, att han **inte** kunde komma.*	It was a pity (that) he couldn't come.
*Jag visste, att han **ofta** sjöng på Operan.*	I knew that he often sang at the Opera.

189. Some Swedish adverbs are used in idiomatic phrases in which they serve to modify a statement in various ways ; the shades of meaning which they convey are often so subtle that it is impossible to give an exact equivalent for each of them in English. The following examples will help to illustrate their use.

*Ja, **då** [dɔ] ; nej, **då**.*	Yes, certainly ; oh no.

(*Note.*—**då** reinforces the sense of the preceding word).

*Han kommer **nog** snart.*	He's sure to come soon.
*Du får **nog** dina pengar tillbaka.*	You'll get your money back all right.

(*Note.*—**nog** usually implies reassurance).

*Han är **allt** godhjärtad. Ja,
det är han.*

I feel sure he is kind-
hearted. Yes, he is.

*Det vore **allt** roligt att resa
dit, men jag har inga
pengar.*

To be sure, it would be nice
to go there; but I
haven't any money.

Note.—**allt** makes an assertion slightly hesitant and is
sometimes followed by a reservation; cf. *visserligen.*

*Jag skall **gärna** hjälpa dig.*

I'll gladly (willingly) help
you.

*Du får **gärna** ta en karamell.*

You're welcome to have a
sweet.

*Du kan **gärna** hjälpa mig
ett tag.*

You might (be a sport and)
lend me a hand.

*Vi kan lika **gärna** gå dit i
kväll, **eller hur**[1] ?*

We might (just) as well go
there this evening, don't
you think ?

*Jag skulle **gärna** vilja resa
till Sverige.*

I should very much like to
go to Sweden.

*Får jag lov att följa med ?
Ja **gärna** för mig[2].*

May I come too ? Yes, I
don't mind.

Note.—When used with the 1st Person of a Verb, **gärna**
usually implies willingness; with the 2nd Person it either
implies permission or attempted persuasion.

*Tycker du om ostron ? Nej,
inte så värst.[3] **Inte jag
heller**.*

Do you like oysters ? No,
not particularly (very
much). Nor do I.

(Cf. French : *ni moi non plus* ; German : *ich auch
nicht*).

*Jag reser **helst** (**hellre**) till
Skottland.*

I prefer to (would rather)
go to Scotland.

*Skall jag betala kontant ? Ni
kan göra det **hur som
helst**.*

Shall I pay in cash ? You
can do it any way you
like.

Note.—In the last example, **som helst** makes the
preceding adverb indefinite ; in most other contexts **hellre**
and **helst** imply degrees of preference.

[1] *eller hur*, lit. ' or how ?' is used in exactly the same way as the
French *n'est-ce pas* ? and the German *nicht wahr* ?

[2] Cf. German *meinetwegen*.

[3] Note : ' very '=*mycket* ; but ' not very ' is translated by *inte
så värst* (sc. *mycket*), roughly equivalent to ' not so frightfully much.'

Ju *längre* **desto** **(dess)** | The longer the better.
bättre.

Jag kunde **ju** *inte vara sam-* | I couldn't be in two places
tidigt på två ställen. | at once, could I ?

Det sade jag **ju.** | That's what I said, you
| know (you will remem-
| ber).

Note.—Except in the first example above, which is a
special idiom, **ju** assumes knowledge or agreement on the
part of the person addressed.

Paketet ligger **kvar** *på pos-* | The parcel remains lying
ten. | (i.e. is still) at the post-
| office.

Är det något té **kvar** *i kan-* | Is there any tea left in the
nan ? | pot ?

Föreställningen var **mindre** | The performance was not a
lyckad. | great success.

Det var **mindre** *artigt sagt.* | That was not a very polite
| thing to say.

Note.—**mindre**, literally ' less,' is often used without any
comparative sense to express a low degree : ' not very, not
particularly.'

Kan jag stå till tjänst ? *Jag* | Can I be of any service ?
är **nämligen** *läkare.* | You see (I may mention)
| I'm a doctor.

Är hon mycket söt ? *Å, hon* | Is she very pretty ? Well,
är inte **precis** *en skönhet.* | she's not exactly a beauty.

Jag hoppas **verkligen**, *att* | I do hope you'll feel better
du blir bättre i morgon. | to-morrow.

Jag vet **verkligen** *inte, vad* | I'm sure I don't know what
jag skall göra. | to (I shall) do.

Detta är min far. **Verk-** | That is my father. (Is it)
ligen ? | really ?

Det är **visserligen** *ingen* | True, it isn't a large sum ;
stor summa, men det är | but it's all I can spare.
allt vad jag kan avstå.

Note.—**visserligen** corresponds to the German *zwar* ; it
has concessive meaning and is always followed by *men*.

*Det är **väl** inte min skuld?*	Surely you don't suggest that it's *my* fault ?
*Ni har **väl** hört, att hon är gift ?*	I suppose you've heard that she is married ?
*Du kommer **väl** till oss i kväll ?*	You'll be coming round to our place this evening, won't you ?

*Note.—**väl** denotes hesitant supposition.*

*Det tycks **ändå** bli regn.*	It seems as if it's going to rain after all.
*Han har **ändå** alltid den ursäkten, att han hade bråttom.*	After all, he can offer the excuse that he was in a hurry.

Passive Forms with Reciprocal Meaning

190. Some verbs with the Passive **-s** ending have reciprocal meaning.

*Vi **träffas** alltså kl. 7.*	We'll meet (each other) at 7 o'clock, then.
*Vi **möttes** på en bal.*	We met at a dance.
*Vi **ses** [se:s] i kväll.*	See you this evening.
*De vill alltid **slåss**[1] [slɔs].*	They're always spoiling for a fight.
*Vi **skildes** på kajen.*	We parted on the quayside.

191. The irregular verb **veta** ' know '[2]

Present	Past	Supine
vet (*pl.* veta)	visste	vetat

Note.— (a) **vet** is the usual form for the entire Present Tense ; the Plural **veta** is only found in literature.

(b) The Present Tense of this verb consists of old Past forms ; hence there is no *-er* termination.

[1] Note the double *-s* with consequent shortening of preceding vowel.

[2] *veta* denotes factual knowledge ; *känna* acquaintance, getting to know by seeing or hearing.

Deponent Verbs

192. Some verbs have only *s*-forms but without passive meaning (cf. Latin *mori*, *conari*). They are called Deponent Verbs because they lay aside any passive meaning. Thus though **passive in form** they are **active in meaning.**

Examples :

*Han **lyckas** i allt.*	He succeeds in everything.
*Jag **hoppas**, att vädret blir vackert i morgon.*	I hope it will be a fine day to-morrow.
*Jag **trivs** mycket bra.*	I am getting on very well.
*Jag **minns** honom väl* [vɛ:l].	I well remember him.
*Han **andades** djupt.*	He took a deep breath.

Other Deponent Verbs are : *brottas* ' wrestle ' ; *kräkas* to be sick (vomit) ' ; *svettas* ' to sweat.'

Some Deponent Verbs denote a natural propensity.

Examples :

*Hunden **bits**.* [biss].	The dog bites.
*Katten **rivs**.* [rifs].	The cat is inclined to scratch.
*Tjuren **stångas**.*	The bull is liable to toss (you).
*Bina **sticks**.*	(The) bees sting.
*Nässlan **bränns**.*	The nettle stings.

Strong Verbs

193. Class II. Vowel change : *y* (or *ju*)—*ö* (or *jö*)—*u* (*ju*).

Present	Past
jag kryper ' I creep '	**jag kröp** ' I crept '
Present Perfect	Past Perfect
jag har krupit ' I have crept '	**jag hade krupit** ' I had crept '
Future	Future in the Past
jag skall krypa ' I shall creep '	**jag skulle krypa** ' I should creep '

Imperative	..	**kryp** ' creep '
Infinitive	..	**att krypa** ' to creep '
Present Participle	..	**krypande** ' creeping '
Supine	..	(*jag har*) **krupit** ' crept '
Past Participle	..	(*hop-*) **krupen** 'huddled, crouched'

194. Other strong verbs of this class are :

bjuda ' offer '	*ljuga* (ˈjuˋ:ga] ' tell a lie '
bryta ' break '	*njuta* ' enjoy '
flyga ' fly '	*skjuta* [ˈʂuˋ:ta][1] ' shoot '
flyta ' float '	*skryta* ' boast '
frysa ' freeze '	*sluta* ' conclude, stop '
klyva ' cleave '	*smyga* ' slip '
knyta ' tie '	*stryka* ' stroke '
ljuda [ˈjuˋ:da] ' sound '	

Two other verbs, which originally belonged to another
class, are now conjugated like those given above, viz. :
sjunga [ˈʂeˋŋŋa] ' sing ' ; *sjunka* [ˈʂeˋŋka] ' sink.' They
retain the *j* in all their forms.

Vocabulary

fotvandring, c. (2) ' walking tour '	*rekommendera*[1] ' recommend '
förträfflig ' excellent '	*semester*, c. (2) ' holiday '
härlig ' glorious '	*stuga*, c. (1) ' cottage '
motorbåt, c. (2) ' motorboat '	*tillgiven* ' devoted, sincere '
nöjd ' contented, pleased '	*trevlig* ' nice, pleasant '
pensionat [paŋsoˈnɑ:t] ' boarding-house '	*utflykt*, c. (3) ' excursion '

Exercise 15
Translate

(*a*)   Stockholm den 18 juli 1940.

Bäste[2] Nils !

Tack för brevet. Jag har varit i Stockholm en vecka,
men jag har inte haft tid att skriva till dig förr. Jag är
mycket nöjd med det[3] pensionat, som du rekommenderade.
Rummen är mycket trevliga, och maten är förträfflig. Vi
trivs mycket bra här på alla sätt (pl. = *in every way*).
I går var hela familjen ute på Lidingö[4] och badade. Vädret
var strålande vackert, och det var mycket folk därute (*a lot
of people out there*). I kväll skall vi gå på teatern, och i
morgon tänker vi göra en utflykt till Drottningholm,[5] om

---

[1] The *j* is dropped before the front vowel in the Past Tense : *sköt.*
[2] See § 107, footnote.   [3] § 177.
[4] *Lidingö* is a large island in the Stockholm district.
[5] *Drottningholm* is the Swedish ' Windsor.'

det inte regnar. Nu måste jag sluta, men nästa vecka skall jag skriva till dig igen. Hjärtliga hälsningar (= *kind regards*) från oss alla.

Din tillgivne[1]

Gunnar.

(*b*)   Malmö, 22nd July, 1940.

Dear Gunnar,

Many thanks for your last letter, which I received (=*fick*, § 159) a week ago (§ 162). It was nice (= *roligt*) to know (transl. : to hear) that you are getting on so well in Stockholm. Last year I stayed with (= *hos*) some friends who have a cottage on a small island near Lidingö, so I know what it is like (transl. : how it is) there. We bathed every morning from the jetty and went for (transl. : made) excursions in a motor-boat. It was a glorious holiday.

This year I am staying at home till (= *till*) the beginning of August. Then I am going on (transl. : I shall make) a walking tour in Småland.

Yours sincerely,

Nils.

(*c*)   **Den svenska nationalsången**
Du gamla, du fria

Du gamla, du fria, du fjällhöga[2] Nord,
du tysta[3], du glädjerika[4] sköna[5] !
Jag hälsar[6] dig, vänaste[7] land uppå[8] jord,
din sol, din himmel, dina ängder[9] gröna,
din sol, din himmel, dina ängder gröna.

Du tronar[10] på minnen[11] från fornstora dar,[12]
då ärat[13] ditt namn flög över jorden.
Jag vet, att du är och du blir, vad du var.
Ack[14], jag vill leva, jag vill dö i Norden !
Ja, jag vill leva, jag vill dö i Norden !

---

[1] See § 109 (*a*).

[2] (poet.) fell-high, i.e. lofty, mountainous ; [3] silent ; [4] rich in gladness, i.e. joyous ; [5] adj. for noun = fair one ; [6] hail, greet ; [7] fairest ; [8] upon ; [9] tracts, regions ; [10] thou art enthroned ; [11] memories ; [12] *forn* = ancient, *dar* = *dagar*, times of former greatness (i.e. the period when Sweden was a Great Power) ; [13] honoured ; [14] oh.

CHAPTER XVI

INDEFINITE AND INTERROGATIVE PRONOUNS AND ADJECTIVES

195. Apart from a few independent pronominal forms the same word serves both as indefinite pronoun and adjective.

Words used as Pronouns only

man is only used as subject (gen. *ens*, obj. *en*). It corresponds to German *man* and French *on*, and has no real equivalent in English. It may be rendered by : one, you, they, or by periphrastic expressions. Examples : *man säger* ' they (people) say, it is said ' ; *man måste leva* ' one must live ' ; *man kan se huset härifrån* ' one (you) can see the house (the house can be seen) from here ' ; *man kan aldrig veta* ' you never can tell, there's no knowing, one never knows ' ; *när ens vänner dör och lämnar en* ' when one's friends die and leave one.'

Note.—The genitive and objective forms are seldom used.

någonting ' something ' ; *ingenting* ' nothing ' ; *allting* ' everything ' are only used as pronouns ; they are neuter. When *någonting* is used in an interrogative or negative statement, it corresponds to English : anything. Examples : *jag har någonting nytt* ' I've got something new ' ; *har du hört någonting om honom* ? ' have you heard anything about him ? ' ; *jag har inte sett någonting dylikt förr* ' I haven't seen anything like that before ' ; *ingenting särskilt* ' nothing special (in particular) '; *jag har glömt allting* ' I've forgotten everything.'

196.   Words used as Pronouns and Adjectives

Common	Neuter	Plural
någon ' some, any, some- body, anybody '	*något*	*några*

Examples : *någon ringde nyss* ' somebody rang just now ' ; *har någon ringt* ? ' has anyone rung ? '; *vi har inte fått*

143

någon mat ' we haven't had any food '; *hörde du något (någonting) därute* ? ' did you hear anything outside ? '; *vi måste skriva några rader* ' we must write some (= a few) lines '; *har du några pengar* ? ' have you any money ? '

ingen ' no, nobody, none ' **intet** **inga**

Examples : *jag känner ingen här* ' I don't know anybody here '; *jag har ingen kniv* ' I haven't got a knife '; *ingen skrev till mig* ' nobody wrote to me '; *ingen rök utan eld* ' no smoke without fire '; *intet blev gjort* ' nothing was done '; *jag har inga* (or : *inte några*) *pengar kvar* ' I haven't got any money left.' (On *inget* see § 73.d).

annan ' other, else ' **annat** **andra**

Examples : *en annan gång* ' another time '; *en annans hustru* ' another man's wife '; *var det någonting annat* ? ' is there anything else (*scil*. I can serve you with[1] ?) '; *andra tider, andra seder* ' other times, other customs.'

Note.—In translating ' another ' into Swedish it is important to decide whether it means ' additional ' or ' different, of another kind,' as this affects the translation. Thus *Kan jag få en kopp till* ? means ' May I have another (i.e. additional) cup ? '; whereas *en annan kopp* means ' a different cup.'

The definite forms are :

den andra ' the other ' **det andra** **de andra**
(masc. **den andre**)

Examples : *den enes död, den andres bröd* ' the one's death the other's bread (one man's meat is another man's poison) '; *det här är fint, men jag vill ha det andra* ' this (one) is fine, but I want the other one '; *de andra stannade hemma* ' the others stayed at home.'

all ' all ' **allt** **alla**

Examples : *all början är svår* ' all (i.e. every) beginning is difficult '; *är detta allt* ? ' is that all ? '; *allt möjligt* ' all sorts (kinds) of things '; *är vi alla här* ? ' are we all here ? '; *alla dagar* ' all days (i.e. every day).'

[1] This expression is heard in shops.

The singular forms of **många** ' many ' are scarcely ever used. Note *många av hans män* ' many of his men '; *många människor* ' many people.'

The word **flera** ' several,' has no singular forms.

Examples : *flera av mina vänner* ' several of my friends '; *på flera ställen* ' in several (various) places.' In comparisons it means ' more,' e.g. *har du några flera* ? ' have you any more (of that sort) ? '; *många flera* ' many more.'

The word **få** ' few,' only occurs in the plural.

Examples : *några få* ' some (= a) few '; *få människor tror det* ' few people believe it '; *i få ord* ' in a few words, briefly.'

The following words have no plural forms :

var ' each, every '	**vart**	—
varje ' each, every '	**varje**	—

Examples : *var och en* ' one and all '; *var* (or *varje*) *dag* ' every day '; *vart tredje*[1] *år* ' every three years '; *de fick var sin* [vɑːsin] *karamell*[2] ' they each received a sweet '; *litet av varje* ' a little of everything.'

Note.—' Few ' is translated by *få* ; ' a few ' by *några*.

' Little ' is translated by *föga* ; ' a little ' by *litet* [ˈliˈːtə]

' Somewhat ' is translated by *något* or *tämligen*.

' Any ' before a Comparative is not translated.

Föga kunde jag ana det.	Little did I suspect (realize) it.
Han hade lite pengar i alla fall.	He had a little money after all.
Han kom något tidigt.	He arrived somewhat early.
Jag hinner inte skriva mera.	I haven't time to write any more.

[1] Note the Ordinal where English has the Cardinal Numeral.

[2] *var sin* is invariable ; hence ' We were each given a sweet ' is *Vi fick var sin* (not : *vår* !) *karamell*.

197. Interrogative Pronouns and Adjectives

The principal interrogative pronouns and adjectives are:

Common	Neuter	Plural
vem ' who, whom '	*vad* ' what '	(wanting)
vilken ' what, which '	*vilket*	*vilka*

Note.—(*a*) As pronouns these words have the genitive forms *vems*, *vilkens*, *vilkets*, *vilkas*.

Note.—(*b*) *Vem* refers only to persons and is seldom used adjectivally; it has the same form whether used as subject or object.

Note.—(*c*) *Vad* refers only to things and is not used adjectivally; it has the same form whether used as subject or object.

Note.—(*d*) *Vilken* serves both as pronoun and adjective.

Examples : Subject.—*Vem är det ?* ' Who is it ! ' Object—*Vem träffade du i parken ?* ' Whom did you meet in the park ? ' Genitive.—*Vems hatt är det här ?* ' Whose hat is this ? '

Subject.—*Vad är det ?* ' What is it ? (or : what is the matter ?).'

Object.—*Vad säger du ?* ' What do you say ? '

A preposition is usually placed at the end of the sentence, e.g. *Vem talade du med ?* ' Whom were you speaking to ? ' *Vem fick du den presenten av ?* ' From whom did you get that present ? '

The missing plural of *vem* is supplied by *vilka*, e.g. *Vilka är de där människorna ?* ' Who are those people ? ' Apart from this, *vilken*, *vilket*, *vilka* are mostly used like English ' which ' in a distinguishing or selecting sense.

Examples : *Vilken av bröderna tycker du bäst om ?* ' Which of the brothers do you like best ? ' *Vilken stig skall jag ta ?* ' Which path do I take ? '

A further use of *vilken* is in exclamations corresponding to English ' what ': *Vilken dåre jag har varit !* ' What a fool I have been ! ' *Vilken hjälte !* ' What a hero ! ' *Vilket elände !* ' What a sorry state of affairs (mess, nuisance, bother) ! ' But in these expressions *vilken* can be replaced by *en sådan* (cf. § 201).

198. **Note.**—When the interrogative pronouns are used as the subject in a dependent question, they are followed by **som.**

Examples :

Vet du, **vem som** *ringde ?*   Do you know who (it was who) rang ?

(But : *Vet du,* **vem** *det var ?*   Do you know who that was ?)

In the second example the subject of the dependent clause is *det* ; hence *som* is omitted.

Säg mig, vilken hatt som kläder [klæ:r] *mig bäst.*   Tell me which hat suits me best.

(But : *Jag undrar, vilken hatt du vill ha.*   I wonder which hat you would like).

Jag vet inte, vad som är sant.   I don't know what is true (the truth of the matter).

199. Swedish has several ways of saying 'What sort (kind) of . . .,' viz. :

Common	Neuter	Plural
vad för en hurudan	**vad för ett hurudant**	**vad för hurudana**

or the invariable **vad för slags** [va fœ ṣlaks].

Examples :

Vad för en människa är hon ?   What sort of person is she ?

Vad för ett djur är det här ?   What sort of animal is this ?

Vad för folk är de ?   What sort of people are they ?

Hurudan mössa hade han ?   What sort of cap had he got (on) ?

Hurudant väder är det ?   What's the weather like ?

Vad för slags folk är Carlssons ?   What sort of people are the Carlssons ?

T.Y.S.—6

200. There are several ways of saying '**I** beg your pardon ; what did you say ? ' in Swedish. The most polite expression is *Förlåt* ; *jag hörde inte*, but *Hur sade* [hur̩ˈʂaː] *ni* ? is also frequently used. Other phrases heard are : *Vad för slag* ? *Vad befalles* ? *Vafalls* ? ' Beg pardon ? ' or just *Vad* [va] ? but the latter is vulgar and should be avoided. *Vilket* ? is occasionally used.

201. The words *sådan* and *dylik*, meaning ' such, like that ' are used both as Adjectives and Pronouns[1] ; their forms are as follows :

Common	Neuter	Plural
(*en*) *sådan*	(*ett*) *sådant*	*sådana*
(*en*) *dylik*	(*ett*) *dylikt*	*dylika*
[ˈdyˈːliːk]	[ˈdyˈːli(k)t]	[ˈdyˈːlika]

Examples :

Sådan herre sådan dräng.	Like master, like man.
Sådant är livet.	Such is life.
En sådan bok vill jag ha.	That's the kind of book I want.
Sådana människor tycker jag inte om.	I don't like such people.
Kan jag få två sådana ?	May (Can) I have two of those ?
I sådant (or *I så*) *fall.*[2]	In that case.
Dylikt väder är vanligt.	Such weather is usual.
Han sade något dylikt.	He said something like that.
Dylika böcker är billiga.	Such books are cheap.

Note.—*Sådan* is also used in exclamations :

En sådan dumbom !	What a blockhead !
Ett sådant väder vi får !	What weather we're having !
En sådan syn det var !	What a sight it was !

---

[1] *sådan* literally means ' so-done, so-fashioned ' ; and *dylik* means ' that like ' or ' like that ', *dy* being a survival of the old dative case of *det*. It is rather formal and not often used nowadays.
[2] *I så fall* is much more usual.

Strong Verbs

202. Class III. Vowel-change : (short) *i—a—u*.

<table>
<tr><td>Present</td><td>Past</td></tr>
<tr><td>*jag binder* ' I bind '</td><td>*jag band*[1] ' I bound '</td></tr>
<tr><td>Present Perfect</td><td>Past Perfect</td></tr>
<tr><td>*jag har bundit* ' I have '
bound '</td><td>*jag hade bundit* ' I had
bound '</td></tr>
<tr><td>Future</td><td>Future in the Past</td></tr>
<tr><td>*jag skall binda* ' I shall
bind '</td><td>*jag skulle binda* ' I should
bind '</td></tr>
</table>

Imperative .. .. *bind* ' bind '
Infinitive .. .. *att binda* ' to bind '
Present Participle *bindande* ' binding '
Supine .. .. (*jag har*) *bundit* ' bound '
Past Participle .. *bunden* ' bound '; neut. : *bundet*;
plur. : *bundna*.

203. Other strong verbs of this class are :

<table>
<tr><td>*brinna* ' burn '</td><td>*rinna* ' run, flow '</td></tr>
<tr><td>*brista* ' burst '</td><td>*spinna* ' spin '</td></tr>
<tr><td>*dricka* ' drink '</td><td>*spricka* ' burst, crack '</td></tr>
<tr><td>*finna* ' find '</td><td>*springa* ' run '</td></tr>
<tr><td>*försvinna*[2] ' vanish '</td><td>*sticka* ' stick, prick '</td></tr>
<tr><td>*hinna* ' have time '</td><td>*vinna* ' win '</td></tr>
</table>

204. Other Vowel Changes

Infinitive	Past	Supine	Past Part.
1. *bära* ' bear, carry '	*bar* (*buro*)	*burit*	*buren*
stjäla ['sɛ`:la] ' steal '	*stal* (*stulo*)	*stulit*	*stulen*
skära ['sæ`:ra] ' cut '	*skar* (*skuro*)	*skurit*	*skuren*
2. *dra*(*ga*) ' draw '	*drog* (*drogo*) [dro:g]	*dragit*	*dragen*
ta(*ga*) ' take '	*tog* (*togo*) [to:g]	*tagit*	*tagen*

[1] The Past Plural form *bundo* only occurs in literature.
[2] See § 206.

fara ' go '	*for (foro)* [fo:r]	*farit*	(*hädan*)*faren*[1]
hålla ' hold '	*höll (höllo)*	*hållit*	*hållen*
falla ' fall '	*föll (föllo)*	*fallit*	*fallen*

(3)   **Irregular Changes**

ge [je:] (*giva*) ' give '	*gav (gåvo)*	*givit* (*gett*)	*given*
gråta ' weep '	*grät (gräto)*	*gråtit*	(*be*)*gråten*[2]
låta ' let '	*lät (läto)*	*låtit*	(*över*)*låten*[3]
komma ' come '	*kom (kommo)*	*kommit*	*kommen*
sova ['so`:va] ' sleep '	*sov (sovo)*	*sovit*	—
svära ' swear '	*svor (svoro)* [svo:r]	*svurit*	*svuren*
äta ' eat '	*åt (åto)*	*ätit*	*äten*

Note.—(*a*) The bracketed disyllabic forms are only used in literature.

Note.—(*b*) The Present Tense of *bära, stjäla, skära, fara* and *svära* is formed by dropping the *-a* termination of the Infinitive. All the other verbs above drop the *-a* and add *-er*, e.g. *hålla— håller* ; the monosyllabic verbs *dra, ta, ge*, form their Present Tense by adding *-r*.

Note.—(*c*) The Present Participle of all the above verbs is formed by adding *-nde* to the Infinitive (e.g. *bärande, givande*).

Note.—(*d*) On the declension of the Participles see §§ 172—176.

Note.—(*e*) The Imperative consists of the bare stem of the verb, that is, it is formed by dropping the *-a* of the Infinitive. Special forms to be noted are : *dra, ta, ge, kom* !

---

[1] *hädanfaren*=' departed hence,' i.e. ' departed this life, deceased' ; some Past Participles are only rarely used and then mostly in compound forms.

[2] *begråten*=bewailed, lamented.

[3] *överlåten*=transferred, made over.

Vocabulary

armband, n. (5) ' bracelet ' *lass*, n. (5) ' load '
bit, c. (2) ' piece ' *ljud*, n. (5) ' sound '
bänk, c. (2) ' seat ' *lycka*, c. ' fortune '
exemplar, n. (5) ' copy (of a *ro*, c. ' rest, repose '
book) ' *skarp* ' sharp '
frukt, c. (3) ' fruit ' *smutsig* ' dirty '
författare, c. (5) ' author, *tanke*, c. (2) ' thought '
writer ' *väg*, c. (2) ' road, way '
först, adv. ' first ' *å*, c. (2) ' (small) river '

Exercise 16

Translate

(a) Det är någon som ringer på (= *at*) dörren. Hörde ni
något ? Nej, jag hörde ingenting. Det är ingen hemma.
Finns det (= *is there*) något te kvar ? Vilken av de här
böckerna har ni läst ? Kan jag få en annan bok ? Vad för
en bok vill ni ha ? Vi har inga andra. Kan jag få ett
exemplar till ? Har ni några flera böcker av den sorten ?
Nej, alla de andra är utsålda (= *sold out*). Vi fick var sin
bok som present. Tåg går (= *leave*) var tjugonde minut.
Hon talade om allt möjligt. Säg mig, i få ord, hur ni hade
det (= *get on*) på landet. Vem var Strindberg ? Strindberg
var en känd svensk författare. Vad är klockan ?

(b) Has anybody seen my brother ? Which brother ?
My eldest brother. No, I haven't seen anyone here. Whom
were you ringing up (= *till*) ? What did he say ? Nobody
knows anything about it (= *därom*). Did you meet anybody ? Can nobody help me ? Which road do (= *skall*) I
take ? There is (= *det finns*) no water in the glass. Have
you any left ? This glass is dirty. Please (= *var snäll och*)
give me another. Can you tell (*säga*) me which train leaves
first ? I don't know what he said. What was the weather
like yesterday in Stockholm ? What sort of hat would you
like (= *vill ni ha*) ? One like that. May I have (= *Can I*

get) six of those (please[1]). Some other time. Every other (*Varannan*) week. Every other year. Every three weeks. Another town.

(c) Jag drack en kopp kaffe. Han hann inte läsa mera,[2] han måste springa till stationen. Han hinner alltid med (=*is always in time for, always catches*) tåget. Han sprang allt, vad han kunde. När Adam plöjde (=*ploughed*) och Eva spann, en var (*everyone*) var då en adelsman (*nobleman*). Vem har stulit mitt armband ? Nära huset rann en liten å. Lyckan kommer, lyckan går. Glaset sprack i tusen bitar. Har ni sovit gott ?—Ja, tack. Jag sov som en stock (*like a log*). Tankarna låter honom inte finna någon ro. Ett skarpt ljud for genom luften och skar i (= *grated on*) hans öron. En gammal man for omkring (= *around*) på landet.

(d) I have cut the apple in two pieces. He fell down-stairs (= *nedför trappan*). I found your book on the table. The horse is coming down (= *nedför*) the street. It (= *Den*) is drawing a heavy load. The girls were sitting on the seat. Tell me what you have given him. I have eaten too much (= *för mycket*[3]) fruit. He swore that he would (= *skulle*) help her. He was holding the parcel under his arm (*transl. the* arm). I took my holidays (*transl.* holiday) in August. When do we have (*transl.* shall we eat) lunch ?

---

[1] Note : ' please ' is not translated in making requests.

[2] In a negative or interrogative sentence *mera* can mean ' any more.'

[3] ' much ' is nearly always translated by *mycket* in the neuter form because it has substantival force ; *mycket frukt* really means ' much of fruit.'

CHAPTER XVII

COMPOUND VERBS—REFLEXIVE VERBS—IMPERSONAL VERBS

205. In Swedish, as in German and, to a lesser extent, English, there are a number of Compound Verbs formed by combining a simple verb with a Prefix, a Noun, an Adjective, an Adverb or a Preposition. In some cases this latter element is detached from the verb proper and occupies an independent position in the sentence, in others it is fused with the verb. These two types are known as **Separable and Inseparable Verbs.** In English the verbs *beset, forget, misuse* have inseparable prefixes; the verb *uphold* is also inseparable, while *to hold up* has a different meaning and is separable. We may compare the sentences ' He has always *upheld* these principles,' ' The highwaymen *held up* the stagecoach,' and ' The boy *held up* his hand.' There are similar variations in Swedish. The verbal part of the word is conjugated in exactly the same way as when it occurs in isolation, e.g. *söka, sökte, sökt* ; *undersöka, undersökte, undersökt.*

206. Verbs having the following Prefixes or an Adjective or Noun as first element are **inseparable** :

> *an-, be-, bi-, er-, för-, här-. miss-, sam-, um-, und-, van-, å-.*

Most of these prefixes are borrowed from the German (cf. Introduction, page xi) and their meanings will generally be apparent to students of German ; *för-* corresponds to *ver-, här-* to *her-, sam-* is connected with *zusammen, und-* corresponds to *ent-, van-* (which is rare in German, cf. *Wahnsinn*) has the sense of English *un-,* and *å-* represents a variant of *an-.*

Examples : *angripa* ' attack ' ; *begrava* ' bury ' ; *biträda* ' assist ' ; *erhålla* ' receive ' ; *förbjuda* ' forbid ' ; *härleda* ' deduce ' ; *missbruka* ' misuse ' ; *samverka* ' cooperate ' ; *umgås* ' associate ' ; *undvika* ' avoid ' ; *vanära* ' dishonour ' ; *åkalla* ' invoke.'

Note.—(*a*) The prefixes *be-* and *för-* are unstressed and verbs formed with these prefixes have Tone I (cf. § 69. *g*). An exception is the verb *bearbeta* ' to work upon, elaborate,' which has stress on the *be-* and Tone II.

Note.—(*b*) Compound Verbs formed with any of the other prefixes in the above list have a full stress on the prefix and Tone II (cf. § 70. *g*).

Examples of Compound Inseparable Verbs having a Noun or Adjective as first element are : *rådfråga* ' consult ' ; *tjuvlyssna* ' keep a wireless receiving set without taking out a licence ' (similarly *tjuvläsa* ' read a book which one does not intend to buy and then return it to the bookseller ', such compounds corresponding to German verbs with *schwarz-* as first element) ; *fullända* ' complete ' ; *godkänna* ' approve, pass ' (e.g. a candidate in an examination) ; *grovhacka* ' rough-hew, chop coarsely.' All Compound Verbs of this type have Tone II with principal stress on the first element.

Some Compound Verbs having an Adverb (often a Prepositional Adverb) as first element are **inseparable**, e.g. *framhäva* ' emphasize ' ; *infria* ' redeem (one's word, a promise) ' ; *övergiva* ' abandon ' ; *förebåda* ' forebode ' ; *emotse* ' await ' ; *förbise* ' overlook.' These, too, have Tone II with principal stress on the first element.

207. Most Compound Verbs not included in the above-mentioned categories have a **Separable** and an **Inseparable** form. The separable forms are the more usual in everyday speech.

Examples :

koppla in or *inkoppla* ' plug in, connect (electrically).'

skära till or *tillskära* ' cut out (e.g. cloth).'

smutsa ner or *nersmutsa* ' make dirty[1].'

söka upp or *uppsöka* ' seek out, go to see.'

---

[1] There are a number of compound verbs in which the prefix *ner-* gives the sense of ' making a mess,' e.g. *svärta ner* ' blacken,' *sota ner* ' cover with soot,' *tjära ner* ' soil with tar,' *smörja ner* ' smear all over,' *blöta ner* ' make all wet, soak.'

Thus *Han sökte upp mig* and *Han uppsökte mig* are both possible and mean ' He looked me up (came to see me) ' ; but the former is more usual.

Note.—(a) In the separable forms the adverbial element usually has a full stress and the verbal element is more weakly stressed (cf. the English ' looked me up ' in the above example).

Note.—(b) The inseparable forms have a strong stress on the first element and are pronounced with Tone II.

208. Some Compound Verbs have separable and inseparable forms with different meanings (cf. English ' look over ' and ' overlook '). Compare the following examples :

Jag går av vid nästa station.	I am getting out at the next station.
Tåget avgår kl. 3.	The train leaves at 3 o'clock.
Han bröt av en gren.	He broke off a branch.
Han avbröt resan.	He broke his journey.

Note.—In the sentence *Han hälsade på oss* ' He called on us, came to see us,' the verb is *hälsa på* with the stress on *på* ; but in *Han hälsade på oss* ' He greeted (saluted) us,' the verb is *hälsa*, and *på* is a preposition not connected with the verb, so the stress falls on the latter. The stress indicates the difference in meaning.

It will be seen that a Separable Verb usually has physical meaning, whereas the corresponding Inseparable Verb is used in a more figurative sense.

209. The Present Participle and Past Participle of all

Compound Verbs are **inseparable**. Compare the following examples :

Solen gick upp tidigt.	*Den uppgående solen.*
The sun rose early.	The rising sun.
Rasen dog ut.	*Den utdöende rasen.*
The race died out.	The race that is dying out.
Han kastade bort nyckeln.	*Den bortkastade nyckeln.*
He threw the key away.	The key which had been thrown away.
Han bröt av en gren.	*Den avbrutna grenen.*
He broke off a branch.	The broken branch.

Reflexive Verbs

210. The Reflexive Pronouns *mig*, *dig*, *sig*, etc., have already been given in § 141, together with the forms of *tvätta sig* ' to wash oneself.' Other reflexive verbs in common use are :

raka[I] *sig* ' shave '	*gifta*[II] *sig* ' get married '
bry[III] *sig* ' bother '	*lära*[II] *sig* ' learn '
klippa[II] *sig* ' get one's hair cut[1] '	*ändra*[I] *sig* ' change one's mind '
kläda[II] [klɛ:] *på sig* [2] ' get dressed '	*förändra*[I] *sig* ' change ' (intr.)
lägga[II] *sig* ' lie down, go to bed '	*röra*[II] *sig* ' move '
känna[II] *sig* ' feel '	*blamera*[I] *sig* ' make a fool of oneself '
försova[IV] *sig* ' oversleep '	*roa*[I] *sig* ' amuse oneself '
sätta[II] *sig* ' sit down '	*visa*[I] *sig* ' appear (prove) '

Examples :

Jag rakar mig i badrummet.	I shave in the bathroom.
Jag måste snart klippa mig.	I shall soon have to get my hair cut.
Jag bryr mig inte om det.	I won't bother about that.
Han klädde på sig så fort som möjligt.	He got dressed as quickly as possible.

[1] *Jag skall klippa mig* does not imply cutting one's own hair ; it is short for *jag skall låta klippa mig* ; see § 255. [2] Stress on *på*.

Jag känner mig trött ; jag måste lägga mig.	I feel tired ; I must lie down.
Hon förklarade, att hon hade försovit sig.	She explained that she had overslept.
Han satte sig på klippan.	He sat down on the rock.
Hon gifte sig med en sjö-kapten [**kap'te:n**]	She married a sea captain.
Vi har svårt[1] att lära oss ryska.	We have difficulty in learning Russian.
Jag har ändrat mig ; jag skall inte gå dit i kväll.	I've changed my mind ; I'm not going there this evening.
Han har förändrat sig[2] mycket, sedan jag såg honom sist.	He has changed a great deal since I last saw him.
Det rör sig.	It's beginning to move.
Jag blamerade mig förfärligt.	I made an awful fool of myself.
Hur skall vi roa oss i kväll ?	How shall we amuse ourselves this evening ?
Det visade sig vara ett misstag.	It proved to be a mistake.

Note.—In English expressions like ' He did it himself ' the word ' himself ' is not a reflexive pronoun ; it merely serves to emphasize the pronoun to which it refers. This is rendered by the Swedish *själv*, neut. *självt* (rarely used), pl. *själva*.

Examples :

Det var jag själv, som såg honom.	I saw him myself.
Konungen själv (formal). *Själva kungen.*	The King himself.
Själva hovet.	The very court.
I själva verket.	As a matter of fact.
Vi köpte det själva.	We ourselves bought it.

[1] This is short for *Vi har det svårt* ; cf. *ha roligt* ' enjoy oneself, have a good time ' ; *ha trevligt* ' have a pleasant time ' ; *ha tråkigt* ' be bored.'

[2] Cf. the opposite : *Han är sig lik* ' He's just the same as he always was (hasn't changed a bit).'

211. In some Reflexive Verbs the pronoun represents a Dative, although this does not affect its form, e.g. *föreställa sig* and *inbilla sig*. Both these verbs mean 'to imagine,' the former with the sense 'call up to one's imagination, picture to oneself,' and the latter with the sense of imagining something that is not true, conceit.

> *Man kan lätt föreställa sig*   You may easily imagine
> *hans förtvivlan.*   (picture) his despair.

> *Hon inbillar sig vara vacker.*   She imagines (thinks) she is
>   beautiful.

Other examples are : *skaffa sig* 'procure (for oneself)'; *beställa sig* 'order (from a shop)'; *ådraga sig* 'incur'; *åta(ga) sig* 'take upon oneself'; *tänka sig* 'think to oneself.'

Impersonal Verbs

212. Impersonal Verbs are those which can only have the subject *det* 'it.' Many of them refer to the weather, e.g. *det regnar*[I] 'it is raining'; *det blåser*[II] 'it is windy'; *det haglar*[I] 'it is hailing'; *det blixtrar*[I] 'there is a flash of lightning'; *det åskar*[I] ['o`skar] 'it is thundering'; *det snöar*[I] 'it is snowing'; *det fryser*[IV] 'it is freezing'; *det töar*[I] 'it is thawing'; *det mulnar*[I] 'it is becoming cloudy'; *det klarnar*[I] 'it is clearing'; *det drar*[IV] 'there is a draught.' Various degrees of rain are expressed by *det duggregnar* 'it is drizzling' (*duggregn* 'drizzle'); *det ösregnar* (*hällregnar, störtregnar*) 'it is pouring with rain'; *det forsar*[I] *ner* or *ned* 'it is coming down in buckets (*fors*, torrent).'

213. In other cases English uses personal forms :
> *Det gläder*[II] *mig* 'I am glad (lit. it gladdens me).'

> *Det lyckas* (§ 192) *mig* 'I succeed (lit. it succeeds to me).'
> *Det förvånar*[I] *mig* 'I am surprised.'

Notice also the following impersonal constructions with the **Past Tense** where English has the Present :

> **Det var roligt** *att träffas.*   I am pleased to meet you.

> **Det var synd**, *att han är*   It's a pity he's ill.
>   *sjuk.*

Det var tråkigt, *att tåget*   (It's a pity) how annoying
   är försenat.   that the train is delayed
                                    (late).

Det var tur att du kom.   It's lucky you've come.

Note.—The Swedish for 'I remember' was formerly
Det kommer mig i håg lit. ' It comes to me into the mind, i.e.
into my mind.' This, by an illogical transposition, has now
become *Jag kommer ihåg det.*

Vocabulary

kaffepanna, c. (1) ' coffee pot '
kök [çøk], n. (5) ' kitchen '
mjölkbud, n. (5) ' milkman,
   milkgirl '
liter, c. (2) ' litre '
grädde, c. ' cream '
färsk ' fresh '
franskbröd n. (5) ' roll '
frukost ['frøˈkɔst], c. (2)
   ' breakfast '
lyssna[1] ' listen '
nyheter ' news '
brevbärare, c. (5) ' postman '

gröt, c. (2) ' porridge '
gaffelbit, c. (2) ' titbit[1] '
limpa, c. (1) ' spiced bread '
knäckebröd[2], n. (5) ' crisp
   bread '
städning, c. (2) ' tidying
   up[3] '
disk, c. ' dish washing '
diskning, c. 'washing up[4]'
färdig ' ready ' (also :
   ' finished ')
uppköp, n. (5) ' purchase '
göra uppköp ' go shopping '

---

[1] *gaffelbit* literally means ' fork bit '; it consists of a strip of
pickled herring.
[2] Also called *hårt bröd* ' hard bread (made of rye).'
[3] *städa ett rum* ' to tidy up a room '; *städerska* ' charwoman.'
[4] *diska* ' to wash the dishes, wash up.'

Exercise 17

Translate

Fru Svensson går upp.

(*a*) Fru Svensson börjar dagen tidigt. Hon går upp kl. 7 och sätter på kaffepannan. Medan (=*Whilst*) kaffet kokar, går hon in i badrummet och gör sin morgontoilett[1]. Sedan dricker hon en kopp kaffe i köket. Det ringer på dörren. Det är mjölkbudet med 2 liter mjölk, 2 dcl. (= deciliter) grädde samt (=*together with*) färska franskbröd till (=*for*) frukost. Kl. 8 lyssnar Fru Svensson på (= *to*) nyheterna i radio. Så kommer brevbäraren med posten. Så är det tid att väcka barnen och att laga frukost. I dag serveras gröt och mjölk, kokta ägg med gaffelbitar, kaffe, smör och flera sorters (=*sorts of*) bröd såsom (=*such as*) franskbröd, limpa och knäckebröd. Vid 10-tiden är städning och disk över, och Fru Svensson är färdig att gå ut och göra uppköp.

(*b*) He sat down on a seat. I go to bed at 11 o'clock every evening. I feel rather queer (*inte riktigt bra*). He shaved very quickly. She married for money. They felt extremely happy. I feel better now. I don't care (*bry*) what he says. I couldn't imagine that it was true. You must get yourself a copy of this book. As a matter of fact I have one (= *ett sådant*). I myself saw the king.

---

[1] See alternative Swedified spelling in § 77; pronunciation as in French.

CHAPTER XVIII
WORD ORDER
I—Inversion

214. The principal rules for Inverted Word-Order have already been given (see § 148). Inversion is also used in many Interrogative Sentences. Since Swedish has no auxiliary corresponding to the English ' do ' in formulating questions, inversion is used in Interrogative Sentences where the Subject is not an Interrogative Pronoun.

Examples :

Sjunger hon bra ?	Does she sing well ?
Hade jag inte rätt ?	Wasn't I right ?

The inverted word-order is also used in Conditional Clauses where the Conjunction *om* ' if ' is omitted (cf. the English ' Should he come . . . ' used instead of ' If he should come ').

Example :

Hade jag *bara anat det, så kunde jag ha kommit tidigare.*	If only I had had an inkling of it, I could have come sooner.

Note.—The rules for inverted word-order apply in the main to Principal Clauses. As a rule the normal (uninverted) word-order is used in Subordinate Clauses.

Contrast :

När **går tåget** ?	When does the train start ?
Jag skall höra, när **tåget går.**	I will enquire (ask) when the train starts.

II—Position of the Adverb

215. In Principal Clauses the Adverb is placed **after** the Verb (in Compound Tenses immediately after the Auxiliary Verb, cf. § 188), e.g. :

Jag **röker aldrig.**	I never smoke.
Jag **har aldrig rökt** *en pipa.*	I have never smoked a pipe.

The position of the negative *inte* 'not' usually follows the above rule ; but sometimes in the colloquial language it is used twice, in the head position and again at the end, for the sake of emphasis, e.g. :

Inte vet jag någonting om   I don't know anything *den saken inte.*   about that, really I don't.

In Subordinate Clauses the following Adverbs are placed **before** the Verb (in Compound Tenses immediately before the Auxiliary Verb) : *aldrig, alltid, bara, ej, icke, inte, ingalunda, ofta, snart, sällan, antagligen, förmodligen* and a few others.

Examples :

*Jag sade, att jag **aldrig***   I said I never smoked. ***rökte**.*

*Han frågade, om jag **snart***   He asked if I were coming ***skulle** komma hem.*   home soon.

Demonstrative Adverbs and Adverbs expressing a more or less definite time are placed **after** the Verb.

Examples :

Jag tror, att tåget stannar   I believe the train stops ***här**.*   here.

*Om du köper biljetterna **nu**,*   If you get the tickets now, *kan vi gå ut i stan.*   we shall be able to go out into the town.

III—Position of the Verb

216. In the older periods of the language the Finite Verb was placed last in a Subordinate Clause ; many examples can be found in Biblical Swedish and there are survivals in legal and official style.

. . . på sex dagar gjorde Her-   . . . in six days the Lord *ren himmelen och jorden*   made heaven and earth, *och havet och allt vad i*   the sea and all that in *dem är.*   them is.

*Alla de som i Sverige **bygga***   All those who dwell in *och **bo**.*   Sweden.

Gustav Vasa är den som   Gustav Vasa is the man
   vårt Sverige **murat** (=   who built up our Sweden.
   har murat).

A few examples of this construction are to be found in everyday usage, e.g. *Vi måste rädda det, som räddas* **kan** (instead of : *som kan räddas*) ' We must save what can be saved ' ; and the expressions *som sagt var* (lit. ' as said was') =' as already stated ' ; *som skick är* ' as is customary ' ; *vad mig själv beträffar* ' as far as I myself am concerned.'

Similarly there are a few survivals of the final position of the Infinitive in the sentence, e.g. the old legal saying *Land skall med lag* **byggas** ' the country is to be organized according to law.' Further examples are :

Jag vill inte ha någonting   I don't want to have any-
   med honom **att göra**   thing to do with him.
   (**skaffa**).

Sanningen **att säga** . . .   To tell the truth . . .

The above examples are given as a record of Swedish usage. The student should note them ; but for all practical purposes it may be said that, apart from inversion, the Verb occupies the same position in the sentence as in English.

IV—Position of the Adjective

217. Occasionally the Attributive Adjective follows the Noun, e.g. *Fågel Blå* ' the blue bird ' ; *på böljan blå* ' on the blue billow(s).' Note that when the Possessive Adjective is placed after the Noun, the latter is usually in the **definite** form : *vännen min* ' my friend, friend o' mine ' ; *kärasten min* ' my beloved.' Occasionally the Possessive Adjective before the Noun is preceded by an Attributive Adjective, e.g. *Käraste min syster* ' My dearest sister.'

Where English has ' nice and warm ' Swedish has *varmt och skönt*.

A Genitive can be inserted between the Indefinite Article and the Noun, e.g. *Ett Herrans väder* ' awful weather ' ; *en bygdens dotter* ' a daughter of the countryside.'

A mass of words, adjectival in nature, may stand between the Article and Noun ; this construction is found where relative clauses are used in English, e.g. :

En i skriftspråket vanlig, men i ledigt umgängestal knappast förekommande **konstruktion.**	A construction which is usual in the written language but scarcely ever occurs in easy conversational language.

This construction, known as Incapsulation, is due to German influence and is frequently found in official notices. It should be noted, but the student should never try to imitate it. The above example could be re-cast in a much more natural style to read : *En konstruktion som är vanlig i skriftspråket men knappast förekommer i ledigt umgängestal.*

V—Position of the Object

218. The Indirect Object, when used without a Preposition, is placed before the Direct Object, e.g. :

Ryssland förklarade Bulgarien krig.	Russia declared war on Bulgaria.
Han gav honom det.	He gave it to him.

Greetings and Polite Expressions

219. Up till about 10 a.m. it is usual to greet a person with the words *God morgon* [gɔ'mɔ`rrɔn] ' good morning ' ; from then on the greeting becomes *God dag* [gɔ'dɑ:g] ' good day.' This greeting extends over the period when English people would say ' Good afternoon,' as there is no exact equivalent of this in Swedish. If one meets a person about the time when dinner (*middag*) is taken—and this varies very considerably in Sweden—it is usual to say *God middag* [gɔ 'mi'dda] as a kind of greeting, even though one is not dining with him. Thus it is used between colleagues or between a shop assistant and customers. During the evening the greeting becomes *God afton* [gɔ'a`ftɔn] ' good evening,' and the last greeting of the day is *God natt* [gɔ'nat]. The parting greeting for any time of day is *Adjö* [a'jø:].

Repetition of the word or phrase makes it more cordial, e.g. *God dag, god dag ! Adjö, adjö !*

A familiar greeting, used between young people at any time of day and roughly corresponding to ' Cheerio ! ' is *Hej* ! [hɛj] or *Hej, hej* ! or *Hej på dig* ! [hɛj po dɛj]. Students and, occasionally, elderly friends, use the words *Tjänare*, *tjänare* ' your servant ' (like the German student greeting *Diener* or the Austrian *servus*) in acknowledging greetings.

A welcome is expressed by the simple word *Välkommen* ! ['vɛˋːlkommən] or by *Välkommen till oss* (to us), *till stan* (to this town), *till Sverige* (to Sweden), *hem* (home), *hit* (hither, i.e. to this place) ; and on saying good-bye to a person going on a journey the expression *Välkommen tillbaka* (*åter*) ' You know you are always sure of a welcome ' is used. Other wishes expressed to a departing friend are : *Sköt om dig väl* ! ' Take care of yourself,' *Må[1] så gott* ! ' Farewell,' and *Lycklig resa* ! (' I wish you) a safe journey.' The phrase *På återseende*, which corresponds to the French *au revoir* and German *Auf Wiedersehen* is seldom used in the spoken language but occasionally written at the end of letters.

Perhaps the best-known word in the Swedish language is that used in drinking a person's health : *Skål* ! (literally : ' bowl ') ; it is invariably answered by repetition of the word. A phrase used in offering a person a present is *Håll till godo[2]* ! or *Slit den* (*det*) *med hälsan* ' You're welcome to it.'

In begging pardon for having trodden on a person's toe it is usual to say *Å förlåt* ! [fɔˋloːt] or *Ursäkta mig* ! [uːˈsɛˋkta mɛj] or, more profusely, *Jag ber så mycket om ursäkt* ! ; and the reply ' Don't mention it ' is *Ingen orsak* ['oˋʂaːk] or *För all del*.

How to address People in Letters

220. On an envelope a man is addressed as *Herr*. Usually the name of his occupation is added as a title,

[1] See § 153.
[2] See § 122 (*b*).

e.g.: *Herr direktör K. E. Svensson, Herr ingenjör* (engineer) *K. E. S., Herr kyrkoherde* (rector, vicar) *K. E. S.* Alternatively, the title may be used without *Herr*, e.g.: *Direktör K. E. S.* When a man and his wife are addressed jointly, the word *Fru* is not placed before the husband's title; the address is either written as *Herr och Fru K. E. S.* (omitting the title), or alternatively as *Herr direktör K. E. S. med fru.* When a letter is addressed to a married lady independently, she does not, as a rule, take her husband's title; thus: *Fru Greta Svensson*; but in a few cases special feminine forms of the title are used, e.g. *Fru Professorskan G. S., Fru Doktorinnan G. S.* A lady who holds a professorship is addressed, for example, as *Professor Greta Svensson*; and the same thing applies to a lady doctor. An unmarried lady is addressed as *Fröken* if she has no other title; e.g. *Fröken Dagmar Svensson.* Women belonging to the learned professions usually prefer the words *fru* or *fröken* to be omitted from their titles. An academic degree is written before the name, e.g. *Fil. mag.* (=*Filosofie magister,* roughly the equivalent of B.A.) *Sven Larsson*; *Jur. kand.* (= *Juris kandidat*) *S. L.*

Swedish has no equivalent of ' Messrs.' in writing to a firm, although the word *Firma* is sometimes prefixed to the name, especially when the firm is not registered as a joint stock company; thus *Firma P. Andersson & Söner* (Messrs. P. Andersson & Sons). The word *Aktiebolaget* (joint stock company), abbreviated to *A/B,* is usually placed before the name in the same way as ' Ltd.' is placed after the name in English; thus *A.-B. P.A. Norstedt & Söner* (P. A. Norstedt & Sons, Ltd.).

The word *aktiebolag* is, however, not always placed before the name; occasionally it follows it, e.g. *Munkedals Aktiebolag Brukskoncernen A.-B.*

A complete address is written as follows:

A.-B. Spik och Bult,

Kungsgatan 7,

Gävle.

Notice that the street name is fused with *gatan* (in the Definite Form) and that the number is placed after the name of the street.

In summer many Swedish families spend their holidays
in villas or cottages situated on islands served by small
steamers. As the mails are sorted on board the steamer, the
name of the latter and that of the nearest jetty are given
in the address, e.g. :

> *Familjen Bratt,*
> *Kolsviks brygga*
> *per S/S Blidösund*
> *Stockholm.*

The English abbreviations *S/S* and *c/o* are freely used in
Sweden. If a letter is to be re-directed, the word *Eftersändes*
is written at the top of the envelope.

In writing addresses Swedes never bother to put the
name of the province (*landskap*) after a place-name ; the
latter is considered sufficient, even though it be a tiny
hamlet.

221. Since the word *kär* ' dear ' implies affection, it can
never be used in writing to a stranger. Relatives writing to
each other use such forms as :

Käre[1] *Johan* !	Dear John.
Kära Maria !	Dear Mary.
Käre Far (Pappa) !	Dear Father (Papa).
Kära Mor (Mamma) !	Dear Mother (Mamma).
Älskade Mamma !	Darling Mamma.
Min egen älskling !	My own Darling.
Snälla[2] *Faster* !	Dear Aunt(ie).

Girl friends writing to each other also use *Kära* with the
first name, whereas boys generally use the more formal
Bäste, even though they have *lagt bort titlarna* (see § 94).

Thus :

Bäste (or : *Bästa*) *Fredrik* !   Dear Frederick.

---

[1] On the termination *-e* in the masculine see page 68, footnote.
[2] Lit.: ' kind.'

As already mentioned the *-a* ending is tending to displace the old masculine *-e* ending of the adjective. Students and male friends of all ages who are *du* with each other often begin letters with *Bäste Bror* ! or simply *Broder* ! There is no feminine form corresponding to this.

In writing to a stranger (or strangers), Dear Sir (or ' Dear Sirs ') is not translated in formal style ; the name is written instead, e.g. *Herr Arvid Johansson, Herrarna Arvid och Magnus Johansson.* Less formally, it is possible to write :

Bäste Herr Johansson !   Dear Mr. Johnson.

222. The usual way of ending a business letter or any letter to a stranger is :

Högaktningsfullt (literally : ' Respectfully ' but corresponding in usage to ' Yours faithfully ').

The phrase *På förhand tackande* corresponds to the English ' Thanking you in anticipation.'

In concluding a letter to a friend one uses *Er* (or : *Din*) *tillgivne* (fem. *tillgivna*) for ' Yours sincerely.' Typical conclusions of letters to relatives are :

> Mammas tillgivne
> Edvard.

> Din tillgivne broder
> Hjalmar.

Words of greeting used in concluding letters are : *Hjärtliga hälsningar* or *Många varma hälsningar* ' Kind regards ' ; *Pappa och mamma ber hälsa* ' Papa and Mamma send their love ' ; *Hälsa dina föräldrar från mig* ' Please remember me to your parents ' ; *Många hälsningar till Lennart och Henrik* ' Kind regards to Leonard and Henry.'

Vocabulary

torg, n. (5) ' market place '
bjuda[IV] *på* ' offer '
välja[II] *på* ' choose from '
kronärtskocka, c. (1) ' globe artichoke '
päron, n. (5) ' pear '

kantarell, c. (3) ' chanterelle[1] '
sallad ['sa'llad], c. (3) ' lettuce '
passa[I] ' suit '
se[III] *ut* ' look, appear '

[1] A yellow mushroom.

skyldig ' owing, in debt '
tillsammans ' together '
lämna[1] ' hand over, deliver, leave '
sedel, c. (2) ' note '
turist, c. (3) ' tourist '
förening, c. (2) ' association'
tacksam ' grateful, obliged '

godhetsfullt ' kindly '
broschyr, c. (3) ' booklet '
rad, c. (3) ' line '
anlända[11] ' arrive '
bekväm ' comfortable '
plats, c. (3) ' seat '
underbar ' wonderful '

Exercise 18

Translate

Fru Svensson går på torget.

(*a*) Det är en vacker lördagsmorgon i augusti. Fru Svensson går tidigt på (=*to*) torget.

Fru Svensson : God morgon ! Vad har fru Andersson att bjuda på i dag ?

Fru Andersson : God morgon, god morgon ! I dag har jag mycket för lilla frun[1] att välja på. Vad skall det vara ?

Fru Svensson : Jag skulle vilja ha[2] ett halvt kilo tomater, sex kronärtskockor, två liter päron och en liter kantareller. Har Fru Andersson ett vackert och fast (= *a nice firm*) salladshuvud ?

Fru Andersson : Ja visst har jag det[4]. Passar detta här ? Det kostar 20 öre[5].

Fru Svensson : Ja tack, det ser bra ut. Hur mycket är jag skyldig nu ?

[1] *lilla frun* is a form of address that cannot be rendered in English : translate : ' you.'

[2] ' I should like '. [4] See § 149 (*e*). [5] Currency : the Swedish crown (*krona*) is divided into 100 *öre*.

Fru Andersson :	Tomaterna kostar 1.50 kr. (read as : *en och* [o] *femti,* omitting the word *krona*); kronärtskockorna kostar 25 öre styck[1] ; det blir[2] också 1.50 kr. Päronen kostar 50 öre, kantarellerna 60 öre och salladshuvudet 20 öre. Det blir tillsammans 4.30 kr.
	(Fru Svensson lämnar en 5-kronors sedel och får 70 öre tillbaka).
Fru Svensson :	Adjö, Fru Andersson.
Fru Andersson :	Adjö, snälla frun, och tack så mycket !

(b)   London, 3rd August, 1945.

The Swedish Tourist Association,

   Stockholm.

Dear Sirs[3],

I should be[4] obliged if you would kindly send me a copy of your booklet " Holidays in Sweden."

Thanking you in anticipation,

Yours faithfully,

N. N.

(c)   Stockholm, 30th August, 1945.

Dear Auntie,

Just a few lines to let you know (=*för att låta Faster veta*) that I arrived home yesterday evening after a good journey. There were a lot of people (=*mycket folk*) on the boat, but I got a comfortable seat.

My best thanks (=*Ett varmt tack*[5]) for the wonderful time (I spent[6]) in Kolsvik. Papa and Mamma send their love.

Yours sincerely,

Henry.

---

[1] Short for *per styck* ' apiece.'   [2] See Ex. 13 (a).   [3] Omit.
[4] Use *vore,* the Past Subjunctive of *vara.*
[5] See § 150.
[6] Omit.

CHAPTER XIX

PREPOSITIONS

223. The principal Prepositions are :

av ' of, by '
bakom ' behind '
bland ' among '
bortom ' behind, beyond '
bortåt ' getting toward '
bredvid [brə'vi:d] ' beside '
efter ' after '
emot, mot ' towards,
 against '
enligt ' according to '
framför, före ' before '
från, ifrån ' from '
frånsett ' apart from '
för ' for '
förbi ' past '
genom, igenom ' through '
gentemot ' as opposed to '
hos ' at, with '
i ' in '
innan ' before '
inom ' within '
intill ' up to, till '
jämte ' together with '
kring, omkring ' round,
 about '

med ' with '
medelst ' by means of '
mellan ' between '
nedanför ' below '
nedåt ' down '
nedför ' down '
nära ' near '
om ' round, about '
ovanför ' above '
på ' on, upon '
samt ' together with '
sedan ' since '
till ' to, till '
under ' under '
uppför ' up '
uppåt ' up '
ur ' out of '
utan ' without '
utanför ' outside '
utmed ' (all) along '
utom ' except '
vid ' at, on, close to '
å ' at, on, to '
åt ' to '
över ' over '

Note (1).—In certain fixed expressions some Prepositions are placed after the word they govern, e.g. *Oss emellan* ' between ourselves '; *tiderna igenom* ' through the ages '; *gata upp och gata ner* ' up and down the street '; *dygnet om* ' all round the clock, all day and night '; *jorden runt* ' round the world.'

Note (2).—Formerly the Prepositions *till* and *i* governed a following noun in the Genitive Case ; there are a few phrases which preserve this construction, e.g. *till bords* ' at table ' ; *till fots* ' on foot ' ; *till sängs* ' to bed ' ; *i fredags* ' last Friday ' ; *i somras* ' last summer ' ; *i julas* ' last Christmas.' (See § 103 *b*).

224. The correct use of the Prepositions can only be acquired by constant practice and by noting examples in reading. The following examples illustrate some of the principal uses of the Prepositions :

Av

En ring av guld.	A ring of gold (*origin*).
Konungen av Sverige.	The King of Sweden.
En roman av Strindberg.	A novel by Strindberg (*author*).
Rummet upplyses av en lampa.	The room is lit by a lamp (*instrument*).
Hon darrar av spänning.	She is quivering with excitement (*cause*).
Av allt mitt hjärta.	With all my heart.

Bakom

Mannen bakom disken.	The man behind the counter.

Bland

Bland mina vänner.	Among my friends.
En bland hundra.	One in a hundred.

Bortom

Huset låg bortom skogen.	The house lay beyond (on the further side of) the forest.
Bortom graven.	Beyond the grave.

Bortåt

Bortåt 50 år gammal.	Getting on for 50 years old.

Bredvid

Hon satt tätt bredvid mig.	She sat (close) beside me.
Prata bredvid munnen.	To make an unguarded statement.

Efter

Han sprang efter mig.	He ran after me.
Efter några timmar.	After some hours.
Efter vad jag hört.	From what I have heard.
Han längtade efter freden.	He longed for peace.
Dag efter dag.	Day by day.

Emot, mot[1]

Hon gick emot mig.	She came towards me.
Han har alltid varit vänlig emot mig.	He has always been kind to(ward) me.
Har ni någonting emot det ?	Do you mind (Have you any objection) ?
Huset ligger mitt emot vårt.	The house lies directly opposite ours.
Tio mot en.	Ten to (against) one.
Mot kvällen.	Towards evening.
Mot betalning.	On payment.
Mot kuponger.	In exchange for coupons.

Enligt ['e`:nlikt]

Enligt paragraf 12.	According to paragraph 12.
Enligt min mening.	In my opinion.
Enligt överenskommelse.	As agreed.

Framför, före

Han red framför oss.	He rode ahead of us (*place*).
Framför dörren.	In front of the door (*place*).
Jag föredrar té framför kaffe.	I prefer tea to coffee.
Framför allt.	Above all.
Före kl. 10.	Before 10 o'clock (*time*).

[1] The question of using the monosyllabic or disyllabic forms is mainly governed by sentence stress. But when the preposition is used as a particle in conjunction with a verb, the disyllabic form is always used, e.g. *gå emot någon, ha någonting emot.* Sometimes the preceding sound is the deciding factor, e.g. *mitt emot,* not *mitt mot,* because the latter would be awkward to pronounce.

Från, ifrån

Ett brev från far.	A letter from father (*person*).
Ett brev från Oslo.	A letter from Oslo (*place*).
Från tid till annan.	At times.
Gå inte ifrån mig !	Don't leave me !

Frånsett

Frånsett denna summa.	Apart from this sum (cf. German *abgesehen von*).

För

Betala för mig, är du snäll.	Please pay for me (*on behalf of*).
Du kan få det för 1 kr.	You can have it for 1 crown (*price*).
Ett skåp för porslin.	A cupboard for china (*purpose*).
För alltid.	For good.
För vidare befordran.	To be sent on.
För en vecka sedan.	A week ago.
Tala inte om det för någon.	Don't tell anybody.
Han stängde dörren för mig.	He shut the door on me.
I stället för mig.	Instead of me.

Förbi

Han gick förbi huset.	He walked past the house (*place*).

Genom, igenom

Vi vandrade genom skogen.	We wandered through the forest (*place*).
Genom min syster har jag hört.	I have heard through my sister (*agency*).
Vi har mycket att gå igenom.	We have a lot to go through.

Gentemot

Hans skyldighet **gentemot** *barnen.*	His duty towards the children.
Skriftspråk **gentemot** *talspråk.*	The written language as against (compared with) the colloquial.

Hos

Han bor **hos** *oss.*	He is living with us.
Boken kan fås **hos** *Lindströms.*	The book is obtainable at Lindström's.
Hos *grekerna.*	With (Among) the Greek (cf. French *chez*).

I[1]

Han bor **i** *London.*	He lives in London (*rest*).
Han steg in **i**[2] *rummet.*	He stepped into (entered) the room (*motion*).
Universitetet **i** *London.*	The University of London.
I *trappan ;* **i** *mörkret.*	On the stairs ; in the dark.
I *regel.*	As a rule.
I *samma anda.*	In the same spirit.
Han rökte sex cigaretter **i** *ett sträck.*	He smoked six cigarettes right off (at a stretch).
Han dog **i** *influensa.*	He died of influenza.
Barn **i** *första giftermålet.*	Children of (by) the first marriage.
Tala med någon **i** *telefon.*	To speak to someone on the telephone.
Den strängaste vintern **i** *mannaminne.*	The severest winter within the memory of man.
Han skall stanna där **i** *sex veckor.*	He is going to stay there for six weeks.
Skall vi ta lite olja **i** *håret*[3] *?*	Shall I put a little oil on your hair ?

[1] In older Swedish *uti* is used instead of *i* when rest is indicated, e.g. *uti världen* ' in the world '; *uti vår hage* ' in our paddock, meadow.'

[2] Some Prepositions are reinforced by a preceding cognate Adverb.

[3] This is a barber's phrase and illustrates the tendency to avoid the use of the Pronoun in the Second Person.

Tre pund i veckan.   Three pounds a week.

Jag träffade honom i söndags.   I met him last Sunday.

I samma ögonblick.   At that moment.

Innan

Innan *jul.*   Before Christmas (*time*).

Innan *dess.*   By then, before that (*time*).

Inom

Inom *räckhåll* ; **inom** *syn-håll.*   Within reach ; within sight (*place*).

Inom *en vecka* ; **inom** *kort.*   Within a week ; before long (*time*).

Intill

Båten låg tätt **intill** *bryggan.*   The boat lay close up to the jetty.

Jämte

Ett boningshus **jämte** *anläggningar.*   A dwelling house together with (and) grounds.

Kring, Omkring

De satt **kring** (**omkring**) *bordet.*   They were sitting round the table (*place*).

Runt **omkring** *huset.*   All round the house (*place*).

Omkring *100.*   About 100.

Omkring *sekelskiftet.*   About the turn of the century.

Med

Med *eller utan mat.*   With or without food.

Med *största nöje.*   With the greatest of pleasure.

Det var fullt **med** *folk.*   It was crowded with people.

En säck **med** *stenkol.*   A sack of coal.

Han reste **med** *tåg.*   He went by train.

Med *anledning av (hänsyn till).*   With reference to.

Med långa mellanrum.	At long intervals.
Kan jag få tala med kaptenen[1] ett ögonblick ?	May I speak to you a moment, captain ?
Gifta sig med ; gift med.	To marry (trans.); married to.
Att multiplicera (dividera) med.	To multiply (divide) by.
Hunden viftade med svansen.	The dog wagged its tail.
Med tiden.	In course of time.
Med flit.	On purpose.

Medelst

Han öppnade lådan medelst en hammare.	He opened the box by means of a hammer (*instrument*).

Mellan

Mellan Köpenhamn och Malmö.	Between Copenhagen and Malmö (*place*).
Allt mellan himmel och jord.	Everything under the sun.

Nedanför

Kvarnen ligger nedanför slussen.	The mill lies below the lock (*downstream*).

Nedför

Han gick nedför trappan.	He went down the stairs.
De körde nedför backen.	They drove down (the) hill.

Nedåt

Han gick nedåt gatan.	He went down the street.

Nära

Huset ligger nära bron.	The house is situated near the bridge.

[1] Usually pronounced [kap'te:n] owing to assimilation of the Article to the preceding *-en*.

Om

Han gick **om** *hörnet.*	He went round the corner (*place*).
En uppsats **om** *brevskrivning.*	An essay on letter-writing (*concerning*).
Om *en vecka (liten stund).*	In a week's time (a little while (*time*)).
Om *dagen.*	In the daytime (*time*).
Tre gånger **om** *dagen*[1].	Three times a day (*time*).
Om *vintrarna;* **om** *lördagarna.*	In the winter; on Saturdays.
Med önskan **om** *ett gott nytt år.*	With (best) wish(es) for a Happy New Year.
På andra sidan **om** *ån*[2].	On the other side of the river.
Våra brev gick **om** *varandra.*	Our letters crossed in the post.
Norr **om** *Stockholm.*	North of Stockholm.
Be (drömma, fråga, tigga) **om** *en sak.*	To ask for (dream of, ask about, beg for) a thing.
Han har en hög tanke **om** *sig själv.*	He has a good opinion of himself.

Ovanför

Reading ligger **ovanför** *Richmond.*	Reading is situated above Richmond (*upstream*).

På

På *taket (gatan, torget).*	On the roof (In the street, market (*place*)).
På *sista dagen,* **på** *onsdag.*	On the last day, on Wednesday (*definite time*).
På *återseende.*	Au revoir.
På *avbetalning.*	On the instalment system (hire purchase).

[1] Note also: *tre gånger* **om** *året* ' a year '; but *tre gånger* **i** *veckan (månaden)* ' a week, a month.'

[2] Swedish has three words for ' river ': *å* for a small river; *älv* for a river of medium size (including most Swedish rivers); and *flod* for a large river, e.g. *Rhenfloden* ' the Rhine.'

På inga villkor.	On no account.
På grund av.	On account of (by reason of).
Blind på ena ögat.	Blind in one eye.
På förekommen anledning.	Cases having occurred (in view of past occurrences).

Note.—This phrase is often found at the beginning of official notices containing prohibitive warnings.

Till på köpet.	Into the bargain.
Var inte ond på mig.	Don't be angry (cross) with me.
Lita (svara, vänta) på.	To rely on (reply to, wait for).
Vara på dåligt humör.	To be in a bad temper.
Knacka (ringa) på dörren.	To knock (ring) at the door.
Få syn (Se) på något.	To catch sight of (look at) something.
Kom hit på ögonblicket !	Come here this very instant !

Samt

Ert brev samt en kopia av mitt svar.	Your letter and a copy of my answer.

Sedan

Sedan början av veckan.	Since the beginning of the week.
Sedan dess (den tiden).	Since then (that time).
Sedan urminnes tider.	From time immemorial.

Till

Håll till vänster.	Keep to the left (*place*).
Tåget går till Stockholm.	The train is going to Stockholm (*place*).
Jag skriver till far.	I am writing to father (*person*).
Jag har inte råd till det.	I cannot afford it.
Från morgon till kväll.	From morn till eve (*time*).
En vän till mig.	A friend of mine.

Till min förvåning.	To my surprise.
Vi fick lax till lunch.	We were given (served with) salmon for lunch.
En dumbom till karl.	A blockhead of a fellow.
Kan jag få lämna det här till tvätt ?	May I leave this to be washed ?
Han är kort till växten.	He is short in stature.
Han är läkare till yrket.	He is a doctor by profession.
Till tack för ; till minne av.	In gratitude for ; in memory of.
Nu till saken.	Now to come to the point.
Han översatte det till engelska.	He translated it into English.
Vattnet förvandlades till vin.	The water was changed into wine.
Han anlände till Göteborg i morse kl. 7.	He arrived in Gothenburg at 7 o'clock this morning.
Hälsa så mycket till Britta !	Remember me (give my kind regards) to Britta.

Trots

Trots *det dåliga vädret.*	In spite of the bad weather.
Trots *allt.*	In spite of everything.

Uppför

Han gick **uppför** *trappan.*	He went up (the) stairs.
De seglade **uppför** *älven.*	They sailed up the river.

Uppåt

Han vandrade långsamt **uppåt** *gatan.*	He strolled slowly up the street.

Ur

*Han gick ut **ur**[1] rummet.*	He went out of the room.
Ur *askan* **i** *elden.*	Out of the frying pan (lit.: ' ashes ') into the fire.
Ur *denna synpunkt.*	From this point of view.
Ur *minnet.*	From memory.

Utan

*Han är alldeles **utan** vänner.*	He is entirely without friends.
*Prov **utan** värde.*	Samples without value.
Utan *tvivel.*	Without a doubt.
Utan *vidare.*	Without further ado.

Utanför

*Bilen stannade **utanför** stationen.*	The car stopped outside the station.
*Hans stuga ligger strax **utanför** stan.*	His cottage is situated just outside the town.
*Båten låg **utanför** Themse-mynningen.*	The boat lay off the Thames Estuary.

Utmed

*De vandrade **utmed** älven.*	They strolled along by the river.

Utom

*Alla **utom** mig.*	All but (except) me.
*Han var **utom** sig av vrede.*	He was beside himself with rage.

[1] See p. 175, footnote 2.

Vid

Hon satt **vid** *brasan.*	She was sitting by the fire (*place*).
Han stod **vid** *dörren.*	He was standing at the door (*place*).
Båten ligger **vid** *kajen.*	The boat is alongside (the quay) (*place*).
Vid *den här tiden i morgon är ni hemma.*	By this time to-morrow you will be home (*time*).
Hon omkom **vid** *en bilolycka.*	She perished in a motor accident.
Likna . . . **vid.**	To compare . . . with.
Van **vid** *. . .*	Used (Accustomed) to . . .
Vid *det laget.*	By that time (By then) (*time*).
Vid *närmare undersökning.*	On closer enquiry.

Å

Å *andra sidan.*	On the other hand.
Som (*Till*) *svar* **å** *Eder skrivelse.*	In reply to your letter.

Åt

Han bor **åt** *Majorna till.*	He lives out in the Majorna[1] direction.
Jag måste köpa en hatt **åt** *Torsten.*	I must buy a hat for Torsten.
Säg **åt** *honom, att jag är ute.*	Tell him I'm out.
Jag kan inte göra någonting **åt** *saken.*	I can't do anything in the matter.
Skratta (*Nicka*) **åt** *någon.*	To laugh at (nod to) a person.
Det var rätt (*lagom*) **åt** *dig !*	It serves you right.

[1] *Majorna* is a part of Gothenburg.

Över

Han gick **över** *torget.*	He walked across the square (*place*).
Fågeln flög **över** *huset.*	The bird flew over the house (*place*).
Han har en våning just **över** *vår.*	He has a flat just above ours (*place*).
Hon stannade **över** *lördag-söndag.*	She stayed for the Saturday and Sunday (*time*).
Över *6 veckor* (6 *kg.*).	Over 6 weeks (6 kg.) (*more than*).
Det gick **över** *hans för-måga* (*krafter*).	It was beyond his powers.
Paket [pa'ke:t] *går* **över** *Tilbury.*	Parcels go via Tilbury.
En karta **över** *Sverige.*	A map of Sweden.
Klaga (*Sörja*) **över**.	To complain about (grieve over).
Ledsen (*Tacksam*) **över**.	Sorry because of (grateful for).

225.   Colours

(*Färger*)

röd ' red '	*brun* ' brown '
blå ' blue '	*svart* [svaʈ] ' black '
gul ' yellow '	*vit* ' white '
orange [o'raŋʂ] ' orange '	*grå* ' grey '
violett ' violet '	*skär* ' pink '
grön ' green '	*mörkblå* ' dark blue '
grönaktig ' greenish '	*ljusblå* ' light blue '
gredelin ' greyish violet '	

On the Neuter Forms of these Adjectives see § 108.

226.   The Cardinal Points
(*Väderstrecken*)

nord [**no:d**]	} 'north'	*ost* [**ost**]	} 'east'
norr		*öster*	
syd	} 'south'	*väst*	} 'west'
söder		*väster*	

i norden ' in the North '

Nordsjön ' The North Sea '

norra Sverige ' the North of Sweden '

norr om Stockholm ' north of Stockholm '

tåg norrut ' trains to the North '

nordlig vind 'northerly wind'

nordväst ' north-west '

Sydengland; *södra England* ' the South of England '

Söderhavet ' the South Seas'

Österlandet ' the Orient '

Östersjön ' the Baltic '

Vocabulary

omfatta(¹) ' comprise '

bred ' wide, broad '

halvö, c. (2) ' peninsula '

sträcka(¹¹) *sig* ' extend '

polcirkel, c. (2) ' Arctic Circle '

breddgrad, c. (3) 'degree of latitude '

skog, c. (2) ' forest '

avlopp, n. (5) ' outlet '

mynna(¹) *ut* ' flow out '

sönderskuren ' indented '

kanta(¹) ' border, fringe '

skär, n. (5) ' skerry, rocky islet '

grupp, c. (3) ' group '

kedja, c. (1) ' chain '

skärgård, c. (2) ' archipelago '

gles ' sparse '

befolka(¹) ' populate '

område, n. (4) ' district, region '

snöbetäckt ' covered with snow '

lapp, c. (2) ' Laplander '

ren, c. (2) ' reindeer '

hjord, c. (2) ' herd '

flod, c. (3) ' river '

rinna(¹ᵛ) *upp* ' rise '

strid ' swift, rapid '

lopp, n. (5) ' flow, course '

lämplig ' suitable '

sjöfart, c. ' navigation '

använda(¹¹) ' use '

timmer, n. ' timber '

flottning, c. ' floating '

talrik ' numerous '

utnyttja[I] ' exploit, utilize '
förse[III] [fo'ṣe:] ' provide '
hästkrafter, pl. ' horse-
power '
viktig ' important '
elektrifiera[I] ' electrify '
bördig ' fertile '
lågland, n. (5) ' lowlands '
idka[I] ' carry on '
lantbruk, n. ' agriculture '
Skåne ' Scania '
jämförelsevis ' comparatively '
tät ' dense '
mellersta ' midmost, central'
kungahuset[1] ' Royal House,
Family '
bestiga tronen ' to ascend the
throne '
regera[I] ' rule, reign '
nuvarande ' present '

omkomma[IV] ' perish, die '
flyg, n. (5) ' aeroplane '
katastrof, c. (3) ' disaster '
kronprins, c. (2) ' Crown
Prince '
senare ' later '
dåvarande ' then ' (adj.)
engelska, c. (1) ' English-
woman '
drottning, c. (2) ' queen '
denne, ' the latter '
dansk ' Danish '
ex-kung, c. (2) ' ex-king '
Belgien ' Belgium '
bilolycka, c. (1) ' motor
accident '
Schweiz [ṣvɛjts] ' Switzerland '
Eugen [eu'ṣe:n] ' Eugene '
berömd ' famous '
konstnär, c. (3) ' artist '

Exercise 19

Translate

(*a*)   Sveriges geografi [jeogra'fi:]

Sverige omfattar den bredare östra och södra delen av
Skandinaviska halvön samt öarna Öland och Gotland i
Östersjön. Det sträcker sig från norr om polcirkeln till
ungefär samma breddgrad som Edinburgh. Landet är
mycket rikt på (*rich in*) sjöar och skogar. De största
sjöarna är Vänern, Vättern och Mälaren. Huvudstaden
Stockholm ligger där (=*at the point where*) Norrström,
avlopp för Mälaren, mynnar ut i Östersjön. Den svenska

---

[1] *kunga-* represents an old gen. pl. ; see § 103. *d.*

kusten är starkt sönderskuren och kantas av många tusen öar, som kallas ' skär.' En hel grupp eller kedja av skär kallas ' skärgård,' t. ex. Stockholms skärgård, den Bohuslänska[1] skärgården.

I landets norra del finnes fjäll och glest befolkade områden, som är snöbetäckta den största delen av året. Här lever c:a 7,200 lappar, som sköter sina renhjordar. De flesta floderna rinner upp i fjällen och mynnar ut i Botniska viken (=*the Gulf of Bothnia*) eller Östersjön. De har ett stritt lopp och är ej lämpliga för sjöfart men användes för timmerflottning. De talrika vattenfallen i norra Sverige utnyttjas för att förse industrin med vattenkraft (c:a $1_{,5}$ million HK[2]), och alla viktiga järnvägar är elektrifierade.

Landets södra del omfattar det bördiga låglandet. Här idkas mycket lantbruk, särskilt i Skåne. Låglandet är jämförelsevis tätt befolkat. Sveriges största städer är Stockholm (c:a 1.160.000 invånare), Göteborg och Malmö.

Landets norra del kallas Norrland, den mellersta delen kallas Svealand,[3] och den södra delen heter Götaland[3].

(b)   **The Swedish Royal Family**

King Gustaf VI Adolf was born in 1882 (*föddes* 1882 or *år* 1882)[4] and ascended the throne in 1950. His father, Gustaf V, was born in 1858 and reigned for (*i*) nearly 43 years.

In 1905 the present king married Princess[5] Margaret of Connaught. The children of this marriage were[6] : Prince Gustaf Adolf, Prince Bertil, and Princess Ingrid. Prince Gustaf Adolf perished in (*vid*) an aeroplane disaster in 1947; his son, Carl Gustaf, is now the Crown Prince of Sweden. Princess Ingrid is married to the King of Denmark. Her mother died in 1920, and three years later the then Crown Prince again married an English-

---

[1] *Bohuslän* is a coastal province extending from Gothenburg to the Norwegian frontier.

[2] *hästkrafter*.

[3] These are old tribal names in the gen. plur. form (cf. § 103. *d*).

[4] See § 157.

[5] Titles are spelt with small letters : see § 74.

[6] There are two further sons, Sigvard and Carl Johan, but they have both married commoners and renounced their royal titles.

woman, Lady Louise Mountbatten. Queen Louise died in 1965.

King Gustaf V had three brothers. The eldest was Prince Bernadotte. His second brother (*Hans näst äldste bror*) was Prince Charles. The latter had three daughters. One of them is still living (*lever ännu*). The eldest, Princess Margaretha, married a Danish prince ; the second, Princess Märtha, was married to Olav, now king of Norway. The third was Princess Astrid, the first wife of ex-King Leopold of Belgium. She perished in (*vid*) a motor accident in Switzerland in 1935. King Gustaf's third brother, Prince Eugene (*note the Swedish spelling above*), died in 1947. He was a famous artist.

Notes.—Names of princesses are preceded by *prinsessan* in the Definite Form ; names of princes by *prins* in the Indefinite Form.

Names of professions preceded by the verb ' to be ' are used without the Indefinite Article unless qualified by an Adjective. Thus ' He is an artist ' is *Han är konstnär* ; but ' He is a famous artist ' is *Han är en berömd konstnär*.

CHAPTER XX
TO DO—USE OF THE TENSES

227. The Swedish verb *göra* is used only as a verb of full meaning, not as an auxiliary :

Vad gör du här ?	What are you doing here ?
Vi gjorde det för honom.	We did it for him.
Han har gjort det.	He has done it.
Det är gjort.	It is done.

228. ' To do ' is not translated in negative and interrogative sentences :

Säg inte det.	Do not say that.
Bor han här ?	Does he live here ?

229. Emphatic ' to do ' is usually replaced by an adverb :

Jag såg honom verkligen. I did see him.

Du kan väl stanna en liten stund.
Stanna en liten stund, är du snäll. } Do stay a little while.

230. In sentences like ' Will this do ? ' in which ' do ' means ' be sufficient,' ' be suitable,' other verbs are used in Swedish, according to the context, e.g. :

Räcker det här ?	Will this be sufficient ?
Duger det här ?	Will this meet the case ?
Passar det här ?	Will this be suitable ?

Use of the Tenses
Present

231. Swedish has no progressive form :

Barnet sover fridfullt. The child is sleeping peacefully.

Jag skriver ett brev. I am writing a letter.

In translating from Swedish into English it is important to decide from the context whether the progressive present or the indefinite present is required. If the action is continuous or in progress, the former will be required ; if it is customary or repeated, the latter, e.g. :

Jag skriver varje vecka till mina föräldrar. — I write to my parents every week.

232. Where it is necessary to emphasize that the action is in progress, the verb *hålla på att* (lit. ' keep on to ') is used with a following infinitive (cf. § 129).

Jag håller på att skriva ett brev. — I am (engaged in) writing a letter.

233. The Present is often used with Future meaning, especially with Verbs of Motion, e.g. :

De kommer tillbaka i morgon kl. 7. — They will return to-morrow at 7 o'clock.

The same thing applies to the verbs *vara* and *bli* when the context indicates future time, e.g. :

Vid den här tiden i morgon **är** *ni nog hemma.* — By this time to-morrow you will be home, I expect.

Det **blir** *ingen föreställning i kväll.* — There will not be a performance this evening.

234. The Present is used instead of the Past in the expressions :

När **är** *ni född ?* — When were you born ?

Han **är** *född år* 1900. — He was born in the year 1900.

This only applies to living persons ; in other cases the Past Passive is used, e.g. :

Karl von Linné föddes 1707. — Karl von Linné was born in 1707.

For examples of Swedish use of the Past where English uses the Present see § 213.

Present Perfect

235. Occasionally Swedish uses the Perfect (like German and French) for an action which took place in the Past, but in such cases the time is not closely defined, e.g. :

Den här överrocken **har** *jag* **köpt** *i London.* — I bought this overcoat in London.

When the time of the action is clearly defined as being entirely in the Past, Swedish (like English) uses the Past, e.g. :

> *Den här överrocken* **köpte**   I bought this overcoat when
> *jag, då jag var i London.*   I was in London.

236.   In cases where there is some connection with the Present (whether implicit or explicit) Swedish agrees with English in using the Perfect, e.g. :

> *Har ni någonsin varit i*   Have you ever been to
> *Tyskland ?*   Germany ?

> *Jag har aldrig hört maken*[1] !   I've never heard of such a
>   thing !

In these examples the words *någonsin* and *aldrig* extend the action up to the present moment. In a few cases where the rule appears to be broken, e.g. :

> *Vem* **har lärt** *dig det* ?   Who taught you that ?

> **Har** *ni* **sovit** *gott i natt* ?   Did you sleep well last
>   night ?

the explanation is that the Swedish vaguely connects up the action with the present moment, whereas the English regards it as an action entirely in the past.

In general it may be stated that Swedish and English agree in the use of the Perfect Tense.

237.   Just as the Present is sometimes used with Future meaning, so too the Present Perfect is sometimes used where English has the Future Perfect, e.g. :

> *Hon* **har** *kanske* **rest**, *innan*   Perhaps she will have left
> *jag kommer tillbaka.*   before I return.

Future

238.   When the Future is used in English with the implied notion of Intention or Determination, it is rendered in Swedish by **skall** + the Infinitive of the Verb, e.g. :

> *Jag skall betala honom snart.*   I'll pay him soon.

> *Du skall få stryk* !   You shall have a good
>   hiding !

[1] Short for *maken till det* lit. ' the match to it,' i.e. ' the like of it.'

But when only Futurity is implied, it is rendered by **kommer att** + the Infinitive, e.g. :

Det kommer att bli en olycka en vacker dag. — One of these fine days there will be an accident.

Han kommer att få en miss-räkning. — He will meet with a disappointment.

Future in the Past

239. This tense corresponds in usage to the English ; but occasionally Swedish uses the Past Subjunctive or Past Perfect Subjunctive instead of the Future in the Past.

Note.—For all practical purposes it may be stated that the only specifically Subjunctive form of any verb used to any extent in Modern Swedish is **vore** ' were.'

*Jag **vore** tacksam för lånet av boken.* — I should be grateful for the loan of the book.

*Det **hade varit** synd, om han hade kommit för sent.* — It would have been a pity if he had arrived too late.

Diminutives

240. Swedish, like English, does not possess one widely used suffix to form diminutives ; it forms them in a number of ways. The young of animals are indicated by adding *-unge* to the root word ; thus *gås—gåsunge* ' gosling '; *anka—ankunge* ' duckling ' ; *björn—björnunge* ' little bear '; *barn—barnunge* ' brat, urchin[1] '. Occasionally the suffix *-ling* is used, e.g. : *kyckling* ' chicken ' (from an old word *kokr* ' cock,' which is no longer extant), *killing* ' kid ' (from an old word *kid* ' kid ' which is archaic). Sometimes this suffix is used with a hypocoristic sense, i.e. to form terms of endearment, e.g. : *älskling* ' darling ' (from *älska* ' to love '). Smallness of size is either indicated by prefixing the word *små-*, as in *småsill* ' small herring,' *småbarn* ' little children, infants,' *småkakor* ' small cakes, sweet biscuits,' *småpengar* ' small change,' or by using the adjective *liten*, e.g. : *en liten bok* ' a booklet,' *ett litet lamm* ' a lambkin.' The prefix *små-* is also used to convey a pejorative sense, e.g. : *småfurste* ' princeling, petty prince.'

[1] The name for ' Cinderella ' (itself a diminutive based on ' cinders ') is formed in this way : *Askungen* (from *aska* ' ashes, cinders ').

This prefix can even be used with adjectives and verbs, though here the sense is purely diminutive : *småprickig* ' covered with small spots,' *smårutig* ' having small panes,' *småvarmt* (adj. used as noun) ' a hot course consisting of a variety of small items ' ; *småprata* ' to chat,' *småle* ' to smile,' *småvissla* ' to whistle softly.'

Terms of endearment are frequently formed by adding *lilla* (the definite form of *liten*) after a word, e.g. : *Pappa lilla* 'Daddy dear,' *Mamma lilla*. Some pet names are formed with *-lill* as a suffix, e.g. : *Ingalill, Annalill* ; on the other hand *Lill-* as a prefix conveys a purely diminutive sense : *Lillanna* ' Little Ann,' *Lilljan* ' Little John.'

Just as in English familiar forms of names are formed by adding *-ie*, e.g. : *Charlie, Annie*, so Swedish uses a shortened form of the name, doubling the final consonant and adding *-e* or *-a* ; thus masc. : *Karl—Kalle, Lars—Lasse, Olaf—Olle, Nils—Nisse, Per—Pelle, Pål—Pålle* ['pɔ'llə] (used as a name for a horse, cf. English *Dobbin*), *Ragnar—Ragge, Sigfrid (Sigurd, Sixten)—Sigge* ; fem. : *Amalia (Malvina)—Malla, Gunilla (Gunhild)—Gullan, Hedvig—Hedda, Ulrika—Ulla*. Similarly *Musse Pigg* ' Micky Mouse ' (from *mus*).

Feminine Forms

241. English has a variety of ways of expressing sex. Thus we say ' king—queen,' ' lion—lioness,' ' he-bear—she-bear.' Swedish has similar forms, such as *kung—drottning, lejon—lejoninna, björn—björnhona* or *björninna*. The main difference between the two languages is that, whereas in English the name of the male person is freely applied to females, either because there is no special form or because the meaning is sufficiently clear without any addition, this is rarely the case in Swedish. The feminine ending must be added whenever possible.

242. In some cases the feminine is not formed by derivation from the masculine but consists of an entirely different word.

Examples :

bock	' he-goat '	*get*	' she-goat '
oxe	' ox '	*ko*	' cow '
tupp	' cock '	*höna*	' hen '
munk	' monk '	*nunna*	' nun '
gubbe	' old man '	*gumma*	' old woman '

243. The principal Germanic suffixes used to form feminines are -*inna* and -*ska*[1].

gud	' god '	*gudinna*
skald	' poet '	*skaldinna*
författare	' author '	*författarinna*
vän	' friend '	*väninna*[2]
greve	' count '	*grevinna*
hertig	' duke '	*hertiginna*
poststations-	' postmaster '	*poststations-*
föreståndare		*föreståndarinna*
lärare	' teacher '	*lärarinna*
student	' student '	*studentska*
arbetare	' workman '	*arbeterska*
kock	' male cook '	*kokerska*
engelsman	' Englishman '	*engelska*
stockholmare	' Stockholmer'	*stockholmska*
värmlänning	'native of Värmland '	*värmländska* [-lɛ`nska]
lundensare	' inhabitant of Lund '	*lundensiska*
fransman	' Frenchman '	*fransyska*
parisare	' Parisian '	*parisiska*
ryss	' Russian '	*ryska*
uppassare	' waiter '	*uppasserska*[3]
kassör	' cashier '	*kassörska*
maskinskrivare	' typist '	*maskinskriverska*

From an Advertisement :

Kokerska

m. bästa rek., fullt kunnig i matlagning, erhåller väl avlönad plats i Gbg. Eget rum, ordnad ledighet. —Tel. 16 49 34.

[1] Plural forms : -*innor*, -*skor*.
[2] *vän* is often used as an epicene form, that is without distinction
[3] For the masculine *kypare* is more usual. [of sex.

Translation:
Cook

With best recommendations (references), fully conversant with (qualified in) cooking will receive (offered) well paid situation in Gothenburg. Own room, free time arranged. —Phone 16 49 34.

———

Sometimes a masculine word ending in *-e* changes it to *-a*, or an *-a* is added to the masculine word, with or without a change of root vowel.

Examples:

make	'husband'	*maka*
hane	'male animal' (biology)	*hona*
katt	'cat'	*katta*
hund	'dog'	*hynda*
dansk	'Dane'	*danska*
svensk	'Swede'	*svenska*

This change is also found in names, e.g.:

Ebbe	*Ebba*
Helge	*Helga*
Tore	*Tora*

244. Swedish also uses adapted forms of Romance suffixes to form feminines: *-issa, -essa, -ess, -tris, -ös*[1].

Examples:

profet [pro'fe:t]	'prophet'	*profetissa* [profe'ti`ssa]
abbot	'abbot'	*abbedissa*
diakon	'deacon'	*diakonissa*
baron	'baron'	*baronessa*
prins	'prince'	*prinsessa*
neger	'negro'	*negress*
direktör	'director'	*direktris*
inspektör	'inspector'	*inspektris*
redaktör	'editor'	*redaktris*
dansör	'dancer'	*dansös*
massör	'masseur'	*massös*

[1]Plurals in *-issor, -essor, -esser, -triser, -öser*.

245. The following compound words, in which the second element either changes or disappears, should also be noted :

fästman	'fiancé'	*fästmö*
änkeman	'widower'	*änkefru* (or : *änka*)
brudgum	'bridegroom'	*brud*

246. Some feminine words have no masculine counterpart. Such are *jungfru* 'maid (servant)'; *städerska* 'charwoman (also : hotel chamber-maid)'; *hushållerska* 'housekeeper'; *guvernant* 'governess.'

Vocabulary

förskräckt ' terrified '
bar ' mere '
åsyn (c.) ' sight '
icke bara . . . ' not only '
utan också . . . but also '
elak ' cross, spiteful '
ovänlig[1] ' unkind '
behandla[1] *illa* ' ill-treat, bully '
blek ' pale '
olycklig[1] ' unhappy '
tvinga[1] ' compel '
förrätta[1] ' perform '
grov ' rough '
syssla, (c. 1) ' task '
ensam ' alone, lonely '
otrevlig ' unpleasant '
kläder, pl. ' clothes '
trasig ' ragged '
klänning, (c. 2) ' dress, gown '
slita[IV] *ut* ' wear out '
eftersom ' since, as '
spis, (c. 2) ' grate '

syssla[1] *med* ' be busy with, see to '
knacka[1] *på* ' knock at '
skynda[1] *sig* ' hurry up '
se efter ' find out '
öppna[1] ' open '
page [**pɑːʃ**], (c. 3) ' page '
hov [**hoːv**], (n. 5) ' court '
inbjudning, (c. 2) ' invitation '
buga[1] *sig* ' make a bow '
djup ' deep '
bevista[1] ' attend, go to '
darra[1] ' tremble, quiver '
spänning (c. 2) 'excitement'
tyg (n. 5) ' stuff, material '
följa med ' accompany '
längtansfull ' longing, wistful '
hånskratta[1] ' laugh mockingly '
löjlig ' ridiculous '
färdig ' ready, finished '
gladeligen ' gaily '

[1] The *o*- prefix corresponds to English ' un-.'

brasa (c.1) ' fire '

snyfta[1] ' sob '

röst (c.3) ' voice '

förvåning (c.) ' surprise '

besynnerlig ' queer looking, strange '

rädd[1] ' frightened '

fe (c.3) ' fairy '

gudmor (c. 2) ' godmother '

blyg ' timid '

svänga[11] ' wave '

trollspö (n.4) ' magic wand '

se ! ' behold ! '

glänsa[1] ' gleam, shine '

trasa (c.1) ' rag '

pumpa (c.1) ' pumpkin '

fånga[1] ' catch '

fälla (c.1) ' trap '

vips ! ' hey presto ! behold ! '

gyllene[2] ' golden '

medan ' while '

för (conj.) ' for '

absolut [abso'lu:t] ' entirely, at all costs '

våning (c.2) ' flat '

utmärkt ' excellent '

Note.—For the position of the stress in compound verbs like *se efter*, see § 207, Note (*a*).

[1] Note : *vara rädd* **för** *något* ' to be afraid of something ' ; *vara rädd* **om** *något* ' to be careful (take great care) of something.'

[2] This adjective is indeclinable.

Exercise 20
Translate
Askungen.

(*a*) Det var en gång en flicka, som hette Askungen. Hon hade två systrar, som var mycket äldre än hon och så fula, att folk blev förskräckta vid bara åsynen. De var icke bara fula utan elaka och ovänliga också, och de behandlade sin lilla syster mycket illa. Askungen var mycket söt, d.v.s.[1] hon *skulle* ha varit söt, om hon inte sett[2] så blek och olycklig ut. Hennes systrar tvingade henne nämligen att förrätta de grövsta sysslorna och vara ensam hela dagen i det mörka, otrevliga köket. Hon hade inga vackra kläder utan[3] var alltid klädd i en trasig brun klänning, och på fötterna hade hon ett par utslitna tofflor. Och eftersom hon alltid fick göra ren spisen och syssla med askan, hette hon Askungen.

En dag, då Askungen arbetade som vanligt i köket, knackade det på dörren. " Skynda dig och se efter, vem det är ! " skrek hennes systrar, och Askungen öppnade dörren. Där stod en page från själva hovet[4]. " En

[1] See § 80.   [2] = *hade sett* ; see § 248.   [3] *utan* = ' but ' after a negative when a contrast is implied : see § 285 (7).   [4] See § 210.

inbjudning från H.K.H.[1] prinsen " sade han, lämnade
henne ett brev och bugade sig djupt. " Hit med brevet på
ögonblicket ! " skrek de fula systrarna, och när de såg,
att det var en inbjudning från själva prinsen att bevista
hans bal följande kväll, darrade de av spänning. " Det var
verkligen tur, att vi köpte det nya tyget " sade den ena.
" Nu får Askungen lov[2] att sitta uppe[3] hela natten och sy
oss var sin[4] balklänning."—" Kan inte jag få följa med ? "
frågade Askungen längtansfullt , men hennes systrar bara
hånskrattade åt henne. "Skulle *du* gå på balen, du din
fuling ! " utropade de. " Å, det är löjligt ! Skynda på med
(*hurry up with*) våra klänningar." Så fick Askungen sitta
ett helt dygn för att (*in order to*) få de båda[5] klänningarna
färdiga. När balkvällen kom, körde systrarna gladeligen i
väg. De såg fulare ut än någonsin förr.

Forts.[6] följer (To be continued).

Anmärkningar

Det var en gång. ' *Once upon a time there was.*'

Hennes systrar tvingade henne nämligen ' *For her sisters compelled
her.*' Nämligen *is really an adverb, but is translated by the conjunction
* '*for.*'

Hit med brevet på ögonblicket ! ' *Hand over the letter this very
instant* ! '

Kan inte jag få följa med (*with the stress on* med) ' *Can't I go too*';
the object of följa med *is omitted.*

Skulle *du* gå på balen, du din fuling ! ' **You** *go to the ball, you
fright* ! ' *See* § 106.

Alltså fick Askungen sitta ' *And so Askungen had to sit.*'

Körde systrarna . . . i väg. ' *The sisters drove . . . off.*'

De såg fulare ut än någonsin förr. ' *They looked uglier than ever*
(*before*).'

(*b*) Poor little Cinderella sat down sadly before the fire.
" If only I could have gone too " she sobbed. All at once
a voice said : " Don't cry ! You *shall* go to the ball ! "
To Cinderella's great surprise, a queer-looking little old
woman was standing near the fire. " Don't be frightened,
my dear," she said, " I'm your fairy godmother,[7] and I've

---

[1] *Hans Kungliga Höghet* ' His Royal Highness.' [2] See § 160.
[3] See § 186. [4] See page 145, footnote 2. [5] *de båda* is used for ' the
two ' when they are taken collectively or grouped. [6] Short for
Fortsättning. [7] In Swedish the two words are combined into a
compound.

come to help you." Cinderella smiled timidly. " I would so like to go to the ball, godmother," she said, " but I have only this worn out old dress." Instead of answering, her fairy godmother waved her wand, and behold ! her rags were changed into a gleaming white silk gown and her slippers into small glass shoes. Before she could speak, her god-mother asked her to fetch a pumpkin and six mice,[1] which she had caught in a trap. Cinderella immediately fetched them, the good fairy waved the wand, and hey presto ! the pumpkin became a golden coach, while the mice were changed into six little white horses. " Now you can go to the ball, my child," said the fairy with a smile. " But remember that you must be sure to leave the ball before twelve o'clock, for then your clothes will be changed[2] into rags again."

Notes

Poor little Cinderella. *Use the Definite Article of the Adjective.*

If only I could have gone too. '*Om jag bara finge vara med.*' *Finge* is the Past Subjunctive of *få.*

All at once a voice said. '*Bäst som hon satt där, hördes en röst.*'

Don't cry ! '*Var inte ledsen !*'

You *shall* go to the ball. '*Du* skall *få vara med på balen.*' See § 238.

My dear. '*Kära du* or : *Kära lilla vän.*'

I've come to help you. '*Här är jag för att hjälpa dig.*'

I would so like to go to the ball. '*Jag skulle så hemskt gärna vilja gå på balen.*' See § 183.

Instead of answering. '*I stället för att svara.*'

Before she could speak. '*Innan hon visste ordet av.*'

With a smile. Use the Present Participle of *le.*

Remember that you must be sure to leave. . . . '*Kom ihåg, att du absolut* [abso'lu:t] *måste lämna. . . .*' See § 213.

(c) My sister is a[3] teacher. She knows a Swedish girl whose name is Tora and who works as a typist[3] in Stock-holm. She lives with her aunt; they have a flat in (*på*) Ös-termalm. Her aunt, who is a Dane,[3] is the author of (*av*) several excellent novels. My sister was a student[4] at (*vid*) the University of London.[5] She hopes to be able to go (*hoppas kunna resa*) to Sweden after the war and visit Tora.

---

[1] See § 109 (*b*) and footnote. [2] Use Present Tense.
[3] Omit Article. [4] See § 243. [5] See § 102. *d.*

CHAPTER XXI

USE OF THE AUXILIARY VERBS

247. English frequently repeats the verb ' to have ' or any other auxiliary used in the sentence in order to ask for confirmation of a statement previously made :

He hasn't arrived yet, has he ?

He can do it to-day, can't he ?

As the above examples show, the question is positive when the preceding statement is negative, and vice versa.

For the first of these questions Swedish inserts the word *väl* into the statement, and for the second it adds the words *eller hur* to the end of the statement.

*Han har **väl** inte kommit än ?*

*Han kan göra det i dag, **eller hur** ?*

(See also the examples given in § 189).

Ha

248. The auxiliary verb *att ha* is often omitted in subordinate clauses.

Examples :

*Hon skulle ha varit söt, om hon inte (hade) **sett** så **blek** ut.*	She would have been pretty if she had not looked so pale.
*När hon (hade) **stigit** av, gick hon uppför trappan.*	When she had got out, she went up the steps.
*Trupperna har gjort en fram-stöt som (har) **fört** dem närmare Maas.*	The troops have made an advance which has brought them nearer to the Meuse.

Skall, skulle

249. As stated in § 238, *skall* is used to form the Future Tense with the implied notion of Intention or Determination. *Skall* also has other uses. It is used to indicate an action which is partly or entirely dependent on another person's will or intention.

Examples :

Skall jag gå av här ?	Do I (am I to) get out here ?
Skall jag skaffa biljetterna ?	Shall I get the tickets ?
Du skall gå hem med detsamma.	You are to go home at once.
Vi skall träffas utanför teatern.	(It is agreed then that) we are to meet outside the theatre.
Jag skall vara där kl. 7.	I am (supposed) to be there at 7 o'clock.
Vad skall detta föreställa ?	What is that meant for (supposed to represent) ?
Hur skall man tolka detta ?	How is one (are we) to interpret (take) that ?

Skulle indicates Future in the Past ; it is also used for the English Conditional.

Examples :

Jag skulle skriva i går, men jag hann inte.	I was going to write yesterday, but I didn't get time to.
Om jag vore som du, så skulle jag gå och lägga mig.	If I were you, I should go and lie down.

Vill, ville

250. *Vill* always indicates volition. *Jag vill* has many equivalents in English ; it can be translated as 'I will,' 'I wish to,' 'I want to,' 'I am willing to,' 'I desire to,' 'I like.'

Examples :

Vill ni ha lite mera ?	Will you have (Would you like) a little more ?

Jag vill skicka ett telegram.	I wish (want) to send a telegram.
Jag vill inte resa än.	I don't want to start yet.
Jag vill gärna låna dig 100 *kronor.*	I am willing to lend you 100 crowns.
Talaren ville påpeka . . .	The speaker desired (wished) to point out . . .
Gör, som du vill.	Do as you like (please).

251. The English Accusative and Infinitive construction after ' want,' ' like ' cannot be imitated in Swedish ; it must be rendered by *vill* followed by a Subordinate Clause beginning with *att*.

Examples :

Jag vill inte, att han skall komma hit i kväll.	I don't want him to come here this evening.
Jag skulle inte vilja att han bodde här.	I shouldn't like him to live here.

Note.—Occasionally *vill* is used with a verb of motion understood (cf. Shakespeare : ' Wit, whither wilt ? ') :

Vart vill du (hän) ?	Where do you want to go ?
Jag vill hem.	I want to go home.

Kan, kunde

252. Besides translating English ' can ' with the notion of ability to do something, *kan* sometimes corresponds to English ' may, might.'

Examples :

Jag kan inte komma hem i kväll.	I can't come home this evening.
Det kan vara sant.	It may be true (*Possibility*).
Det kan nog hända.	That may be (*Possibility*).
Klockan kunde väl vara omkring 3.	It might have been about 3 o'clock (*Possibility*).
Någon kunde komma in och se oss.	Somebody might come in and see us (*Possibility*).

*Du **kan** lika gärna komma fram med sanningen.* — You may as well make a clean breast of it (*Request*).

*Du **kan** gärna be honom att komma upp hit.* — You might ask him to come up here (*Request*).

Sometimes *kan* is used to denote a Propensity or Habit where English has ' would,' e.g. :

*Hon **kunde** ofta brista ut i gråt för ingenting.* — She would often burst out crying for nothing (at all).

Occasionally *kan* is used as a verb of full meaning to denote knowledge or skill, e.g. :

*Han **kan** sin sak.* — He knows his business thoroughly.

*Pojken **kunde** sin läxa.* — The boy knew (could say) his lesson.

Måste

253. This verb has the same form for the Present and Past and corresponds in meaning to English ' must,' expressing compulsion. In the Perfect *har måst* is sometimes replaced by *har varit tvungen* ' have been obliged.'

Examples :

*Jag **måste** skriva hem i dag.* — I must write home to-day.

*Jag **måste** skriva hem i går.* — I had to write home yesterday.

*Jag **måste** skriva hem i morgon.* — I shall have to write home to-morrow (Present for Future).

*Jag har **måst** (varit tvungen att) skriva hem.* — I have had (been obliged) to write home.

Sometimes it is used to express a supposition in the same way as English ' must ' :

*Ni **måste** ha tagit fel.* — You must have made a mistake.

*Jag **måste** ha skrivit fel.* — I must have made a mistake (in writing).

Må, måtte

254. This verb usually renders English 'may' in an Optative sense, both *må* and *måtte* being used ; but for the Past Tense 'might' only *måtte* can be used.

Examples :

Ja, må han leva[1] !	(Long) may he live !
Måtte det snart bli fred i världen.	May there soon be peace in the world.
Han önskade, att jag snart måtte bli kry igen.	He expressed the wish that I might soon be well again.

Må is also used to translate 'may' in Concessive Clauses, e.g. :

Hur rik han än må vara ...	However rich he may be. .

Låta

255. Although it differs from the other Auxiliary Verbs in belonging to the Strong Conjugation (see § 204. 3) and is occasionally used as a verb of full meaning, *låta* may be classed as an Auxiliary Verb. It has two different senses : (1) 'to allow, permit' ; (2) 'to cause.'

Examples :

(a)

Låt mig se brevet.	Let me see the letter.
Hoppas att du snart låter höra ifrån dig.	Hope you will soon let (me, us) hear from you.
De lät henne inte följa med på balen.	They did not allow her to go with them to the ball.

(b)

Han lät oss vänta.	He kept us waiting.
Hon lät Askungen hämta en pumpa.	She got (caused) Cinderella to fetch a pumpkin.
Hon lät hämta en pumpa.	She had a pumpkin fetched.
Jag skall låta sy en ny klänning.	I am going to have a new dress made.

Note.—In the last two examples the dependent infinitive acquires a passive sense through the omission of the personal object.

[1] These are the opening words of the Swedish equivalent of 'For he's a jolly good fellow ! '

256.   Adjectives and Nouns of Nationality

Country	Adjective	Inhabitant
Amerika[1] ' America '	*amerikansk*	*en amerikan*
Belgien ' Belgium '	*belgisk*	,, *belgier*
Danmark ' Denmark '	*dansk*	,, *dansk*
England ' England '	*engelsk*	,, *engelsman*
Finland ' Finland '	*finsk*	,, *finne*[2]
Frankrike ' France '	*fransk*	,, *fransman*
Holland ' Holland '	*holländsk*[3]	,, *holländare*
Irland ' Ireland '	*irländsk*[3]	,, *irländare*
Island ' Iceland '	*isländsk*[3]	,, *isländare*
Italien ' Italy '	*italiensk*	,, *italienare*
Kanada ' Canada '	*kanadensisk*	,, *kanadensare*
Kina ' China '	*kinesisk*	,, *kines*
Norge ' Norway '	*norsk*	,, *norrman*
Polen ' Poland '	*polsk*	,, *polack*
Ryssland ' Russia '	*rysk*	,, *ryss*
Schweiz 'Switzerland'	*schweizisk*	,, *schweizare*
Skottland ' Scotland '	*skotsk*	,, *skotte*
Spanien ' Spain '	*spansk*	,, *spanjor*
Sverige ' Sweden '	*svensk*	,, *svensk*
Turkiet ' Turkey '	*turkisk*	,, *turk*
Tyskland ' Germany '	*tysk*	,, *tysk*
Ungern ' Hungary '	*ungersk*	,, *ungrare*
Österrike ' Austria '	*österrikisk*	,, *österrikare*

Note (1).—The name of the language is formed by adding
-*a* to the Adjective, e.g. *Talar ni finska* ? ' Do you speak
Finnish ? ' *Hur heter det på svenska* ? ' What is it called in
Swedish ? '

Note (2).—Plurals of names of inhabitants : if the
Singular ends in -*are* or -*ier*, the word remains unchanged in
the Plural ; if the Singular ends in -*man*, it changes to -*män*
in the Plural ; if it ends in -*sk* the Plural is formed by
adding -*ar* (and this also applies to *finnar, ryssar, skottar,
turkar*) ; in the remaining words above the ending -*er* is
added : *amerikaner, polacker, spanjorer.*

[1] *Förenta Staterna* ' the United States.'
[2] *en finländare* is a Finlander of Swedish descent.
[3] The *d* is not pronounced.

Vocabulary

buss (c.2) ' bus '
förtjäna⁽¹⁾ ' earn '
förare ' driver '
jo ' well '
inom kort ' within a short time '

vricka⁽¹⁾ ' wrick, dislocate '
nacke (c.2) ' neck '
kräva⁽ᴵᴵ⁾ ' demand, require '
en smula ' a little '
eftertanke (c.2) ' reflection '

Exercise 21
Translate
En skotsk historia

(*a*) Två skotska bröder köpte en buss och började köra passagerare mellan två städer för att (*in order to*) förtjäna pengar. Den ene var förare och den andre var konduktör. Men experimentet blev ingen succé. Och varför ? Jo, den som var förare dog inom kort—av en vrickad nacke.

(Obs. : denna historia kräver en smula eftertanke).

Vocabulary

tillräcklig ' sufficient '
upprörd ' excited '
palats (n.5) ' palace '
sal (c.2) ' hall '
hovman (c. § 91. *f*) ' courtier, lord '
färga⁽¹⁾ ' colour '
få syn på ' set eyes on '
gå fram ' walk up '
niga⁽ᴵⱽ⁾ ' curtsey '
graciös ' graceful '
se på ' look on '
se ut ' look '
avundsjuka (c.) 'jealousy'
varenda ' every (single) '
kasta⁽¹⁾ ' cast, throw '
fart (c.) ' haste, hurry '

tappa⁽¹⁾ ' drop '
fastän ' though '
under tiden ' meanwhile '
tankfull ' pensive, wistful '
förklara⁽¹⁾ ' declare '
prova⁽¹⁾ ' try on '
förgäves ' in vain '
klämma⁽ᴵᴵ⁾ 'cram, squeeze'
*jättestor*¹ ' huge '
näpen ' dainty, neat '
usch ! ' pooh ! '
snäsa⁽ᴵᴵ⁾ *av* ' snub, snap up '
ilska (c.) ' rage '
brudklänning (c.2) ' wedding gown '
öm ' tender '
utropa⁽¹⁾ ' exclaim '

Note.—For the position of the stress in compound verbs like *gå fram*, see § 207, Note (*a*).

¹ In the colloquial language *jätte-* ' giant ' is prefixed to Adjectives to intensify the meaning, e.g. *jättefin* ' very fine ' ; *jättelyckad* ' very successful.' The stress falls on *jätte-*.

(b) **Askungen** (*Fortsättning*)

Askungen steg in i vagnen. " Nog skall jag komma ihåg det. Men hur skall jag kunna tacka min kära gudmor tillräckligt ? " ropade hon och viftade[1] upprört med handen, medan hon körde bort. Den gyllene vagnen stannade snart utanför palatset. Askungen steg av och gick blygt uppför trappan. Inne i salen var det fullt med hovmän och hovdamer, alla vackert klädda, men aldrig hade hon sett någon så vacker som prinsen i hans vita och silverfärgade uniform. Han tyckte också, att hon var den skönaste flicka,[2] han någonsin fått syn på. " Vem kan det vara ? " tänkte han. Han gick fram till Askungen och bugade sig djupt. " Får jag be om nästa dans ? " frågade han, och Askungen neg graciöst. Så (*then*) tog han hennes hand och de dansade tillsammans, medan hela hovet såg på[3]. De fula systrarna såg gröna ut av avundsjuka, men föga anade de, att det var Askungen. Prinsen dansade varenda dans med henne och kastade inte ens (*not even*) en hastig blick på någon annan.

Plötsligt började klockan slå. Det var nästan midnatt ! " Jag måste gå genast ", ropade Askungen, och innan prinsen visste ordet av, började hon springa i väg. I farten tappade hon en av sina glasskor i trappan, men fastän prinsen ropade " Stanna ! ", sprang hon bara fortare och fortare. Just som hon kom utanför palatset, slog klockan tolv. Hennes vagn försvann, och hennes kläder förvandlades åter till trasor. Hon sprang hela vägen hem, och strax därefter kom hennes systrar på mycket dåligt humör.

Anmärkningar

Nog skall jag komma ihåg det. '*I'll be sure to remember*.' (*I'll certainly not forget*). See §§ 189 and 213.

Det var fullt med. . . . '*There was a crowd of*. . . .'

Föga anade de. . . . '*Little did they suspect*.' See § 196, *Note*.

I farten. '*In her haste*.'

(c) Meanwhile the prince stood gazing[4] wistfully at the glass shoe. No one could tell him where to find the charming

---

[1] Use the Present Participle.
[2] See § 164 (b).
[3] Translate ' stood and looked on.'   [4] *stod och såg*.

girl he had danced with[1] all the evening. Suddenly he had
a splendid idea. " The girl (*unga flicka*) whom this shoe fits,[2]
shall be[3] my bride ! " he declared. Next day one lady after
another came and tried on the glass shoe, but (all[4]) in vain.
Then[5] the ugly sisters came. What a sight it was when they
tried to[6] cram their huge feet into (*in i*) the dainty little
shoe ! Just at that moment Cinderella came timidly
forward. " Let me try " she begged.[7]

" You ! Pooh ! Ridiculous ! " they snapped, weeping
with rage ; but the prince said kindly : " Let her try."
And so Cinderella tried on the glass shoe, and of course it
fitted her perfectly. And at that moment her rags changed
into a beautiful white wedding-gown.

" I've found you at last ! " exclaimed the prince, and
taking her in his arms, he kissed her tenderly. All the bells
began to ring. They were married[8] the same day and lived
happily ever after.

Notes

No one could tell him where to find. '*Ingen kunde tala om* (with
the stress on *om*) *för honom, var han skulle kunna finna.*'

Suddenly he had a splendid idea. '*Plötsligt fick han en härlig idé.*'

Next day one lady after another came. '*Nästa dag kom den ena
damen efter den andra.*'

What a sight it was. '*En sådan syn det var.*' See § 201, *Note.*

Just at that moment. '*Just då.*'

Ridiculous ! they snapped. '*Det är löjligt ! snäste de av* (with
the stress on *av*) *henne.*'

Weeping with rage. Translate : and wept with rage. In place of
an English verb followed by a Present Participle Swedish often has
two coordinated verbs.

And so Cinderella tried on the glass shoe. '*Och så provade
Askungen glasskon.*'

Of course it fitted her perfectly. '*Den passade henne precis,
förstås.*'

At that moment. '*I samma ögonblick* or *I ett nu.*'

And taking her into his arms, etc. Translate : took her . . . and
kissed (*kysste*) her.

All the bells began to ring. '*Alla klockor började ringa.*'

Lived happily ever after. '*Sedan levde de lyckliga i all sin tid.*'

---

[1] See §§ 164. *b* and 166. [2] *passar åt.* [3] *bli.* [4] Omit. [5] *Sedan.*
[6] Omit *att.* [7] translate ' asked.' [8] *de gifte sig.*

CHAPTER XXII

USE OF THE INFINITIVE AND PARTICIPLES

The Infinitive

257. The Infinitive is usually preceded by *att*, e.g. :

Att stava *rätt är inte alltid lätt.*	It is not always easy to spell correctly.
Jag glömde **att svara.**	I forgot to answer.

258. When the Infinitive is used to express a personal Aim or Intention, it is preceded by *för att* (which corresponds to English ' in order to,' ' so as to,' or ' to ' expressing purpose).

Jag tog en bil **för att komma** *till stationen i god tid.*	I took a taxi so as to reach the station in good time.
Jag gick till stationen **för att hämta** *mitt bagage* [bag'ɑ:ʂ]	I went to the station to fetch my luggago.

259. The Infinitive is preceded by *till att* when it expresses the Utilitarian Purpose of a substance, e.g. :

Fett användes **till att göra** *tvål.*	Fat is used to make (for making) soap.

260. The Infinitive is used without *att* :

(a) In Proverbs and elevated Literary Style :

Tala är silver, **tiga** *är guld.*	Speech is silver ; but silence is gold.

Bättre **fråga** *än vilse* **fara**.	It is better to ask (ones way) than go astray.
Vara eller inte **vara**, *det är frågan*.	To be, or not to be : that is the question.
Mötas och **skiljas** *är världens gång,* **skiljas** *och* **mötas** *är hoppets sång*.	To meet and to part is the way of the world ; to part and to meet is the song of hope.

(b) After the Auxiliary Verbs (**skall, vill, kan, får, måste**, etc.) :

Du **får komma** *igen*.	You will have to come again.

(c) After several other Verbs, e.g. : *behöva* ' need '; *bruka* ' be in the habit of ' ; *synas* ' seem ' ; *tyckas* ' seem ' ; *tänka* ' contemplate, be thinking of ' ; *ämna* ' intend.'

Examples :

Jag **behöver** *inte* **gå** *dit i dag*.	I need not go there to-day.
Hon **brukar ta** *ett varmt bad på kvällarna*.	She usually has a hot bath in the evening(s).
Han **syns** (= *synes*) **vara** *trött*.	He appears to be tired.
Tåget **tycktes röra** *sig*.	The train seemed to be moving.
Vi **tänker ha** *ett litet kalas* [ka'la:s].	We are thinking of having a little party.
Jag **ämnar ta** *min examen på våren*.	I intend to take my examination in the spring.

(d) In the Accusative with Infinitive Construction :

Jag såg honom **dö**.	I saw him die.
Han bad mig **stiga** *in*.	He asked me to come in.
Han sade sig **hoppas** *det*.	He said he hoped so.

And similarly in the Nominative with Infinitive Construction, e.g. :

*Han **hördes säga** ett fult ord.*	He was heard to say a foul word.

Note.—The Accusative with Infinitive Construction is frequently used in Swedish ; when the Verb is put into the Passive Voice, the Nominative with Infinitive results.

Compare the following examples :

*Jag anser **honom vara** mycket samvetsgrann.*	I consider him to be very conscientious.
***Han** anses **vara** mycket samvetsgrann.*	He is considered to be very conscientious.

Swedish Equivalents of the English Infinitive

261. In English the Infinitive is often used in a free and elastic way which has no direct equivalent in Swedish ; in such cases Swedish has a full Subordinate Clause.

(*a*) After verbs of volition such as ' wish,' ' want,' ' desire,' ' expect.'

*Jag vill, **att ni skall lära** er den här dikten utantill.*	I want you to learn this poem by heart.
*Hon väntar, **att vi skall vara** hemma före midnatt.*	She expects us to be home by midnight.

(*b*) When English has an Infinitive after an Interrogative Pronoun or Adverb.

*Han visste inte, **vad han skulle göra**.*	He didn't know what to do.
*Hon visste inte, **var hon skulle finna** dem.*	She didn't know where to find them.

(*c*) When English has an Accusative with Infinitive after the Preposition ' for.'

*Han väntade alltid **på att någonting skulle hända**.*	He was always waiting for something to turn up.

*Det är inte **vanligt, att*** It is not customary for
   gäster skålar med vär-   guests to toast the hos-
   dinnan.   tess.[1]

A similar construction is used when English has 'had better,' e.g. :

*Det är bäst, **att du går nu**.*   You had better go now.

(*d*) When English has an Ordinal Numeral followed by an Infinitive.

*Han var **den första, som*** He was the first to set foot
   satte sin fot på fransk   on French soil.
   mark.

*Han var **den sista**[2], som* He was the last to arrive.
   kom.

Note also the following expressions :

*Jag var **dum, som trodde*** I was a fool to believe it.
   det.

*Det är inte troligt, **att han*** He is not likely to come.
   kommer.

*Det är säkert, **att han har*** He is sure to have passed
   klarat sin examen.   his examination.

Swedish Equivalents of the English Gerund

262.   In English the Gerund, a Verbal Noun ending in -*ing*, is frequently used to denote the name of an action. In form it is identical with the Present Participle ; but its function is that of a Noun. In some cases Swedish has corresponding nouns formed by adding -*ing* or -*ning* to the root of the verb ; in others the infinitive is used as a verbal noun.

Examples :

*Rök**ning** (Parkering, Spott-* Smoking (Parking, Spit-
   ning) förbjuden.   ting) prohibited.

---

[1] i.e. individually ; for obvious reasons it is undesirable for guests to drink to the hostess's good health in sequence.

[2] Here *sista* is tantamount to an Ordinal Numeral.

*Jag tycker om **att simma**.*	I like swimming.
*Låt bli **att skratta**.*	Stop (leave off) laughing.
*Hon fortfor **att skriva** brev.*	She went on writing letters.
*Det tjänar ingenting till **att gråta**.*	It's no use crying.

263. When the English Gerund is preceded by a Possessive Adjective, a Genitive, or a Noun governed by a Preposition, it is usually translated by a full clause in Swedish.

Examples :

*Vi tycker inte om, **att hon stannar så sent ute**.*	We don't like her staying out so late.
***Att Ingrid gifte sig så tidigt**, gjorde det lättare för hennes far att dra sig tillbaka från affärerna.*	Ingrid's marrying so early made it easier for her father to retire from business.
*Jag gillar inte, **att barn alltid får sin vilja fram**.*	I don't approve of children always having their own way.

264. Infinitives are often governed by Prepositions in Swedish :

*Han reste **utan att betala** sin räkning.*	He left without paying his bill.
*Pojken roade sig **med att kasta** stenar i dammen.*	The boy amused himself by throwing stones into the pond.
***Efter att ha tillbringat** tolv år i Fjärran Östern återvände han till Sverige.*	After having spent twelve years in the Far East he returned to Sweden.

265. Subordinate clauses are often governed by Prepositions in Swedish.

*Jag är säker **på att** han **kommer snart**.*	I am sure he will arrive soon.
*Kan jag räkna **med** (**lita på**) att du hjälper mig i morgon ?*	Can I count (rely) on your helping me to-morrow ?

*Han klagade **över att de** He complained that they
    hade lurat honom.* had cheated him.

Note.—A preposition which governs a following full
clause is sometimes combined with *där-*, which represents a
pronoun and serves as provisional object to the preposition
(cf. German *darin, dass* ; *darauf, dass*), e.g. :

Hans enda anspråk på rykt- His only claim to fame
    *barhet bestod **däri, att han*** consisted in his once
    en gång hade räddat having saved a drowning
    ***ett drunknande barn**.* child (lit. ' therein that
                            he had once saved, etc.').

It is more usual, however, for the plain preposition to
govern a following clause, e.g. :

*Jag tänkte aldrig **på, att du*** I never thought of your
    ***skulle komma**.* coming.

The Present Participle

266.   The Present Participles of Deponent Verbs are rarely
used ; when they do occur the *-s* is sometimes dropped,
e.g. *åldras* ' to age,' but *en åldrande man* ' an ageing man.'
In other cases the Participle is replaced by a Finite Verb or
a periphrastic construction. Thus the English phrase
' Hoping to see you soon ' is either rendered by *(Jag)
hoppas att snart få se dig* or by *I förhoppningen* (' In the
hope ') *att snart få se dig.*

267.   English often uses a verb followed by a Present
Participle. In such cases Swedish uses either two coordinated verbs or the Accusative with Infinitive.

*Han **satt och läste** en bok.*   He sat reading a book.
*Jag hörde **honom skratta**.*   I heard him laughing.

The participial construction is used, however, after the
verb **komma**, and occasionally after *bli(va)*.[1]

*Han **kom åkande** på lands-*   He came driving along the
    vägen.   highway (road).
*Han **blev liggande** på trot-*   He remained lying on the
    toaren.   pavement.

[1] In this construction *bliva* has the same meaning as *förbliva* ' to
remain.'

268. Participial constructions which are equivalent to contracted sentences cannot be used in Swedish; they must be replaced by full sentences.

Då jag märkt er annons i Morgonbladet, tillåter jag mig fråga. . . .	Having seen your advertisement in ' Morgonbladet,' I beg to enquire. . . .
Han skickade mig ett brev och erbjöd sina tjänster.	He sent me a letter offering his services.
Om väder och vind tillåter.	Wind and weather permitting.

The Past Participle

269. The Past Participle is used as an Attributive or Predicative Adjective. For examples of its attributive use see §§ 174–175. When used predicatively the Past Participle is declined like an Adjective.

Examples :

*Dörren är **stängd**.*	The door is closed.
*Han blev mycket **förvånad**.*	He was very much surprised.
*Böckerna är **tryckta**.*	The books are printed.

Vocabulary

styv i ' good at '
rita[(1)] ' draw, design '
ordbok (c.3) ' dictionary '
laga[(1)] ' prepare, mend '
skepp (n.5) ' ship '
gå[(IV)] *under* ' founder '
pjäs (c.3) ' play '
värd ' worth '
resväska (c.1) ' suit-case '
ro[(III)] ' row '
fiska[(1)] ' fish '
chans [ʃaŋs] (c.3) ' chance '
åka[(II)] *skidor* ' ski '

nybörjare (c.5) ' beginner '
besvara[(1)] ' answer (trans.) '
supé (c.3) ' supper (party) '
gruffa[(1)] ' grumble '
gå[(IV)] *galet* ' go wrong '
frånvaro (c.) ' absence '
matros [maˈtroːs] (c.3) ' sailor '
tala[(1)] *om* ' mention, tell '
flytta[(1)] 'move (intrans.) '
en massa pengar ' a lot of money '
ta[(IV)] *betalt* ' charge '

Note.—Tala om with the stress on *om* = ' mention, tell,' but with the stress on *tala* = ' talk about'.

Exercise 22
Translate

(a) Han är mycket styv i ritning. Han är mycket styv i att översätta. Han visste inte, vart han skulle gå. Jag har inte råd att köpa en sådan ordbok. Jungfrun håller på att laga mat. Kaptenen hade mycket litet hopp om att kunna rädda skeppet från att gå under. Finns det något hopp om att få träffa fröken igen ? Hennes dotter fick aldrig lov att vara sent uppe. Det tjänar ingenting till att försöka. En pjäs av Strindberg är väl värd att se. Jag har mycket bråttom med att packa min resväska. Erik kommer till stationen för att möta oss. Jag är rädd för att träffa honom. Var så goda[1] ; middagen är serverad ! Jag vill inte, att hon skall finna mig här. Han satt och skrev. Vad man ser, det tror man.

(b) My brothers like rowing and fishing. Have we any chance of getting a seat ? I am fond of reading. She is tired of (*trött på*) waiting. We were surprised to hear that he was ill. Learning to ski is not easy for older beginners. I am sorry (*ledsen över*) that I forgot to answer your letter. He has been saving up (use : *spara pengar*) so as to be able to buy this book. It is too good to be (*för att kunna vara*) true. We want you to come to a little supper party. We cannot help (*låta bli*) liking him. Uncle is the first to grumble when anything goes wrong. Are you ready to start out (*gå*) ? We are longing to see you again. Can I rely on your taking great care[2] of the money ? I am afraid of the car being stolen in my absence. The sailors saved their lives (transl. : *the* life) by swimming to the shore. He wrote a letter saying (use : *tala om*) that he was married. He went out of[3] the room without begging my pardon (*be mig om ursäkt*). After having lived in the country for (=*i*) ten years, he suddenly moved to Stockholm. He got (*fick*) me to write the letter for him. I am sorry to have kept you waiting. His father does not approve of boys having a lot of money. He complained of their having charged so much for a glass of brandy (*konjak*).

Note.—A Noun Clause is always marked off from a Main Clause by a comma (cf. § 78.*b*). Be careful to apply this rule in translating the above exercise.

[1] See page 12, footnote. [2] See page 196. [3] See *ur*, page 181.

Vocabulary

väderlek (c.) (used in compounds) 'weather'
rapport (c.3) 'report'
tillta[IV] 'increase'
avta[IV] 'decrease'
måttlig 'moderate'
frisk 'fresh'
styv 'stiff'
efterhand 'by degrees'
mestadels 'for the most part'
uppehållsväder 'fair weather'
i huvudsak 'in the main'

oförändrad 'unchanged'
opålitlig 'unreliable'
fjälltrakt (c.3) 'mountain region'
flerstädes 'in several places'
uppmäta[II] 'record (by measuring)'
tidvis 'at times'
storm (c.2) 'gale'
varning (c.2) 'warning'
utfärda[I] 'issue, publish'
kuststräcka (c.1) 'coastline'
kultje (c.) 'persistent wind'

Note.—The following passage is based on the weather reports published twice every evening by the Swedish Broadcasting Company immediately after the news bulletins (for times see Preface, page v). It contains many of the words most frequently used, and is intended to assist students who wish to listen in regularly to these reports for ear-training purposes; but it is *not* an exact reproduction of an actual broadcast.

(c) En väderleksrapport

Väderlekstjänstens[1] eftermiddagsrapport har följande utsikter för landdistrikt :

För västkust- och Vänerområdet : måttlig till frisk, efterhand [ɛftər'hand] något avtagande vind ; mestadels uppehållsväder ; i huvudsak oförändrad temperatur.

Övriga (= *the rest of*) Götaland, nordöstra Svealand med Gotland : svag till måttlig vind ; opålitligt för något regn ; oförändrad temperatur.

För Bergslagsområdet, hela Norrlands inland och fjälltrakter : måttlig till frisk vind, till en början något tilltagande ; tidvis något regn eller duggregn ; fallande temperatur.

För hela Norrlands kustland. . . . Regn har under dagen fallit flerstädes i landet ; således uppmättes i Stockholm 3 millimeter, i Göteborg 4, i Karlstad 3, etc.

[1] This may be translated as ' The Meteorological Bureau.'

Utsikter för sjödistrikt:

För västkustens farvatten (*waters*): frisk till styv vänstervridande vind. . . .

Stormvarning har utfärdats i kväll för kuststräckan mellan Hälsingborg och Landsort för styv till hård kultje.[1]

Anmärkningar

Vänerområdet, The region round *Vänern* (see page 185).

Bergslagsområdet. Bergslagen is a collective name for the mining districts of *Värmland, Västmanland* and *Dalarna* (Dalecarlia).

Vänstervridande vind, wind turning to the left, i.e. backing. During the war the exact direction of the wind was not announced. Detailed reports have now been resumed.

[1] **A** *kultje* corresponds to degrees 6–8 in Beaufort's wind scale.

CHAPTER XXIII
USE OF THE ARTICLES—CONJUNCTIONS—INTERJECTIONS— WORD FORMATION
Definite Article

270.   Abstract nouns used in a general sense usually take the definite article in Swedish, but not in English :

Tiden läker alla sår.	Time heals all scars.
Tappa inte modet.	Don't lose courage.

The article is frequently omitted, however, in proverbs, in groups of words, in headings and in prepositional phrases.

Examples :

Ärlighet varar längst.	Honesty lasts longest (is the best policy).
Tid är pengar.	Time is money.
Krig och fred.	War and peace.
Om konst och industri.	On art and industry.

Note.—Material nouns used in a general sense do not always take the definite article, as in some languages :

Guld är mjukare än silver.	Gold is softer than silver.
Trä har ett relativt högt bränslevärde.	Wood has a relatively high fuel value.

But the use of such words with the article is also possible, especially when a contrast is implied :

Brännvinet är den fattiges champagne.	Gin is the poor man's champagne.

271.   The names of seasons, days and festivals usually take the definite article :

Jag tycker om våren.	I like spring.
Om lördagarna gör vi utflykter.	On Saturdays we go on excursions.
Påsken kommer tidigt i år.	Easter comes early this year.

272. Names of meals usually take the definite article :

Frukosten serveras kl. 8.	Breakfast is served at 8 o'clock.
Jag brukar vila mig efter lunchen.	I usually have a rest after lunch.
Middagen är serverad.	Dinner is served.

After prepositions, however, the article is sometimes omitted :

Jungfrun dukade[1] till lunch.	The maid was laying the table for lunch.

273. Names of streets, parks, squares, bridges, etc., take the definite article :

Södra Hamngatan.	South Harbour Street.
Sture-parken.	but : Hyde Park.
Hötorget.	but : Haymarket.

Similarly with much frequented public places :

Hon går i kyrkan (skolan).	She goes to church (school).

274. Names of Swedish rivers, lakes, mountains, etc., take the definite article :

Lagan, Vättern, Storsylen, Ljungdalen.

275. Nouns denoting measure take the definite article, where English has the indefinite article or *per* :

Ägg kostar 25 öre stycket[2].	Eggs cost 25 öre apiece.
Dessa strumpor kostar 4 kr. paret.	These stockings cost 4 kronor a pair.

Similarly in phrases expressing rate or frequency nouns denoting time are used in the definite form, preceded by the prepositions *i* or *om* :

Han kommer hem två gånger i veckan (om året).	He comes home twice a week (year).

[1] The object *bordet* is omitted.

[2] *styck* is very usual in the colloquial.

T.Y.S.—8*

276. The definite article is used in Swedish, as in French and German, with parts of the body, clothing, etc., where English uses a possessive adjective :

Jag har fått någonting i ögat.	I've got something in my eye.
Han lyfte på hatten.	He raised his hat.

277. Some adjectives are followed by a noun in the definite form. Note the following examples :

Båda (or : *Bägge*) *bröderna var hemma.*	Both brothers were home.
Det hände förra veckan.	It happened last week.
Jag var ute hela dagen.	I was out all day.

Omission of Definite Article

278. The definite article is not used with names of families, hotels and ships (nor with names of some foreign rivers and newspapers).

Hälsa så mycket till Anderssons.	Give my kind regards to the Anderssons.
Vi reste till Göteborg med Britannia.	We went to Gothenburg by the Britannia.
De tog in på Savoy.	They put up at the Savoy.
Han satt och läste " Times."	He sat reading " The Times."

Notice also the following expressions in which a definite form in English corresponds to a form without article in Swedish :

Vi gick av på fel station.	We got out at the wrong station.
Hotellet ligger på höger (vänster) sida.	The hotel is on the right (left) hand side.

Indefinite Article

279. In general the indefinite article is used in Swedish where it would be used in English.[1]

[1] Note the occasional use of the article with an abstract noun in expressions like *ett härligt väder* ' glorious weather ' ; *en verklig tur* ' real good luck ' ; *en underbar musik* ' wonderful music.'

It is placed **before** and not **after** the adjective in expressions like *en halv timme* ' half an hour ' ; *ett så stort hus* ' such a big house ' ; *en sådan karl* [kɑːr] ' such a fellow ' ; *en alltför stor summa* ' too large a sum,' etc.

Omission of Indefinite Article

280.   The indefinite article is not used before predicative nouns denoting profession, trade, nationality, rank, religion, etc.

Examples :

Hans far var läkare.	His father was a physician.
Är ni engelsman ?	Are you an Englishman ?
Levertin var jude.	Levertin was a Jew.

Note.—The indefinite article is usually inserted if the noun is qualified.

Hans far var en berömd läkare.	His father was a famous physician.
Han var en författare, som var verksam under 80-talet.	He was an author who was active in the eighties.

281.   The indefinite article is omitted after *som* in the sense of ' as,' ' in the capacity of.'

Redan **som** *student skrev han många dikter.*	Even as a student he wrote many poems.

282.   The indefinite article is not used after *vilken* in exclamations.

Vilken utmärkt idé !	What a splendid idea !

283.   The indefinite article is sometimes omitted before nouns denoting concrete things used as the object of a verb.

Han röker pipa.	He smokes a pipe.
Jag har fått brev från Sverige.	I have had a letter from Sweden.
Skall jag ta paraply med mig ?	Shall I take an umbrella ?
Hon väntar på svar.	She is waiting for an answer.
Huset hade platt tak.	The house had a flat roof.

Relics of Older Constructions

284. Modern Swedish writers occasionally use both articles in juxtaposition, followed by a superlative, e.g.: *Hon var ett det vackraste barn*, literally: ' She was one the fairest child ; i.e. ' the fairest child you could find (imaginable).' Here *ett* has its older semi-demonstrative force. There are parallels to this construction in Shakespeare, e.g.: ' One the wisest prince.'

The use of a plural form of the indefinite article, *ena*, for emphasis cannot be rendered exactly in English, e.g.: *Ni är **ena** rediga rackarungar*. This can only be translated by disregarding the article and saying ' You are (a pair, gang of) real young rascals.' Similarly *Vad är ni för **ena***? may be rendered ' What sort of fellows are you ? '

Conjunctions

285. The most important conjunctions are:

A—Co-ordinating Conjunctions

These are used to join words or sentences of equal value.

1. *och* ' and.'
2. *både . . . och* ' both . . . and.'
3. *såväl . . . som* ' as well as.'
4. *eller* ' or.'
5. *antingen . . . eller* ' either . . . or.'
6. *varken . . . eller* ' neither . . . nor.'
7. *men* ' but.'
8. *för* $\left.\right\}$ ' for '[1]
   ty
9. *inte bara* (or *endast*) . . . *utan* (*också*) ' not only . . . but (also).'
10. *dels . . . dels* ' partly . . . partly.'[2]
11. *än . . . än* ' now . . . now.'

Examples :

(1) *Jag adresserade brevet och lade det i brevlådan* ' I addressed the letter and put it into the letter-box.';

---

[1] *för* is colloquial ; *ty* is only used in the written language.

[2] *dels . . . dels* can also mean ' on the one hand . . . on the other . . . '; ' for one thing . . . for the other. . . . '

kvinnor och barn ' women and children ' ; *svart och vit* ' black and white.'

(2) *Han älskade både sitt land och sitt folk.* ' He loved both his country and his people ' ; *både stora och små* ' both large and small.'

(3) *Han var en skräck för såväl vänner som fiender* (or : *för vänner såväl som fiender*) ' he was a terror to friends as well as foes.'

(4) *Vill ni ha te eller kaffe ?* ' Would you like tea or coffee ?' *Ja eller nej ?* ' yes or no ? '

(5) *Antingen du eller jag* ' either you or I ' ; *du kan få antingen en smörgås eller en kaka* ' you can have either a slice of bread and butter[1] or a cake.'

(6) *Han varken stal eller ljög* ' he neither stole nor lied.'

(7) *Solen sken från en klar himmel, men det var bitande kallt* ' the sun was shining from a clear sky, but it was bitterly cold.'

Note.—**men** is used after an affirmative, **utan** is used after a negative phrase or clause when a contrast is implied (cf. *aber* and *sondern* in German).

Example : *Han kan inte gå i skolan utan måste stanna hemma.* ' He cannot go to school but has to stay at home (instead) ' ; *inte rik utan fattig* ' not rich but (on the contrary) poor.'

(8) *Du kan behålla pengarna, för du är en hederlig karl* [kɑ:r]. ' You can keep the money, for you are an honest fellow.'

Gubben satte sig att vila, ty han orkade icke gå längre. ' The old man sat down to rest, for he hadn't the strength to go any farther.'

(9) *Hästen var inte endast halt utan också mager.* ' The horse was not only lame but thin.'

(10) *Han kommer inte, dels därför att han inte vill och dels därför att han inte kan.* ' He isn't coming, partly because he doesn't want to and partly because he cannot.'

(11) *Än kommer han för sent, än för tidigt.* ' Now (At one time) he arrives too late, now (at others) too early.'

---

[1] A *smörgås* often has something on it (*ett pålägg*), e.g. meat, cheese, etc. It is then a kind of one-sided sandwich.

B.—Subordinating Conjunctions

These conjunctions introduce various kinds of subordinate clauses.

286. **Noun clauses** are introduced by *att* ' that ' and by *om* ' if, whether.'

Examples:

Jag trodde, att hans sista stund var kommen. ' I thought (that) his last hour had come.'

Jag frågade honom, om han ville komma. ' I asked him whether he wished to come.'

The remaining Subordinating Conjunctions may be classified as follows :

287. **Temporal Conjunctions**

då ' when '	
när ' when '	*sedan* ' after '
närhelst ' whenever '	*allt sedan* ' ever since '
förrän ' before '	*medan* ' while '
innan ' before '	*tills*
så länge som ' as long as '	*till dess* } ' until '
så snart som ' as soon as '	

Note.—(a) **När** and **då** are used without distinction as temporal conjunctions, but **när** is more common in the spoken language.

(b) **Innan** and **förrän** both mean ' before,' but the latter is more usual after a negative, e.g. : **Innan** han *visste ordet av, började hon springa i väg.* ' Before he could speak, she started to run away ' ; but : *Jag kan väl inte besvara din fråga,* **förrän** *jag läst brevet.* ' I can't answer your question before I've read the letter, can I? ' Similarly after a main clause containing *knappt* or *knappast* ' scarcely ' (which is equivalent to a negative), e.g.: *Knappast hade jag hört musiken, förrän hela processionen kom i sikte.* ' Scarcely had I heard the music before the whole procession came in sight.'

(c) **Tills** is the most usual word for ' until ' in the spoken language ; **till dess** is more usual in the written language.

288.   Causal Conjunctions

då ' as, since '	*eftersom* ' since '
därför att ' because '	*emedan* ' as, because '

Note.—(*a*) *Då* (which, as stated above, is also a temporal conjunction) and *eftersom* are used without distinction to render English ' as, since,' e.g. :

Då (*Eftersom*) *jag var genomvåt, måste jag stanna hemma.*	As (Since) I was wet through, I had to stay at home.

(*b*) *Därför att* is much more usual than *emedan* ; the latter is never used in the spoken language.

289.   Conditional Conjunctions

om ' if '	*antaget att* ' supposing '
om . . . bara ' as long as '	*förutsatt att* 'provided that'
om . . . . inte ⎫ ' unless ' *med mindre* ⎭	*i fall (att)* ⎫ ' in case ' *i händelse (att)* ⎭
bara ' if only '	

Note.—(*a*) *Om* is both an interrogative conjunction, used to introduce a Noun Clause (see above), and a conditional conjunction, e.g. :

Om jag vore som du, skulle jag inte anta hans inbjudan.	If I were you, I shouldn't accept his invitation.

(*b*) *Om . . . inte* is much more usual than *med mindre.*

(*c*) When a Conditional Clause is followed by a Principal Clause, the latter is often introduced by *så* ' then.' The *så* is more usual in Swedish than *then* in English.

Example :

Om du väntar ett tag, så följer jag med.	If you wait a bit, I'll come with you.

Similarly *så* is occasionally (but less frequently) used to introduce a Principal Clause after a preceding Causal Clause.

Example:

Eftersom de var vana vid det därhemma, så började de göra det också här.	Since they were used to it at home, they began to do it here too.

Så, corresponding to English 'and,' is used after a clause expressing a Command, Promise, etc., e.g.: *Var en snäll gosse, så ska' du få en karamell.* 'Be a good boy and you shall have a sweet.'

In many cases the *så* may be omitted.

290. Concessive Conjunctions

ehuru		*även om*	
fast	'though, although'	*om än*	'even though'
fastän		*oaktat*	
hur . . . än 'however'		*vare sig . . . eller* 'whether . . . or'	

Note.—(a) **Fast** is the most usual word for 'although'; *ehuru* is never used in the spoken language, e.g.:

Partisanerna hade framgång, fast de var illa utrustade.	The partisans were successful, although they were poorly equipped.

(b) *Även om* is more usual than *om än* and *oaktat*.

291. Final Conjunctions

These denote an end or purpose:

att 'that'
för att 'so that'
på det att . . . icke 'lest, so that . . . not'

på det att 'that, in order that'

Note.—The most usual final conjunction is **för att**, e.g.:

Jag skickade honom ett telegram, för att han inte skulle göra resan förgäves.	I sent him a telegram so that he should not make the journey to no purpose (in vain).

The other final conjunctions above are only used in the written language.

292. **Consecutive Conjunctions**

These denote a consequence : *så att* or *så ... att* ' so that.'

The two particles are sometimes used together and sometimes split up, e.g. :

Båten var inne tidigt, så att vi kunde fortsätta resan till Stockholm.	The boat was in early, so we were able to continue our journey to Stockholm.
Snön låg så djupt att det var omöjligt att komma fram.	The snow lay so deep that it was impossible to make (any) headway.

293. **Conjunctions of Comparison**

som ' as '	*så ... som*[1] ' as ... as '
som om ' as if '	*allt efter som* ' (according) as '
lika ... som ' (just) as ... as '	*ju ... dess (desto)* ' the ... the '

Examples :

Som man bäddat, får man ligga.[2]	As you have made your bed (so) you must lie on it.
Han såg ut, som om han vore full.	He looked as if he were drunk.
Hon är lika vacker som förr.	She is just as beautiful as before (ever).
Han är inte så dum som han ser ut.	He isn't as stupid as he looks.
Han blev tröttare allt efter som arbetet ökades.	He became more fatigued as the work increased.
Ju mera han arbetar, dess (desto) mindre tycks han lära sig.	The more he works, the less he seems to learn.

[1] The *som* is sometimes omitted, e.g. *Han sprang så fort han kunde.* ' He ran as fast as he could.'

[2] See § 248.

Note.—The particle **än** is used as a conjunction of comparison after a clause containing *annan* or a comparative, e.g. :

> *Detta är en **annan** bok **än** den som du lovade mig.*
>
> This is a different book from the one you promised me.

> *Han ville **hellre** gå till fots **än** åka taxi.*
>
> He would rather go on foot than take a taxi.

Interjections

294. The principal Swedish interjections are :

ack ! ' oh ! ah ! alas ! '
ah, aha ! ' oh ! oho ! '
aj, aj ! ' oh dear ! '
asch ! ' pooh ! '
bums ! ' plomp ! plonk ! '
fy (skäms) ! (fie) ' for shame ! '
hallå ! ' hallo ! '
hu ! ' ugh ! '
hysch ! ' hush '
jaså ! ' (oh) indeed ! '
ja, ja män ! ' yes, indeed ! '
ja visst ! ' (why) yes, of course ! '

klatsch ! ' crack ! '
oj, oj, oj ! ' oh ! oh ! '
pang ! ' bang ! '
prat ! ' (stuff and) nonsense ! '
strunt ! ' rubbish ! '
topp ! ' done ! agreed ! '
tyst ! ' be quiet ! '
usch ! ' huh ! how horrid ! '
vyss ! ' hushaby '
å, åh ! ' oh ! '
äsch ! ' pooh ! '

Note.—(a) *ack* ! corresponds exactly to the German *ach* !

(b) *aj, aj* ! and *oj, oj, oj* ! express pain or regret.

(c) *asch* ! *usch* ! and *äsch* ! express varying degrees of disparagement.

(d) *jaså* ! has a great variety of meanings according to its intonation. It may be used to express acceptance of a fact, surprise or (ironically) disbelief.

(e) In *ja, ja män*, which expresses emphatic corroboration, the word *män* is an obscured oath ; it stands for ' the holy men,' i.e. ' the saints.' Similarly in expressions like *nej men se* ! ' just look at that ! ' though the spelling *men* conceals the origin of the word.

Word Formation

295. The Swedish language abounds in compound and derivative words, many of them based on German originals (see Introduction). As soon as the student has acquired a small vocabulary of ' root ' words, he will at once see the meaning of a large number of compounds and derivatives, e.g. :

dag ' day '	*dagbok* ' diary ' *daglig* ' daily ' (adj.) *dagligen* ' daily ' (adv.)
tro (verb) ' believe ' (noun) ' belief, faith '	*trohet* ' fidelity ' *trofast* ' loyal, trusty ' *trolös* ' faithless ' *trovärdig* ' credible '

296. When two nouns form a compound, there may be a connecting link *-s*, *-a* or *-e* :

arbetslön ' wage '   *läsebok* ' reading book '
jordagods ' landed property '

Derivative Nouns[1]

297. *Nomina agentis*, i.e. names of persons performing a certain activity, are usually formed with the suffix *-are*, more rarely with *-när* :

arbetare ' workman '	*konstnär* ' artist '
bagare ' baker '	*gäldenär* ' debtor '

The *-are* suffix is also used to form names of Instruments :

ångare ' steamer '   *hammare* ' hammer '

298. Names of trades or places where trades are carried on are formed with the suffix *-eri* :

bageri ' bakery '   *tryckeri* ' printing works '

[1]See also Diminutives, § 240 and Feminine Forms, §§ 241—246.

299. The chief suffixes used to form abstract nouns are -a, -ja, -ma, -ad, -nad, -an, -ande, -d, -e, -else, -sel, -ende, -het, -lek, -ning, -dom, -skap, -t.

Examples :

stark ' strong '	styrka ' strength '
lat ' lazy '	lättja ' laziness '
fet ' fat '	fetma ' corpulency '
ledsen ' sad '	ledsnad ' regret, sorrow '
lyda(II) ' obey '	lydnad ' obedience '
längta(I) ' long '	längtan ' longing '
bibehålla(IV) ' retain '	bibehållande ' retention '
lång ' long '	längd ' length '
varm ' hot '	värme ' heat '
fresta(I) ' tempt '	frestelse ' temptation '
viga(II) ' marry (them) '	vigsel ' wedding '
avse(IV) ' refer to '	avseende ' respect '
häftig ' violent '	häftighet ' violence '
kär ' dear '	kärlek ' love '
laga(I) mat ' prepare food '	matlagning ' cooking '
vis ' wise '	visdom ' wisdom '
vän ' friend '	vänskap ' friendship '
skriva(IV) ' write '	skrift ' writing '

As will be seen from the above examples, the root vowel is sometimes changed in the derivative word.

Derivative Adjectives

300. The chief adjectival suffixes are :
-ig, -lig, -isk, -bar, -sam, -aktig, -full, -rik.

Examples :

prakt ' splendour '	präktig ' splendid '
hus ' house '	huslig ' domestic '
hygien ' hygiene '	hygienisk ' hygienic '
frukt ' fruit '	fruktbar ' fruitful '
verka(I) ' act '	verksam ' active '
fabel ' fable '	fabelaktig ' fabulous '
hopp ' hope '	hoppfull ' hopeful '
kunskap ' knowledge '	kunskapsrik 'well-informed'

Adjectives are sometimes formed from foreign words by means of the Romance suffix -iell, e.g. finanser ' finances ' —finansiell ' financial.'

Derivative Adverbs

301. Most adverbs are formed from the corresponding adjectives by adding *-t* (see § 182) ; but in some cases there are special forms. Thus a few adverbs are formed by adding *-lunda* to the root, e.g. : *annorlunda* ' differently ' ; *ingalunda* ' by no means ' ; *sålunda* ' thus.' The ending is really the genitive plural of an extinct feminine noun *lund* ' manner,' so adverbs of this type are ' obscured compounds.' Other genitival endings used to form adverbs are : *-dels*, e.g. : *mestadels* ' for the most part ' ; *-deles*, e.g. : *alldeles* ' entirely, quite ' ; *särdeles* ' especially ' ; *-ledes* e.g. : *annorledes* ' differently ' ; *likaledes* ' likewise ' ; *således* ' thus ; (and, popularly, *brevledes* ' by letter ') ; *-städes*, e.g. : *därstädes* ' at that place ' ; *härstädes* ' at this place ' ; *flerstädes* ' in several places.'

When the corresponding adjective ends in *-lig*, some adverbs are formed by adding *-en*, e.g. : *muntligen* ' orally ' ; *nyligen* ' recently ' ; *ursprungligen* ' originally.'

Others, in imitation of German adverbs like *glücklicherweise*, add *-vis* to the root, e.g. : *delvis* ' partly ' ; *lyckligtvis* ' fortunately ' ; *parvis* ' in pairs ' ; *undantagsvis* ' by way of exception.'

Derivative Verbs

302. The suffix *-era*, used to form verbs from foreign roots —e.g. : *promenera* ' to stroll ' ; *studera* ' to study '—has already been mentioned.

Some native verbs are derived from nouns and adjectives by adding the suffix *-ja*, which usually causes mutation of the root vowel.

Examples :

sorg ' sorrow '	*sörja* ' to lament '
svalg ' throat '	*svälja* ' to swallow '
tam ' tame '	*tämja* ' to tame '

In some cases the *-j-* has now disappeared but the mutation of the vowel remains, e.g. : *krav—kräva* ' demand,' *varm—värma* ' heat.'

Inchoative verbs, i.e. those denoting ' entering into the state expressed by the root-word ', are formed from adjectives by adding the suffix *-na* (cf. English *deepen, lengthen,* etc.).

Examples :

hård ' hard ' *hårdna* ' to harden '
blek ' pale ' *blekna* ' to become pale '

A few verbs are formed by means of a *-ka* suffix, e.g. : *jaka* ' to affirm ' ; *neka* ' to deny ' ; *dyrka* ' to adore.'

Vocabulary

ha lust att . . . ' feel inclined to . . . '
komma överens ' agree '
ingång (c.) ' entrance '
överenskommelse (c.3) ' agreement '
aptit (c.) ' appetite '
varg [**varj**] (c.2) ' wolf '
ytterkläder 'outer garments'
garderob [**gaɖə'roːb**] ' cloak room '
sätta sig (*ner*) ' sit down '
ledig ' free, vacant '
ta emot ' take, receive '
snaps (c.2) ' schnapps, dram (of aqua-vitae) '

pilsner (c.2) ' light ale '
matsedel (c.2) ' menu '
avsluta(IV) ' finish, conclude '
måltid (c.3) ' meal '
punsch (c.) ' punch '[1]
göra upp ' settle up '
nota (c.1) ' bill '
brännvin [**'brɛ'nvin**] 'spirits'
öl (n.) ' beer '
växel (c.2) ' change '
drickspengar (pl.) ' tip, gratuity '
bjuda någon på något ' invite someone to something '

Exercise 23
Translate
På restauranten [resto'ra'ŋən]

Hr. Svensson ringer upp sin vän Hr. Johansson och frågar, om han har lust att äta middag (*have dinner*) med honom på Restaurant Viktoria. De kommer överens om att träffas kl. 6 utanför ingången. Kl. 6 träffas de enligt överenskommelse (*as agreed*).

Hr. Svensson : Goddag, kära bror ! Hoppas, du har god aptit. Jag är hungrig som en varg.

Hr. Johansson : Ja, det är jag med. Det ska' bli härligt att få något varmt och gott i sig.

Hr. Svensson : Kom, låt oss gå in.

De lämnar ytterkläderna i garderoben och går in i matsalen.

[1] Swedish punch is a liqueur made of arrack.

Hr. Svensson :   Ska' vi sätta oss vid fönstret där borta (*over there*) ? Jag tror, det finns ett ledigt bord.

De sätter sig ner, och kyparen kommer och tar emot beställningen.

Hr. Svensson (till kyparen) : Vi ska' be att få en stor snaps var (*each*) och två pilsner. Och kanske vi kan se på matsedeln.

Kyparen (lämnar matsedeln) : Var så god !

Restaurant Viktoria

Menu

Diné à kr. 2:75
Smör, bröd och varmrätt[1]
Diné à kr. 3:25
Smör, bröd, ost, sill och varmrätt[2]
Diné à kr. 4:00
Smörgåsbord, soppa eller dessert och
varmrätt[3]

—o—

Champinjonsoppa[4]
Tomatsoppa
Stekt kolja med skarpsås[5]
Kokt sjötunga med musselsås[6]
Hummeromelett[7]
Hackad kalvfilé med svampsås[8]
Stekt fläsk med bruna bönor[9]
Bräckt falukorv med stuvad potatis[10]
Blandade grönsaker i smör[11]
Hallonkräm med vispad grädde[12]
Plättar med sylt[13]
Filbunke[14]

---

[1] Butter, bread and hot course. [2] Butter, bread, cheese, (pickled) herring and hot course. [3] Hors d'œuvres table, soup or dessert, and hot course. [4] Mushroom (champignon) soup. [5] Fried haddock with *sauce piquante.* [6] Boiled sole with mussel sauce. [7] Lobster omelette. [8] (Minced) veal cutlet (*filé*=Fr. *filet*) with mushroom sauce. [9] Roast streaky pork with brown beans. [10] Broiled Falun sausage with stewed potatoes. [11] Assorted vegetables in butter. [12] Raspberry crème with whipped cream (*kräm* is a kind of jelly made by boiling fruit juice with potato flour or arrowroot). [13] Small pancakes with jam. [14] clotted sour milk (similar to *yoghurt*).

Herrarna har avslutat måltiden med punsch och kaffe och önskar göra upp.

Hr. Svensson : Kyparen, får jag be om notan ?

Kyparen : Ja, tack ! Det var två middagar à kr. 4, brännvin, öl, kaffe och en halvflaska punsch. Det blir i allt (*all together*) kr. 21.

Hr. Svensson lämnar tre 10-kronors sedlar, och när han har fått växeln, lägger han kr. 3 på bordet som drickspengar. Sedan går herrarna ut.

Hr. Johansson : Tack ska' du ha för en härlig middag, och nästa gång är det min tur att bjuda dig.

Anmärkningar

Jag är hungrig som en varg. ' *I'm as hungry as a hunter* (lit. *wolf*).'

Det är jag med (*with the stress on* med). '*So am I*.'

Något varmt och gott. '*Something nice and hot*' (see § 217).

Kanske vi kan se. *Note the absence of inversion after the adverb* kanske, *because it is equivalent to a full clause followed by* att. *This word-order is used when* kanske *introduces a polite suggestion. But inversion is used when it indicates a supposition, e.g.* Kanske kommer han snart. '*Perhaps he will come soon*.'

The word smörgås, *originally used for a small pat of butter, is now used for* ' *a slice of bread and butter*,' ' *a slice of bread and butter with something laid or spread on it* ' *and* ' *an hors d'œuvre with or without bread and butter*.' *In Swedish restaurants there is often a central table with a large variety of* hors d'œuvres, *from which diners help themselves before commencing the meal proper. This is called a* smörgåsbord.

In falukorv *the first part of the word is the stem form of* Falun, *a place in the province of* Dalarna (*Dalecarlia*).

Nästa gång är det min tur. ' *Next time it'll be my turn*.'

Vocabulary

flyg (n.5) ' plane '

övernatta⁽¹⁾ ' spend the night '

ämna⁽¹⁾ ' intend '

skott (n.5) ' shot '

buller (n.5) ' noise '

kamrat (c.3) ' comrade '

anta⁽ᴵⱽ⁾ ' accept '

anbud (n.5) ' offer '

somna⁽¹⁾ ' fall asleep '

brevskrivning (c.) ' letter writing '

passa⁽¹⁾ *upp* ' wait on '

sällskap (n.5) ' party '

dålig ' bad '

spela⁽¹⁾ ' play (an instrument) '

förkylning (c.2) ' cold, chill '

äta⁽ᴵⱽ⁾ *lunch* ' have lunch '

promenad (c.3) ' walk '

Translate

(b) The plane does not leave till (*avgår först*) to-morrow, so you will have to (*får*) spend the night here. What would you most like to be (*vill du helst bli*) when you grow up (*blir stor*)? I want to travel. But I don't speak French very well (*inte så värst bra*), nor do I know (*kan jag*) much German. He asked (me) whether I intended to come. She absolutely refused (*ville absolut inte*) to come with us (*följa med*) but wanted to stay at home. I had scarcely gone to bed before I heard a shot. As soon as I heard the noise, I roused my comrades. While we were lying there, we heard several more shots (*flera skott till*). The noise got (*blev*) so loud (*stark*) that we couldn't sleep. We lay there a long time before we noticed that the noise was not coming from the street but from the next house. If I were you (*som du*), I should accept his offer. I can't come and see (*hälsa på*) you this evening, for I have heaps (*massor*) of letters to write. There are so many that I don't know where to start.[1] But you can come and see us as soon as you have finished your letter-writing? Yes, I will (*det skall jag göra*). I stayed at home until I had written all the letters. Afterwards I was so tired that I fell asleep in my chair. I sent the letter off in good time so that he should get it early next morning. Now we must begin our meal (*börja äta*), whether he comes or not. I gave the waiter a kr. 5 note (colloquial *en femma*) because he had waited on the party so well (*bra*). I ran as fast as I could, though I hadn't much hope of catch-

[1]See § 261 (b).

ing[1] the train. The more he works, the less he seems (*tycks*)
to learn. The more he heard the less he said. Next morning
the weather was very bad, so I stayed at home. As the
weather was so bad, I stayed at home. She both sings and
plays very well. My hands were so cold that I couldn't hold
(*hålla i*) the pen. I felt as if I were going to catch (*skulle få*)
a cold. He talked of Stockholm as if he had lived there a
long time. After (*Sedan*) we had had lunch, we took a long
walk. Don't talk about it until he has arrived (*kommit*)
home. I shall not give up all hope until I hear from his
comrades.

Vocabulary

nyheter (pl.) ' news '
front (c.3) ' front '
Moskva ' Moscow '
kommuniké (c.3) ' communiqué '
utkant (c.3) ' outskirts '
strid (c.3) ' conflict '
meddela[1] ' state, report '
allierad ' allied '
högkvarter [kva'ʈeːr] (n.5) ' headquarters '
armé (c.3) ' army '
tillfoga[1] ' inflict '
förlust (c.3) ' loss '
flygministerium (n.3) ' Air Ministry '
utsätta[II] ' expose '
häftig ' violent '
anfall (n.5) ' attack '
driva[IV] ' drive '
kil (c.2) ' wedge '
försvar [fœ'ʂvɑːr] (n.5) ' defence '
ställning (c.2) ' position '
framryckning (c.2) ' advance '

motanfall (n.5) ' counter-attack '
kasta[1] *tillbaka* ' repulse, throw back '
överkommando (n.4) ' Supreme Command '
svår ' difficult, severe '
avvärja[II] ' ward off '
avvisa[II] ' repulse '
upprepa[1] ' repeat '
försök (n.5) ' attempt '
tränga[II] *in* ' penetrate '
likvidera[II] ' liquidate '
rapportera[1] ' report '
landsätta [II] ' land (trans.) '
landsättning (c.2) ' landing '
fartyg (n.5) ' vessel, craft '
igångsätta[II] ' start, set in motion '
påstå [IV] ' maintain, assert '
omringa[1] ' surround '
tyda[II] *på* ' indicate, suggest '
samtliga (pl.) ' all '
flygplats (c.3) ' aerodrome '

[1] See Exercise 16 (c).

obrukbar ' unusable '

upprätta[1] ' set up, establish '

brohuvud (n.5) ' bridgehead '

motstånd (n.5) ' resistance '

hårdna[1] ' harden, stiffen '

verksamhet (c.) ' activity '

tung ' heavy '

mål (n.5) ' objective '

Note.—The following passage contains many of the words used in the Swedish wireless news bulletins during the war. It is *not* a reproduction of an actual broadcast.

(c) **Kvällsnyheter från T.T.**[1]

Ryska trupper på nordfronten står nu, enligt en Moskvakommuniké, i utkanten av Riga.

Om striderna (*transl.* : *the fighting*) i Italien meddelar det allierade högkvarteret, att tyska armén tillfogats stora förluster.

Det brittiska flygministeriet meddelar, att München utsattes för (=*to*) ett häftigt flyganfall natten till i dag.

(END OF HEADLINES)

Vi övergår till (*We now proceed to*) eftermiddagens telegram :

Ryssarnas anfall mot tyskarna vid Östersjöfronten tilltar i häftighet. De har lyckats[2] driva en kil in i de tyska försvarsställningarna och har gjort en framryckning på bortåt 8 kilometer. Alla tyska motanfall har kastats tillbaka.

Det tyska överkommandot meddelar från ostfronten, att den femte tyska armén i svåra avvärjningsstrider avvisat upprepade ryska försök att tränga in i de tyska ställningarna. Flera ryska grupper blev likviderade.

Det allierade högkvarteret i Italien rapporterar, att den åttonde brittiska armén i går med framgång (*successfully*) landsatte trupper med landsättningsfartyg på tre ställen på västkusten. Anfallen till lands (*by land, from the landward side*) igångsattes flera timmar förut, och tyskarna

[1] *Tidningarnas telegrambyrå* (The Newspapers' Telegram Bureau).

[2] See § 192.

påstås vara[1] omringade. Rapporter från Reuters korrespondent tyder på, att samtliga flygplatser i området i förväg (*in advance, previously*) gjorts[2] obrukbara. Amerikanerna har lyckats upprätta brohuvuden norr om Angelio. Längre mot öster har det tyska motståndet hårdnat.

Om det senaste dygnets flygverksamhet meddelas från London, att södra England utsattes för ett flyganfall i eftermiddag. " Faran över " (*the danger over*, i.e. *raiders passed*) gavs efter en kort tid.

Brittiska Lancaster-bombplan gjorde ett häftigt anfall på München natten till i dag. Tunga amerikanska bombplan angrep under förmiddagen militära mål i norra Frankrike.

Så var det slut för dagen (*That is all for to-day*) från T.T.

CHAPTER XXIV

Translations

Passages for Students of Commerce and Economics

Vocabulary

handel (c.) 'trade, commerce'

antyda(II) 'intimate'

brevväxling (c.) 'correspondence'

avdelningskontor (n.5) 'branch office'

steg (n.5) 'step'

byggnad (c.3) 'building'

åta(ga)(IV) *sig* 'undertake'

framtida (indecl. adj.) 'future'

utveckling (c.2) 'development'

visa(I) *sig* 'prove (§ 210), turn out'

motivera(I) 'motivate, account for, justify'

bibehålla(IV) 'retain'

länk (c.2) 'link'

återkomma(IV) 'come back'

förfrågan (c.) 'enquiry'

diverse (indecl. adj.) 'sundry'

samband (n.5) 'connection'

gång (c.) 'course, progress'

uppstå(III) 'arise'

förutse(IV) 'foresee'

behov (n.5) 'need, requirement'

verktyg (n.5) 'tool'

filial (c.3) 'branch'

hålla(IV) 'keep'

vara (c.1) 'commodity'; (pl.= goods, articles)

förråd (n.5) 'stock'

sistnämnd 'last-mentioned, latter'

punkt (c.3) 'point'

upplysningar (pl.) 'information'

Note.—In the more formal style of commercial correspondence the special plural forms of the verb (*vi ha, vi äro, vi taga*, etc.) and the full forms of the pronoun *Ni* (*Eder*, etc.) are used.

(a)   Ett handelsbrev

Aktiebolaget Spik och Bult,
Kungsgatan 7,
Gävle.

Stockholm den 3 januari 1944.

Betr.[1] : Luleåkontoret.

Såsom antytts[2] i tidigare brevväxling ha vi för avsikt[3] att öppna ett avdelningskontor i Luleå. Vi taga detta steg närmast med tanke på[4] ett större[5] byggnadsarbete, som vi åtagit oss i luleåtrakten, men hoppas att den framtida utvecklingen[6] skall visa sig motivera bibehållandet av[7] det nya kontoret som en permanent länk i vår organisation.

Inom de närmaste[8] dagarna ämna vi återkomma[9] med en förfrågan om (*for*) diverse material i samband med luleåkontraktet. Dessutom kommer under arbetets gång förmodligen att[10] uppstå oförutsedda behov av verktyg o. dyl. Så vitt vi veta[11] ha Ni ingen filial i Luleå, men kanske det finnes[12] en agent, som håller Edra varor i förråd.

Det är närmast på den sistnämnda punkten, som vi för närvarande (*at present, now*) äro i behov av upplysningar från Eder.

Högaktningsfullt
A.-B. Byggnadskontrakt.

Notes.—[1]=*beträffar* ' concerns '; transl. : ' re.' [2] *Såsom* (*har*) *antytts* ' as (has been) intimated.' [3] lit. ' we have for intention '='we intend.' [4] lit. ' nearest with thought of ' ; transl. ' primarily with regard to.' [5] See § 114. [6] ' future developments.' [7] lit. : ' will turn out to justify the retention of ' ; transl. : ' will show that we are justified in retaining.' [8] ' next few.' [9] lit. : ' come back ' ; here= ' write to you again.' [10] *kommer att*, see § 238. [11] ' As far as we know.' [12] On the absence of inversion after *kanske*, see Ex. 23 (*a*), Anmärkningar.

Note the absence of a capital letter in *luleåtrakten*, *-kontraktet*, and see § 74.

Vocabulary

rubrik (c.3) ' heading '

rubricera[1] ' quote in a heading '

angelägenhet (c.3) ' matter, affair '

sakna[1] ' lack, be without '

bevaka[1] ' watch over '

därstädes ' in that place '

järnhandel (c.) ' ironmonger's store '

välsorterad ' well assorted '

lager (n.5) ' stock '

föreslå[III] ' suggest '

representant (c.3) ' representative '

uppsöka[II] ' visit, call on '

direktör (c.3) ' director '

diskutera[1] ' discuss '

möjlighet (c.3) ' possibility '

tillfredställa[II] ' satisfy '

brådskande [ˈbrɔˈskandə] ' urgent '

emotse[III] ' look forward to '

stål (c.) ' steel '

detalj (c.3) ' item '

specificera[1] ' specify '

komplex (n.5) ' complex, block (of buildings) '

förhoppning (c.2) ' hope, expectation '

angenäm ' pleasant '

samarbete (n.4) ' collaboration '

känneteckna[1] ' characterize '

mellanhavande (n.4) ' business (relations) '

fruktbringande ' fruitful, profitable '

teckna[1] ' sign '

(b) Svaret

A.-B. Byggnadskontrakt, Stockholm.

Gävle den 5 januari 1944.

Betr : Edert luleåkontor.

Vi tacka för Eder ärade skrivelse (*esteemed favour*) av den 3 ds.[1] i rubricerade angelägenhet[2]. Det är mycket riktigt (*quite correct*) att vi sakna filialkontor[3] i Luleå. Våra intressen bevakas därstädes av firman E. G. Karlssons Järnhandel, som håller ett tämligen välsorterat lager av våra varor. Vi skulle vilja föreslå (*beg to suggest*), att Eder representant uppsöker direktör Karlsson för att diskutera dennes (*his*) möjligheter att tillfredställa de mera brådskande behov, som förutses i Edert brev.

Vi emotse med stort intresse Eder förfrågan om de järn- och ståldetaljer, vilka specificerats[4] för byggnadskomplexet i fråga.

Notes.—[1] See §156 (b). [2] ' on the matter quoted in the heading.' [3] See § 283. [4] See § 248.

I förhoppningen att det angenäma samarbete, som alltid
kännetecknat[1] våra mellanhavanden, skall visa sig fruktbringande även i luleåprojektet,[2] teckna vi[3],

Högaktningsfullt
Aktiebolaget Spik och Bult.

Vocabulary

tillgång (c.2) 'supply, asset'

efterfrågan (c.) 'demand'

tänka[(II)] 'imagine'

procedur (c.3) 'process'

förse[(III)] 'provide'

behov (n.5) 'need'

bränsle (n.) 'fuel'

uppvärmning (c.) 'heating'

matlagning (c.) 'cooking'

elda[(1)] 'make a fire'

numera 'nowadays'

stenkol (c.) 'pit coal'

torv (c.) 'peat'

renlig 'clean'

ved (c.) 'wood[4]'

onekligen 'undeniably'

stapla[(1)] *upp* 'pile up'

fång (n.5) 'armful'

öppen 'open'

härd (c.2) 'hearth'

fordom 'formerly'

bruka[(1)] +Inf. 'to be accus-
tomed to . . .'

flamma[(1)] 'flame'

eld (c.2) 'fire'

spisel (c.2) 'grate'

samlas[(1)] 'foregather, con-
gregate'

uppväga[(II)] 'outweigh'

bekvämlighet (c.3) 'amenity,
comfort'

oskattbar 'invaluable'

avseende (n.4) 'aspect, point
of view'

avlägsen 'remote'

skogsbygd (c.3) 'forest district'

unna[(1)] *sig* 'allow oneself,
afford'

lyx (c.) 'luxury'

förmögen 'wealthy'

gripa[(IV)] *till* 'have recourse
to'

besparing (c.2) 'saving'

vadan 'whence'

växa[(II)] 'grow'

gåva (c.1) 'gift'

tillstädja[(II)] 'sanction,permit'

envar 'everyone'

hugga[(IV)] 'hew'

släpa[(1)] 'drag, carry'

förmå (aux. vb.) 'be able'

ersättning (c.) 'remunera-
tion, payment'

självfallen 'obvious'

uthugga[(IV)] 'hew down'

inskränkning (c.2) 'limitation'

ovillkorligen 'absolutely,
unconditionally'

ske[(III)] 'happen, take place'

[1]See § 248. [2]*även i luleåprojektet* 'in the Luleå project, too'. [3]cf.
German *zeichnen wir*. [4]Swedish has three words for 'wood': *trä*
(n.), the general term; *virke* (n.) wood in the mass, timber; *ved*
(c.) fuel wood.

(c) Tillgång och Efterfrågan

Tänkom[1] oss t. ex. den procedur, genom vilken vi alla
förses med vårt behov av bränsle till uppvärmning och
matlagning. I stora delar av landet eldar man ju numera
med stenkol eller torv; men ett bättre och renligare
bränsle är utan tvivel veden,[2] och allra bäst är onekligen
att få[3] stapla upp det ena vedfånget efter det andra på en
öppen härd, så som fordom brukades.[4] En dylik flammande
eld på spiseln, kring vilken hela familjen om kvällen
samlas, uppväger tjogtals av[5] civilisationens bekvämlig-
heter; den är oskattbar i såväl estetiskt som hygieniskt
avseende.[6] Men numera är det nästan endast i de avlägs-
naste skogsbygderna, som man ännu kan unna sig en dylik
lyx; vi andra, både förmögnare och fattigare, ha för länge
sedan fått gripa till besparingsspislar[7] m.m. Vadan detta[8] ?
Är icke den växande skogen en fri gåva av naturen, varför
kan det då icke utan vidare tillstädjas envar[9] att hugga och
släpa hem så mycket ved som han själv förmår eller mot
ersättning[10] låta andra göra detta åt honom ? Svaret är
ju självfallet: under en sådan regim skulle alla skogar i
landet, åtminstone söder om Dalälven,[11] vara uthuggna
inom några få år. En inskränkning måste således här
ovillkorligen ske.

(Adapted from: Knut Wicksell: *Socialiststaten och
nutidssamhället. Verdandis småskrifter*, 129. *Albert
Bonniers förlag, Stockholm*, 1905).

Notes.—[1]*tänkom* is the Plural Imperative, 1st person, now
seldom used; transl. 'let us consider.' [2]Material nouns used in a
general sense are sometimes used without the article; see §270.
Here, however, the article is used. [3]'be allowed, be able.' [4]'as
was customary in olden times.' [5]'is worth more than scores of.'
[6] both from the aesthetic and the hygienic point of view.'
[7] lit. ' economy stoves '; transl. ' slow combustion stoves.'
[8] lit. ' whence this ? '; transl. ' why should this be so ? '
[9] lit. ' why can it not then be permitted to everyone ?';
transl. ' why then should not anyone have a perfect right
(*utan vidare*) to cut down and carry home ? ' [10] ' for payment.'
[11] a large river flowing through the province of Dalecarlia;
the region south of it is the more populous part of the country.

Chapter XXV

Translations

Extracts from London University Examination Papers

Vocabulary

kyrka (c.1) ' church '	*klockklang* (c.) ' ringing of bells '
fullsatt ' filled, full '	*bölja*[1] ' billow, roll out '
smal ' narrow '	*hav* (n.5) ' sea '
stig (c.2) ' path '	*packa*[1] *samman* ' pack together '
sydväst (c.2) ' sou'wester '	
bredbrättig 'broad brimmed'	*tränga*[II] *sig in* ' squeeze in '
sjöstövel (c.2) ' sea-boot '	*framåt* ' forward '

(a) Söndagen kommer. Och nu minnes varje fiskare, att här finns[1] en kyrka. Det är märkvärdigt, så[2] fullsatt kyrkan blir. Där komma fiskarna en efter en på[3] de smala stigarna i snön. Och i dag ha de inte sydväst[4] utan en bredbrättig hatt. Men en och annan[5] har sjöstövlar, för att han annars inte skulle haft[6] annat än[7] tofflor att ha på. Klockklangen böljar över berg och hav[8] och in i kyrkan stiga männen med snö på stövlarna, och då alla äro vana vid de sista platserna i kyrkan därhemma,[9] så[10] börja de också här att packa sig samman på den sista bänken. Men när det inte är möjligt för fler[11] att tränga sig in där, sjunker man ner på nästa ; och så kryper det framåt, bänk efter bänk.

—Matriculation, Jan. 1941.

Notes.—[1] *här finns* ' there is . . . here.' [2] transl. ' how.' [3] ' along.' [4] See § 283. [5] ' one or two, some of them.' [6] skulle *ha* haft ' ; see § 248. [7] ' anything else but ' ; see § 293, Note. [8] See § 270. [9] ' at home.' [10] See § 289, Note *c.* [11] ' any more.'

Vocabulary

skapa[1] ' create '
rätt ' right '
blick (c.2) ' look '
kund (c.3) ' customer '
påse (c.2) ' bag '
ställe (n.4) ' place '
handel (c.) ' business, trade '
obehaglig ' unpleasant '
envis ['e`:nvi:s] 'obstinate'

köpare (c.5) ' buyer '
råka[1] *på* ' meet with, come across '
pruta[1] ' bargain, haggle '
affär (c.3) ' bargain, piece of business '
hederlig ' honest '
bjuda[IV] *ut* ' offer for sale '
skada[1] ' damage '

(*b*) Anna Svärd var säkert skapad för att gå omkring med varor.[1] Hon hade den rätta blicken för[2] vad som helst[3] borde bjudas kunderna.[4] Det hade aldrig hänt henne, att hon hade lagt i sin påse en vara, som inte gick att sälja.[5] Kom hon[6] in på ett ställe, där man inte ville göra handel, gick hon sin väg[7] utan att vara obehagligt envis. Råkade hon på sådana köpare, som tyckte om att pruta, så[8] lät hon dem få sin vilja fram[9] och såg lagom[10] ledsen ut, för att de skulle tro, att de hade gjort en god affär. Till på köpet[11] var hon fullt[12] hederlig. Hon bjöd aldrig ut ett stycke tyg, som var skadat.

—ibid.

Notes.—[1] ' made for going round with (hawking) goods.'
[2] transl. ' an eye for.' [3] *helst*=' for preference, most of all, especially.' [4] Omit article. [5] *som inte gick att sälja*—' which it was impossible to sell '; transl. ' that wouldn't sell.'
[6] See § 214. [7] *att gå sin väg*=' to go away.' [8] See § 289, Note *c.* [9] ' have their way.' [10] See § 103 *e.* [11] *till på köpet*= ' into the bargain '; here: ' in addition, moreover.'
[12] ' fully, entirely, quite.'

Vocabulary

bortskämd ' spoilt '
neka[1] ' deny '
sak (c.3) ' thing '
sträng ' stern, severe '
kunskapsrik 'well informed, cultured '

ändamål (n.5) ' end, purpose '
anställa[II] ' appoint, engage '
lärd ' learned '
hovdam (c.3) ' lady-in-waiting '

läxa (c.1) ' lesson '

nyttig ' useful '

onödig ' unnecessary '

anslå ' assign, set apart '

läxläsning (c.) ' learning of lessons '

förhör (n.5) ' interrogation '

övrig ' remaining '

hovfröken (c.2) ' maid of honour '

våld (n.5) ' sway, thrall '

brodera[1] ' embroider '

promenera[1] ' go for a stroll '

ta(ga)[IV] *igen* ' recover, make up for '

(c) Prinsessan var bortskämd och vacker. Kungen, hennes fader, kunde knappast neka henne någonting. Endast i en sak var kungen sträng. Han ville,[1] att hans dotter skulle bli världens mest kunskapsrika prinsessa. Och för det ändamålet hade han anställt tre förskräckligt lärda hovdamer, som gåvo henne svåra läxor. Mycket, som var gott och nyttigt, fick prinsessan lära sig men också en hel del,[2] som var onödigt. Fyra av dagens timmar voro anslagna till läxläsning och fyra till förhör[3]. Men de övriga fyra[4] var prinsessan ledig och fick roa sig med sina hovfröknar. Medan hon var i lärda hovdamers och läxors våld, broderade eller promenerade de unga hovfröknarna och hade rätt så tråkigt[5]. Men när prinsessan äntligen blev ledig, togo de skadan igen.[6]

—Matriculation, June 1942.

Notes.—[1] See § 261(a). [2] *en hel del*=' quite a lot.' [3] transl. ' hearing her say them.' [4] *de övriga fyra* expresses duration. [5] *ha tråkigt=ha det tråkigt* ' be bored '; *rätt så=* rather ; cf. *ha roligt=*' have a good time'. [6] ' they made up for the loss.'

Vocabulary

höna (c.1) ' hen '

pinne (c.2) ' perch '

ansikte (n.4) ' face '

vinge (c.2) ' wing '

gård (c.2) ' yard '

faslig ' dreadful, terrible '

väsen (n.) ' fuss, to-do '

blomsterrabatt (c.3) ' flower bed '

sätta[III] *av* ' dash off '

häck (c.2) ' hedge '

hamna[1] ' land, arrive '

ge[IV] *sig till* ' take to, start '

ruta (c.1) ' pane '

riktig ' real '

rackarunge (c.2) ' rascal, imp '

ta[IV] *fast* ' catch '

stuva[1] *in* ' stow away '

bur (c.2) ' coop '

släppa[II] *ut* ' let out '

lova[1] ' promise '

(*d*) När hönan såg, att pinnarna voro borta,[1] flög hon rätt i vädret[2] och hade så när[3] slagit Svante i ansiktet med vingarna. Nästa minut var hon ute[4] på gården.[5] Mamma kom ut. Och bägge jungfrurna kommo ut. Och det blev[6] ett fasligt väsen. Hönan flög genom blomsterrabatterna, satte av över häcken, flög tillbaka igen och hamnade slutligen på verandan, där hon gav sig till att flyga emot fönsterrutorna. Svante sprang efter[7] hela tiden med hjärtat i halsgropen[8] och kände sig som en riktig liten rackarunge, ända till dess[9] hönan blivit[10] fasttagen och lyckligt och väl[11] instuvad i buren igen, ty det var ju han, som hade släppt ut henne. Och nu lovade han mamma, att han aldrig skulle göra så mer.[12]

—ibid.

Notes.—[1] ' were away,' see § 186 ; transl. ' had gone.'
[2] ' up in the air.' [3] *hade* is Subjunctive ; *så när*=well nigh ; transl. ' and nearly hit.' [4] See § 186. [5] ' in the yard.' [6] lit. ' it became ' ; transl. ' there was.' [7] The object is omitted ; supply ' her.' [8] ' with his heart in his mouth.' [9] *ända till dess*=' until.' [10] See § 248. [11] ' well and truly.' [12] *mer* after a negative=' any more, again.'

Vocabulary

trång ' confined, shut in '
orörd ' untouched '
slott (n.5) ' castle '
tillhöra(II) ' belong to '
förnäm ' noble '
mur (c.2) ' wall '
resa(II) *sig* ' rise '
brant ' steep '
klippväg (c.2) ' face of a rock '
port (c.2) ' gate '
synlig ' visible, conspicuous '
tät ' dense '

lyfta(I)*sig* ' rear '
glimma(I) ' gleam '
torn ([to:ɳ] (n.5) ' tower '
blänka(II) ' shine, glitter '
färd (c.3) ' journey '
aning (c.2) ' surmise, idea '
festlig ' festive, magnificent'
pojke (c.2) ' boy '
ta(IV) *sig för* ' proceed to '
klättra(I) ' climb '
speja(I) *efter* ' look (search) for '
strövtåg (n.5) ' ramble, excursion '

(e) Långt borta i skogen, där vägarna äro smala och trånga och träden stå orörda sedan hundratals år, ligger ett slott, som tillhör en förnäm fe. Dess mur reser sig brant och grå. Den som går där förbi, kunde ta den för en klippvägg. Inte heller[1] är porten mycket synlig. Men högt uppe över de täta trädkronorna lyfter sig slottet, och däruppe i ljuset glimma torntaken, och fönstren blänka som kristall. Det är endast fåglarna, som på sina färder över skogen få en aning om feslottets festliga form. Fåglarna—ja—och den lille pojke, som en vacker dag tog sig för att klättra upp i ett av de högsta träden för att speja efter vägen hem, vilken han förlorat[2] under ett av sina strövtåg i skogen.

—Matriculation, June 1943.

Notes.—[1] *inte heller* ' nor ' should only be used after a preceding negative ; here it is equivalent to ' and . . . not.' [2] *(hade) förlorat.*

Vocabulary

enkel ' simple '
trevlig ' pleasant '
envåning (c.2) ' single story'
förstuga (c.1) ' hall '
blyinfattad ' leaded '
tung ' heavy '
möbler (pl.) ' furniture '
ek (c.2) ' oak '
länstol (c.2) ' armchair '
ordning (c.) ' method, regularity '
reda (c.) ' order '
tåla[II] ' tolerate '
slarv (n.) ' untidiness '

nyckel (c.2) ' key '
rätt ' right, correct '
förlägga[II] ' mislay '
klädesborste (c.2) ' clothes brush '
försmädlig ' derisive '
dräpande ' crushing '
ändå ' all the same '
hålla[IV] *av* ' be fond of, attached to '
underlydande ' subordinate, servant '
sträva[I] *efter* ' strive for '

(f) Erik Gustav Geijer, som var[1] född 1783, hade sex yngre bröder och systrar. Enkelt men trevligt hade de det[2] i den lilla envåningsbyggnaden med sin mörka förstuga och sina rum med små blyinfattade fönsterrutor och tunga möbler : massiva ekskåp, djupa länstolar och långa soffor.

Ordning och reda var det också i hela huset, ty husfadern var mycket sträng och tålde ej något slarv. Ve den,[3] som hängt[4] någon av nycklarna på orätt plats eller förlagt klädesborsten! Inte blev han egentligen ond, fadern,[5] men försmädlig och dräpande. Men ändå höllo alla på gården varmt av honom, både den milda, goda hustrun, barnen och de underlydande,[6] ty de visste, att han strävade efter att ställa det[7] så bra[8] han kunde för dem allesammans.[9]

—ibid.

Notes.—[1] *var född* because he is now dead ; *är född* would be used of a living person. [2] lit. ' they had it ' ; *det* refers vaguely to their circumstances. Transl. ' they lived simply but pleasantly.' [3] lit. ' woe to the one ' ; transl. ' woe betide anyone.' [4] (*hade*) *hängt.* [5] The unusual word-order serves to lend emphasis to the statement. [6] *under-lydande* is a participial adjective and is therefore used with the definite article of the adjective. Here it is equivalent to a noun. [7] *det* is an indefinite object ; lit. ' arrange it as well as he could for them ' ; transl. ' do his best for them.' [8] See page 227, footnote 1. [9] *allesammans* is an intensive form of *alla.*

Vocabulary

fiskhandlare (c.5) ' fish-monger '
svag ' weak '
ringa ' humble '
lam ' paralyzed '
duga[II] ' be fit '
fiske (n.) ' fishing '
rodd [rod] (c.) ' rowing '
vinna[IV] ' gain '
uppehälle (n.) ' livelihood '
sälja[III] ' sell '
salta[I] ' salt '
torka[I] ' dry '
landsväg (c.2) ' highway '

på landbacken ' on shore, (dry land) '
språka[I] ' chat, talk '
yvig ' thick, bushy '
päls (c.2) ' coat, pelt '
stilla ' quiet, silent '
nedtrycka[II] ' press down '
behaga[I] ' please '
resa[II]*sig* ' rise, get up, rear '
nos (c.2) ' snout, nose '
tjuta[IV] ' howl '
ulv (c.2) ' wolf '

(*g*) Det bodde en gång i Marstrand en fattig fiskhandlare, som hette Torarin. Han var en svag och ringa man. Hans ena arm var lam, så att han dugde varken till fiske eller rodd. Han kunde inte vinna sitt uppehälle på sjön, utan

han for[1] omkring och sålde saltad och torkad fisk till folk på landbacken.[2] En februaridag kom han åkande på landsvägen. Han hade bredvid sig på lasset en god vän, med vilken han kunde språka. Det var en liten svart hund med yvig päls, som Torarin kallade Grim. Han låg mestadels stilla med huvudet nedtryckt mellan benen. Men om han fick höra något, som inte behagade honom, så reste han sig upp på lasset, satte nosen i vädret[3] och tjöt värre än en ulv.
                           —Matriculation, June 1944.

Notes.—[1] past tense of *fara*.   [2] 'folk on dry land.' [3] 'pointed his nose up into the air.'

Vocabulary

ta[IV] *examen* 'pass an examination'

behöva[II] 'need'

inkomster (pl.) 'income'

erbjuda[IV] 'offer'

biträde (n.4) 'assistant'

släppa[II] *av* 'release, let go'

enda 'only'

närhet (c.) 'neighbourhood'

snarare 'rather'

obekant 'unknown'

locka[I] 'entice, attract'

enformig 'monotonous, tedious'

sjuklig 'infirm'

(*h*) Hulda var så snäll och präktig och bra på alla sätt, men hon fick komma[1] för tidigt ensam ut i världen, stackars[2] barn. Hon hade tagit telegrafistexamen, och som hon behövde få inkomster[3] så fort som möjligt, hade hon tagit den första plats, som erbjöds henne, som post- och telegrafbiträde långt uppe i Norrland.[4] Det var svårt för modern att släppa av sitt enda barn ensam så långt bort, hon hade alltid drömt om en plats för henne i Göteborg eller dess närhet. Men vad Hulda själv beträffar,[5] så[6] tycktes hon snarare glad[7] åt att komma[8] långt bort. Hon var ung förstås, och det som var nytt och obekant lockade henne— och så fann hon väl också livet tämligen enformigt hos sin mor och mormor, som voro gamla och sjukliga bägge två.[9]
                               —ibid.

Notes.—[1] 'she had to go out into the world.' [2] See § 108 (*j*). [3] *få inkomster* 'to gain (earn) an income.' [4] 'far away up in Norrland; see page 186. [5] See § 216. [6] *så* is used to introduce the main clause; omit in translation. [7] Translate as if it were *snarare vara glad*. [8] Here *komma*='go.' [9] *bägge två*=both of them.

Vocabulary

skönskrift (c.) 'calligraphy'
intim 'intimate'
förbunden 'combined, connected'
framstående 'prominent, eminent'
kalligraf (c.3) 'calligraphist'
städse 'always'
skatta[1] 'esteem'
röna[II] 'experience, meet with'
beundran (c.) 'admiration'
vördnad 'respect'
likaväl som 'just as'
målning (c.2) 'painting'
pryda[II] 'adorn, ornament'
citat (n.5) 'quotation'
kraftig 'bold'

tecken (n.5) 'symbol, character'
duk (c.2) 'cloth, canvas'
utföra[II] 'execute'
mästare (c.5) 'master'
extas (ɛks'tɑːs] (c.3) 'ecstasies'
penselföring (c.) 'touch, method of handling a brush'
skrivtecken (n.5) 'written character'
tavla (c.1) 'picture'
medföra[II] 'cause, result in'
infälla[II] 'put in, introduce'
mästerlig 'masterly'

(*i*) Skönskriften har alltid i Kina varit på det intimaste[1] förbunden med målarkonsten, och en framstående kalligraf har städse skattats lika högt och rönt samma beundran och vördnad som en framstående målare. Likaväl som man dekorerar ett rum med målningar, så pryder man det i Kina med citat ur litteraturen, skrivna med stora, kraftiga tecken på vit duk, utförda av någon framstående mästare. En kines kan falla i[2] extas över en skön penselföring likaväl i ett skrivtecken som på en tavla. Den intima förbindelse mellan skrift och målning medför nu,[3] att den kinesiske konstnären, som i regel är både kalligraf[4] och målare,[4] gärna[5] i sin tavla infäller en eller flera rader skrift, vilka han förstår att placera och utföra på ett dekorativt mästerligt sätt.

—External Intermediate Arts, July 1937.

Notes.—[1] See § 184. [2] Here *falla i* = 'go into.' [3] Begin the sentence with *nu*. [4] On the omission of the article see § 280. [5] transl. 'often.'

Vocabulary

ståtlig ' splendid looking, stately '

ända till ' right up to '

lär (aux. vb. only used in the pres.) ' is said (to) '

öde (n.) ' fate, destiny '

oblid ' unpropitious, unkind '

skifte (n.4) ' vicissitude '

bevara[1] ' preserve '

reslig ' erect, towering '

skepnad (c.3) ' form '

hållning (c.) ' bearing '

äga[II] ' own, possess '

fädernearv (n.4) ' inheritance from the father's side '

tör (defective aux. vb.) past *torde*—see notes

storman (c. § 91.*f*) ' great man '

företrädesvis ' especially '

brås[III] *på* (depon. vb.) ' take after '

föräldrahem (n.5) ' parental home '

betydande ' important, influential '

personlighet (c.3) ' personality '

ande (c.2) ' spirit '

samstämmig ' in agreement'

uttalande (n.4) ' pronouncement, statement '

från skilda håll (pl.) ' from different quarters '

sällsynt ' rare '

blid ' mild, gentle '

godhjärtad 'kind-hearted '

känslovarm ' of warm emotions '

djup ' deep, sincere, genuine '

därtill ' in addition '

hurtig ' brisk, active '

vänsäll ' winning '

utomordentlig ' extraordinary '

duglighet (c.) ' ability, efficiency '

förestå[III] ' manage, superintend '

utöva[1] ' exercise, practise '

kall (n.) ' calling, vocation '

omgivning (c.2) ' surroundings, milieu '

föresyn (n.5) ' pattern '

handlingskraftig ' energetic '

plikttrogen ' dutiful, loyal '

(*j*) Till sitt yttre[1] var Johan Rydberg en vacker[2] och ståtlig man. Ända till det sista lär han—trots ödets oblida skiften—bevarat[3] sin resliga, höga skepnad ; och den militäriska hållning, som hans yngste son ägde ännu i ålderns höst,[4] var ett fädernearv. Men i sina inre egen-

Notes.—[1] ' In his exterior.' [2] transl. ' handsome.' [3] (*ha*) *bevarat.* [4] ' in the autumn of his days (evening of his life).'

skaper torde[1] Viktor liksom så många stormän företrädesvis
bråtts[2] på modern, som var föräldrahemmets mest betydande personlighet, dess goda ande. Enligt samstämmiga
uttalanden[3] från de mest skilda håll var hon en kvinna av
sällsynta egenskaper : blid, godhjärtad, känslovarm och
djup, därtill hurtig och vänsäll. Med utomordentlig
duglighet förestod hon sitt hus och utövade hon sitt kall.
För hela sin omgivning stod[4] hon som en ädel föresyn : en
trosvarm, handlingskraftig och plikttrogen kvinna.

—External Intermediate Arts, July 1938.

[1] This auxiliary verb is used like *dürfen* in German to
express a modest assertion of probability; transl. ' he
probably took after his mother.' [2] (*ha*) *bråtts*. [3] Transl. by
the phrase ' by common consent.' [4] Here equivalent to
' was.'

Vocabulary

bäck (c.2) ' brook '
gran (c.2) ' fir '
skugga (c.1) 'shadow, shade'
häll (c.2) ' ledge of rock '
avröja[II] ' clear '
skogshuggare (c.5) ' wood-
cutter '
yxa (c.1) ' axe '
bebygga[II] ' inhabit '
riskoja (c.1) ' hut made of
dried boughs and twigs '
kolare (c.5) ' charcoal bur-
ner '
lämningar (pl.) ' remains '
mila (c.1) ' kiln '
ljung (c.) ' heather '
ormgräs (n.5) ' fern,
bracken '
stake (c.2) ' stake '
slå[III] *ned* ' drive down '
skytt (c.2) ' marksman '
glad[1] (n.5) ' glade '

omtala[I] ' mention, tell '
junker (c.2) ' young nobleman '
hop (c.2) ' crowd '
karl (c.2) ' man, fellow '
hy (c.) ' complexion '
tross (c.) ' baggage '
tält (n.5) ' tent '
slå[III] *upp* ' pitch (a tent)'
svedjeland (n.5) ' clearing '
dröja[II] ' tarry, stay '
förtälja[II] ' relate, tell '
visa[I] ' show, point out '
hjulspår (n.5) ' track of a
wheel '
slingra[I] *fram* 'wind along '
pärla (c.1) ' bead '
lik ' like '
fotvrist (c.3) ' ankle '
uppta[IV] ' pick up '
gömma[II] ' hide, keep '

[1] This word is an archaism, now replaced by *glänta* (c.1).

(*k*) Erland steg upp och följde bäcken in i skogen. Han vandrade i granars skugga, klättrade över stenar och hällar och kom så[1] till ett ställe, avröjt av skogshuggarens yxa, men ännu obebyggt. Endast en riskoja, en sådan som kolare bygga, stod där vid lämningarna av en mila ; ljung, svampar och ormgräs växte runt omkring. Här voro stakar nedslagna i marken, och medan han undrade, vartill de tjänat,[2] kom Rasmus skytt[3] vandrande över gladet och omtalade för junkern, att en hop främmande människor,[4] karlar, kvinnor och barn, bruna till hy[5] och svarta till hår och ögon, underligt klädda och underligt talande, med hästar, vagnar och mycken tross, haft[6] sina tält uppslagna på svedjelandet,[7] dröjt där en dag och sedan vandrat norrut. Mer visste Rasmus icke förtälja,[8] men han visade deras vagnars hjulspår, slingrande fram, där träden stodo längst ifrån varandra.[9] Och medan Erland såg på hjulspåren och tänkte, att Singoalla måste vara en av dessa människor, fann han på marken en röd pärla, lik dem, som prydde flickans armar och fotvrister. Den pärlan upptog han och gömde vid sitt hjärta.[10]

—External B.A. General, June 1940.

Notes.—[1] *så* =' then.' [2] (*hade*) *tjänat.* [3] ' Rasmus the marksman.' [4] ' strange people.' [5] See examples under *till*, § 224 ; lit. : ' swarthy of complexion.' [6] (*hade*) *haft.* [7] *svedjeland* means ' a clearing made in a forest by burn-beating ' ; from *svedja*[(1)] ' to de(vo)nshire, i.e. burn wood-land.' [8] Usually : ' *att förtälja.*' [9] ' farthest apart.' [10] ' kept (it) nearest his heart'.

Alphabetical List of the Principal Strong Verbs

Infinitive	Present	Past Singular	Past Plural	Supine	Past Part.
binda 'bind'	*binder*	*band*	*bundo*	*bundit*	*bunden*
bita 'bite'	*biter*	*bet*	*beto*	*bitit*	*biten*
bjuda 'offer'	*bjuder*	*bjöd*	*bjödo*	*bjudit*	*bjuden*
bli(va) 'become'	*blir*	*blev*	*blevo*	*blivit*	*bliven*
brinna 'burn'	*brinner*	*brann*	*brunno*	*brunnit*	*brunnen*
brista 'burst'	*brister*	*brast*	*brusto*	*brustit*	*brusten*
bryta 'break'	*bryter*	*bröt*	*bröto*	*brutit*	*bruten*
bära 'bear'	*bär*	*bar*	*buro*	*burit*	*buren*
dra(ga) 'draw'	*dra(ge)r*	*drog*	*drogo*	*dragit*	*dragen*
dricka 'drink'	*dricker*	*drack*	*drucko*	*druckit*	*drucken*
driva 'drive'	*driver*	*drev*	*drevo*	*drivit*	*driven*
falla 'fall'	*faller*	*föll*	*föllo*	*fallit*	*fallen*
fara 'go'	*far*	*for*	*foro*	*farit*	*(hädan) faren*
finna 'find'	*finner*	*fann*	*funno*	*funnit*	*funnen*
flyga 'fly'	*flyger*	*flög*	*flögo*	*flugit*	*(bort) flugen*
flyta 'float'	*flyter*	*flöt*	*flöto*	*flutit*	*fluten*
frysa 'freeze'	*fryser*	*frös*	*fröso*	*frusit*	*frusen*
försvinna 'vanish'	*försvinner*	*försvann*	*försvunno*	*försvunnit*	*försvunnen*
giva (ge) 'give'	*giver (ger)*	*gav*	*gåvo*	*givit (gett)*	*given*
gjuta 'cast'	*gjuter*	*göt*	*göto*	*gjutit*	*gjuten*
glida 'glide'	*glider*	*gled*	*gledo*	*glidit*	—

gnida	*gnider*	*gned*	*gnedo*	*gnidit*	*gniden*
' rub '					
gripa	*griper*	*grep*	*grepo*	*gripit*	*gripen*
' seize '					
gråta	*gråter*	*grät*	*gräto*	*gråtit*	(be)*gråten*
' weep '					
hinna	*hinner*	*hann*	*hunno*	*hunnit*	*hunnen*
' get (have) time '					
hugga	*hugger*	*högg*	*höggo*	*huggit*	*huggen*
' hew '					
hålla	*håller*	*höll*	*höllo*	*hållit*	*hållen*
' hold '					
kliva	*kliver*	*klev*	*klevo*	*klivit*	(upp)*kliven*
' stride '					
klyva	*klyver*	*klöv*	*klövo*	*kluvit*	*kluven*
' cleave '					
knipa	*kniper*	*knep*	*knepo*	*knipit*	*knipen*
' pinch'					
knyta	*knyter*	*knöt*	*knöto*	*knutit*	*knuten*
' tie '					
komma	*kommer*	*kom*	*kommo*	*kommit*	*kommen*
' come '					
krypa	*kryper*	*kröp*	*kröpo*	*krupit*	*krupen*
' creep '					
lida	*lider*	*led*	*ledo*	*lidit*	*liden*
' suffer '					
ligga	*ligger*	*låg*	*lågo*	**legat**	(*för*)**legad**
' lie '					
ljuda	*ljuder*	*ljöd*	*ljödo*	*ljudit*	—
' sound '					
ljuga	*ljuger*	*ljög*	*ljögo*	*ljugit*	(be)*ljugen*
' tell a lie '					
låta	*låter*	*lät*	*läto*	*låtit*	(över)*låten*
' let '					
låta	*låter*	*lät*	*läto*	*låtit*	
' sound '					
niga	*niger*	*neg*	*nego*	*nigit*	—
' curtsy '					
njuta	*njuter*	*njöt*	*njöto*	*njutit*	*njuten*
' enjoy '					
pipa	*piper*	*pep*	*pepo*	*pipit*	—
' pipe '					
rida	*rider*	*red*	*redo*	*ridit*	*riden*
'ride '					
rinna	*rinner*	*rann*	*runno*	*runnit*	*runnen*
' run, flow '					
riva	*river*	*rev*	*revo*	*rivit*	*riven*
' tear '					
ryta	*ryter*	*röt*	*röto*	*rutit*	—
' roar '					

sitta ' sit '	*sitter*	*satt*	*sutto*	*suttit*	*(för)sutten*
sjuda ' seethe '	*sjuder*	*sjöd*	*sjödo*	*sjudit*	*sjuden*
sjunga ' sing '	*sjunger*	*sjöng*	*sjöngo*	*sjungit*	*sjungen*
sjunka ' sink '	*sjunker*	*sjönk*	*sjönko*	*sjunkit*	*sjunken*
skina ' shine '	*skiner*	*sken*	*skeno*	*skinit*	—
skjuta ' shoot '	*skjuter*	*sköt*	*sköto*	*skjutit*	*skjuten*
skrida ' slide '	*skrider*	*skred*	*skredo*	*skridit*	—
skrika ' shriek '	*skriker*	*skrek*	*skreko*	*skrikit*	*(ut)skriken*
skriva ' write '	*skriver*	*skrev*	*skrevo*	*skrivit*	*skriven*
skryta ' boast '	*skryter*	*skröt*	*skröto*	*skrutit*	*(om)skruten*
skära ' cut '	*skär*	*skar*	*skuro*	*skurit*	*skuren*
slippa ' slip '	*slipper*	*slapp*	*sluppo*	*sluppit*	*(upp)sluppen*
slita ' tear '	*sliter*	*slet*	*sleto*	*slitit*	*sliten*
sluta ' conclude '	*sluter*	*slöt*	*slöto*	*slutit*	*sluten*
smyga ' slip '	*smyger*	*smög*	*smögo*	*smugit*	*(in)smugen*
snyta ' blow the nose '	*snyter*	*snöt*	*snöto*	*snutit*	*(o)snuten*
sova ' sleep '	*sover*	*sov*	*sovo*	*sovit*	—
spinna ' spin '	*spinner*	*spann*	*spunno*	*spunnit*	*spunnen*
spricka ' burst '	*spricker*	*sprack*	*sprucko*	*spruckit*	*sprucken*
sprida ' spread '	*sprider*	*spridde* (*spred*)	*spredo*	**spritt**	**spridd**
springa ' run '	*springer*	*sprang*	*sprungo*	*sprungit*	*sprungen*
spritta ' start up '	*spritter*	*spratt*	*sprutto*	*(spruttit)*	—
sticka ' stick '	*sticker*	*stack*	*stucko*	*stuckit*	*stucken*
stiga ' rise '	*stiger*	*steg*	*stego*	*stigit*	*stigen*
stjäla ' steal '	*stjäl*	*stal*	*stulo*	*stulit*	*stulen*

strida	*strider*	*stred*	*stredo*	*stridit*	(*be*) **stridd**
' fight '					
stryka	*stryker*	*strök*	*ströko*	*strukit*	*struken*
' stroke '					
supa	*super*	*söp*	*söpo*	*supit*	(*för*)*supen*
' tipple '					
svida	*svider*	*sved*	*svedo*	*svidit*	—
' smart '					
svika	*sviker*	*svek*	*sveko*	*svikit*	(*be*)*sviken*
' betray '					
svär(j)a	*svär*	*svor*	*svoro*	*svurit*	*svuren*
' swear '					
ta(ga)	*ta(ge)r*	*tog*	*togo*	*tagit*	*tagen*
' take '					
tiga	*tiger*	*teg*	*tego*	**tegat**	(*för*)*tegen*
' be silent '				(*tigit*)	
tjuta	*tjuter*	*tjöt*	*tjöto*	*tjutit*	—
' howl '					
vika	*viker*	*vek*	*veko*	*vikit*	*viken*
' fold '					
vina	*viner*	*ven*	*veno*	*vinit*	—
' whiz '					
vinna	*vinner*	*vann*	*vunno*	*vunnit*	*vunnen*
' win '					
vrida	*vrider*	*vred*	*vredo*	*vridit*	*vriden*
' twist '					
äta	*äter*	*åt*	*åto*	*ätit*	*äten*
' eat '					

VOCABULARY
ENGLISH—SWEDISH

A

				Page
about	. . .	om, kring, omkring	.	106, 176
absence	. . .	frånvaro (c.) . .	.	214
accept	. . .	anta . .	.	235
accident	. . .	olycka (c.) .	.	185
after	. . .	efter . .	.	106, 173
afterwards	. . .	sedan, efteråt	.	133, 135
again	. . .	igen . .	.	134
air-borne	. . .	flygburen .	.	128
alarm clock	. . .	väckarklocka (c.)	.	106
answer	. . .	svar (n.) .	.	112
anybody	. . .	någon . .	.	143
apple	. . .	äpple (n.) .	.	52
approve	. . .	gilla . .	.	212
arm	. . .	arm (c.) .	.	207
arrive	. . .	ankomma, anlända	.	169
as	. . .	som, eftersom	.	225
ascend	. . .	bestiga .	.	185
ask	. . .	fråga . .	.	93
association	. . .	förening (c.) .	.	169
aunt	. . .	faster, moster (c.)	.	89
author	. . .	författare (c.)	.	151

B

				Page
bad	. . .	dålig .	.	235
ball	. . .	bal (c.) .	.	131
bathe	. . .	bada .	.	93
beautiful	. . .	vacker .	.	71
become	. . .	bli(va) .	.	88
bed	. . .	säng (c.) .	.	58
before	. . .	före, innan (prep.) ; förr(ut) (adv.)		
				134, 173, 176
beg	. . .	be(dja) .	.	113
beginner	. . .	nybörjare (c.)	.	214
beginning	. . .	början (c.) .	.	45
behold !	. . .	se ! .	.	196
believe	. . .	tro .	.	107
bell	. . .	klocka (c.) .	.	207
bicycle	. . .	cykel (c.) .	.	82
big	. . .	stor .	.	75
bird	. . .	fågel (c.) .	.	46
birthday	. . .	födelsedag (c.) .	.	96
book	. . .	bok (c.) .	.	50

Page

cup				kopp (c.)				58
cupboard				skåp (n.)				53
cushion				kudde (c.)				58
cut				skära, klippa			100,	149
cry				skrika, gråta			120,	150

D

dainty				näpen				205
dance				dans (c.)				206
Dane				dansk (c.)				194
dark				mörk				77
daughter				dotter (c.)				48
day				dag (c.)				82
dead				död				118
dear				kär				105
declare				förklara				205
Denmark				Danmark			77,	204
desert				öken (c.)				46
do				göra				101
dog				hund (c.)				112
door				dörr (c.)				60
draw				dra(ga)				149
dress				klänning (c.)				195
duke				hertig (c.)				193

E

ear				öra (n.)			46,	52
easy				lätt				69
English				engelsk				77
evening				kväll, afton (c.)			129,	164
every				varje				145
everything				allt, allting				144
exact(-ly)				precis				77
example				exempel (n.)				46
excellent				utmärkt			29,	196
exciting				spännande				121
exclaim				utropa				205
excursion				utflykt (c.)				141
eye				öga (n.)			46,	52

F

fairy				fe (c.)				196
fall				falla				150
fall asleep				somna				235
famous				berömd				185
farmer				bonde (c.)				51
fast				fort				133
father				fa(de)r (c.)			53,	60
feel				känna (sig)				98

Page

fetch	hämta		125
few	få		145
film	film (c.)		118
finger	finger (n.)		46
Finland	Finland		77
fit	passa		207
flat	våning (c.)		196
flee	fly		107
floor	golv (n.)		60
flower	blomma (c.)		105
fond of, to be	tycka om		109, 212
foot	fot (c.)		50
forget	glömma		98
fork	gaffel (c.)		60
friend	vän (c.)		66
frightened	rädd		70
from	från		105, 174
fruit	frukt (c.)		151

G

gentleman	herre (c.)		102
germinate	gro		107
get	få		113
get on	må		107, 108
get up	gå upp		114
girl	flicka (c.)		47
give	giva, ge		150
glass	glas (n.)		53
gleam	glimma		247
glorious	härlig		141
go	gå, fara		113, 150
go out	gå ut		114
go to bed	lägga sig		156
godmother	gudmor (c.)		196
gold	guld		77
golden	gyllene		196
good	god, bra		69, 106
gown	klänning (c.)		195
grain	säd (c.)		112
grandfather	farfar, morfar		89
grass	gräs (n.)		105
great	stor		75
green	grön		67
grumble	gruffa		214

H

half	(adj.) halv ; (noun) hälft (c.)		115
hand	hand (c.)		50
handkerchief	näsduk (c.)		106
happen	hända		112
happy	lycklig		207

				Page
have	ha(va)			56
head	huvud (n.)			46
heap	hop, massa (c.)			235
hear	höra			97
heavy	tung			237
help	hjälpa			100
hold	hålla			150
holiday	semester (c.)			141
home	hem (n.)			132
hope	hoppas ; (noun) hopp (n.)		140, 209
horse	häst (c.)			43, 48
hospital	sjukhus (n.)			90
hour	timme (c.)			82
house	hus (n.)			53
how	hur			60
huge	ofantlig, väldig, jättestor			205

I

Iceland	Island			77
idea	idé (c.)			50
if	om			224
ill	sjuk			90
imagine	föreställa sig			158
immediately	genast			134
instead	i stället			198
intend	ämna, tänka			235
iron	järn (c.)			77
island	ö (c.)			48

J

jetty	brygga (c.)			118
journey	resa (c.)			165
just	just			134

K

kilometre	kilometer (c.)			115
kind	snäll		167, 173
kindly	godhetsfullt			169
king	kung, konung (c.)			62
kiss	kyssa ; (noun) kyss (n.)			207
knife	kniv (c.)			60
know	veta, känna	5, 98, 139, 210

L

lady	dam (c.)			49
lake	sjö (c.)			48
large	stor			75
last	(vb.) vara ; (adj.) sist		73, 118
later	senare			185
latter	senare, denna			185

						Page
lay	.	.	.	.	lägga . . .	. 101
lazy	.	.	.	.	lat . . .	70, 96
lead	.	.	.	.	bly (n.) . .	. 77
leaf	.	.	.	.	löv (n.); blad (n.) .	. 128
learn	.	.	.	.	lära sig . .	. 156
leave	.	.	.	.	lämna . .	. 169
left	.	.	.	.	vänster; (remaining) kvar	70, 138
less	.	.	.	.	mindre . .	. 134
let	.	.	.	.	låta . .	. 150
letter	.	.	.	.	brev (n.) . .	. 90
lie	.	.	.	.	ligga . .	. 181
life	.	.	.	.	liv (n.) . .	. 96
like	.	.	.	.	(adj.) lik; (vb.) tycka om	. 100
live	.	.	.	.	leva, bo . .	98, 107
load	.	.	.	.	lass (n.) . .	. 151
long	.	.	.	.	lång . .	. 70
look at	.	.	.	.	se på, titta på .	93, 128
lot	.	.	.	.	massa (c.) . .	. 214
lunch	.	.	.	.	lunch (c.) . .	. 118

M

make	.	.	.	.	göra . .	. 101
man	.	.	.	.	man (c.) . .	. 45
marriage	.	.	.	.	giftermål (n.) .	. 175
marry	.	.	.	.	gifta sig . .	. 156
meal	.	.	.	.	måltid (c.) .	. 232
mean	.	.	.	.	mena . .	. 118
means	.	.	.	.	medel (n.) . .	. 46
meanwhile	.	.	.	.	under tiden .	. 205
meet	.	.	.	.	träffa(s), möta(s) .	. 139
metre	.	.	.	.	meter (c.) . .	. 46
Miss	.	.	.	.	fröken . .	. 90
moment	.	.	.	.	ögonblick (n.) .	177, 197
money	.	.	.	.	pengar (pl.) . .	. 214
month	.	.	.	.	månad (c.) .	51, 82
more	.	.	.	.	mer(a) . .	. 75
mother	.	.	.	.	mo(de)r (c.) .	. 60
motor-boat	.	.	.	.	motorbåt (c.) .	. 141
motor(-car)	.	.	.	.	bil (c.) . .	. 105
move	.	.	.	.	flytta (trans.); röra sig (intrans.)	214
much	.	.	.	.	mycket . .	. 60
mushroom	.	.	.	.	svamp (c.) .	. 96
must	.	.	.	.	måste . .	. 202
my	.	.	.	.	min, (nt.) mitt; (pl.) mina	. 64

N

name	.	.	.	.	namn (n.) . .	. 53
near	.	.	.	.	nära . .	. 66

Page

new	.	.	.	.	ny	.	.	.	.	.	68
next	.	.	.	.	näst	.	.	.	.	.	74
no	.	.	.	.	nej ; (adj.) ingen, inget, inga			58, 144
nobody	.	.	.	.	ingen	.	.	.	.	.	144
noise	.	.	.	.	buller (n.)	.	.	.	.	235
Norway	.	.	.	Norge	.	.	.	.	.	77
not	.	.	.	.	icke, (coll.) inte	.	.	.	134
note	.	.	.	.	sedel (c.)	.	.	.	.	169
nothing	.	.	.	intet, ingenting	.	.	.	112
novel	.	.	.	.	roman (c.)	.	.	.	.	172
now	.	.	.	.	nu	.	.	.	.	.	134

O

obliged	.	.	.	tacksam, förbunden	.	.	169
of	.	.	.	.	av	.	.	.	.	.	172
offer	.	.	.	.	anbud (n.)	.	.	.	.	235
old	.	.	.	.	gammal, (pl.) gamla	.	.	71
old woman	.	.	.	gumma (c.)	.	.	.	193
only	.	.	.	.	bara, endast	.	.	106, 133
other	.	.	.	.	annan, (nt.) annat, (pl.) andra		144
own	.	.	.	.	egen, eget, (pl.) egna ; (vb.) äga		68

P

page	.	.	.	.	sida (c.) ; (court-) page (c.)		82, 195
painter	.	.	.	målare (c.)	.	.	.	106
paper	.	.	.	.	papper (n.)	.	.	.	.	82
parcel	.	.	.	.	paket (n.)	.	.	.	.	183
pardon	.	.	.	förlåt ; förlåtelse	.	.	105, 113
party	.	.	.	.	sällskap (n.)	.	.	.	235
past	.	.	.	.	förbi	.	.	.	.	128, 174
peel	.	.	.	.	skala	.	.	.	.	.	128
pen	.	.	.	.	penna (c.)	.	.	.	.	58
pencil	.	.	.	(blyerts-)penna (c.)	.	.	58
people	.	.	.	folk (sg.)	.	.	.	.	35, 141
perish	.	.	.	omkomma	.	.	.	.	185
person	.	.	.	person (c.)	.	.	.	.	118
pick	.	.	.	.	plocka	.	.	.	.	.	93
piece	.	.	.	.	bit, stycke (n.), styck (n.)		151, 170
plane	.	.	.	.	flyg (n.)	.	.	.	.	235
play	.	.	.	.	(vb.) leka ; (noun) pjäs (c.)		100, 214
plate	.	.	.	.	tallrik (c.)	.	.	.	.	60
pneumonia	.	.	.	lunginflammation (c.)	.	.	118
pooh !	.	.	.	usch !	.	.	.	.	.	205
poor	.	.	.	.	fattig ; (pity) stackars	.	.	70
potato	.	.	.	potatis (c.)	.	.	.	.	128
president	.	.	.	ordförande (c.)	.	.	.	53

W

									Page
wait				vänta				93,	179
wait on				passa upp					235
waiter				kypare (c.)				53,	118
wake up				vakna					93
walk				promenad (c.); (vb.) promenera					235
wall				vägg (c.)					60
wand				spö (n.)					196
war				krig (n.)					105
warrior				krigare (c.)					128
wash				tvätta					93
water				vatten (n.)					46
wave				svänga					196
way				väg (c.)					151
weather				väder (n.)					70
wedding gown				brudklänning (c.)					205
week				vecka (c.)					82
weep				gråta					150
well				väl, bra				106,	130
well known				känd					98
what				vad				90,	146
when				när					134
where				var					60
which				vilken, vilket, (pl.) vilka					146
who				vem				66,	146
why				varför					96
wife				fru, hustru				48,	51
window				fönster (n.)					58
winter				vinter (c.)					77
wistful				längtansfull					195
woman				kvinna (c.)					60
wonderful				underbar					169
word				ord (n.)					70
work				arbete (n.); (vb.) arbeta					128
worn-out				utsliten					195
write				skriva					120
writer				skriftställare (c.), författare (c.)					151
wrong				fel					220

Y

year				år (n.)					82
yes				ja					58
yesterday				i går				96.	134

VOCABULARY

SWEDISH—ENGLISH

A

			Page
absolut	entirely, at all costs		196
agent	agent		50
aldrig	never		133
alldeles	completely		133
allierad	allied		236
alltså	consequently		133
anbud	offer		235
anfall	attack		236
annan, (n.) annat, (pl.) andra	other		144
anta	assume, accept		235
aptit	appetite		232
arbete	work		128
armé	army		50, 236
aska	ashes		191
askungen	Cinderella		191
avlopp	outlet		184
avsluta	conclude		232
avta	diminish		216
avvisa	repulse		236
avvärja	ward off		236

B

			Page
bad	bath		52
bada	bathe (also : to bath)		93
badrum	bathroom		156
bal	ball		131, 198
bank	bank		118
bara	only		106
barn	child		53
be(dja)	ask, request, beg		113
befolka	populate		184
bekväm	comfortable		169
Belgien	Belgium		185
belgisk	Belgian		204
berg	mountain		82
berömd	famous		185
bestiga	climb, ascend (the throne)		185
besvara	answer		214
besynnerlig	strange		196
betala	pay		190, 212
betäckt	covered		184

271

Page

frukt	. . . .	fruit ; fear	. .	151, 230
frysa	. . .	freeze, feel cold	. .	141, 158
fråga	. . .	ask a question	. .	93
från	. . .	from . .	.	105, 174
frånsett	. . .	apart from	.	. 174
frånvaro	. . .	absence	. .	214
fröken	. . .	Miss . .	.	90
ful	. . .	ugly . .	.	82
få, färre	. . .	few, fewer	.	75, 145
få	. . .	get, receive	.	. 113
fågel	. . .	bird . .	.	. 46
fånga	. . .	catch . .	.	. 196
fånge	. . .	prisoner	.	. 112
färdig	. . .	ready, finished	.	. 159
födelse	. . .	birth . .	.	. 96
fönster	. . .	window .	.	. 58
före	. . .	before .	.	. 173
förening	. . .	association	.	169
författare	. . .	author, writer	.	151, 193
förfärlig	. . .	awful .	.	. 131
förhand, på	. . .	in advance	.	. 168
förklara	. . .	declare, explain	.	. 205
förkylning	. . .	chill, cold	.	235
förlåt	. . .	pardon (me) .	.	. 105
förlåta	. . .	pardon, excuse	.	148, 165
förr	. . .	before, previously	.	134
förut	. . .	before, previously, in advance		134
förrätta	. . .	perform .	.	. 195
förskräckt	. . .	terrified	.	. 195
förstås	. . .	of course	.	. 134
försvar	. . .	defence .	.	. 236
försök	. . .	attempt .	.	. 236
förträfflig	. . .	excellent	.	. 141
förtjusa	. . .	charm .	.	. 131
förvandla	. . .	change, transform .		. 180
förvåna	. . .	surprise, astonish .		. 158
förvåning	. . .	surprise, astonishment		. 196
föräldrar	. . .	parents	. .	48, 66

G

gaffel	. . .	fork .	. .	. 60
galen, (n. galet)	. .	wrong .	. .	. 214
ganska	. .	quite, rather	. .	. 134

Page

kort	short		109
krig	war		105
krigare	warrior		128
krona	crown		169
kronärtskocka	globe artichoke		163
kudde	cushion, pillow		58
kultje	persistent wind		216
kung	king		62
kusin	cousin		89
kust	coast		216
kvar	left (behind, over)		138
kvart	quarter; quarter of an hour		115
kvinna	woman		60
kyckling	chicken		128, 191
kypare	waiter		53, 118
känd	known, well known		98
känna	feel, know		98
kär	dear		230
kärlek	love		230
kärleksfull	affectionate		131
kök	kitchen		159
köld	cold		105
köpa	buy		99
köra	drive		97
kött	meat		82

L

laga	prepare; mend		93, 160
lampa	lamp		58
land	land, country		35, 50
landskap	province		167
landsätta	land		236
landsättning	landing		236
lantbruk	agriculture		185
lapp	Laplander		184
lass	load		151
le	smile		113
ledig	disengaged, vacant		232
ledsen	sad		18, 230
lik	like		10, 157
likvidera	liquidate		236
lite	a little		134
liten (n.) litet	little, small		68, 75
liter	litre		159
liv	life		96
ljus	light		53, 60
luft	air		77
lunginflammation	pneumonia		118
lunch	lunch		118
lust	desire, inclination		232

Page

morgon	.	.	.	.	morning	.	.	48, 164
mormor	.	.	.	.	grandmother (maternal)	.	.	89
Moskva	.	.	.	.	Moscow	.	.	236
motanfall	.	.	.	.	counter-attack	.	.	236
motstånd	.	.	.	.	resistance	.	.	237
mus	.	.	.	.	mouse	.	.	53
mycket	.	.	.	.	much ; very	.	.	60
mynna ut	.	.	.	flow into	.	.	184
mynning	.	.	.	.	estuary	.	.	181
mål	.	.	.	.	goal, aim	.	.	237
målare	.	.	.	.	painter	.	.	106
måltid	.	.	.	.	meal	.	.	232
månad	.	.	.	.	month	.	.	51, 82
måne	.	.	.	.	moon	.	.	17
många (pl.)	.	.	.	many	.	.	60, 75
måttlig	.	.	.	.	moderate	.	.	216
människa	.	.	.	.	human being	.	.	58
märke	.	.	.	.	mark	.	.	52
mörk	.	.	.	.	dark	.	.	77
möta	.	.	.	.	meet	.	.	99

N

namn	.	.	.	.	name	.	.	53
natt	.	.	.	.	night	.	.	50
naturligtvis	.	.	.	naturally, of course	.	.	112
nedför	.	.	.	.	down	.	.	177
neger	.	.	.	.	negro	.	.	51, 194
nej	.	.	.	.	no	.	.	58
nog	.	.	.	.	enough	.	.	136
nord	.	.	.	.	north	.	.	184
norr	.	.	.	.	north	.	.	184
nota	.	.	.	.	bill	.	.	232
nu	.	.	.	.	now	.	.	134
ny	.	.	.	.	new	.	.	68
nyheter	.	.	.	news	.	.	159
någon, (n.) något, pl. några	some, any, (-body, -thing)	.	143
när	.	.	.	.	when	.	.	134
nära	.	.	.	.	near	.	.	66, 177
närmare	.	.	.	.	nearer	.	.	132
näsduk	.	.	.	.	handkerchief	.	.	106
nästan	.	.	.	.	nearly, almost	.	.	134
nöjd	.	.	.	.	satisfied, pleased	.	.	141
nöje	.	.	.	.	pleasure	.	.	52, 79

O

o- (prefix)	.	.	.	un-	.	.	195
observatorium	.	.	observatory	.	.	45, 51
och	.	.	.	.	and	.	.	46

Page

					Page
påstå	assert	.	.	.	236
påron	pear	.	.	.	168

R

rad	row, series, line	.	.	169
radio	radio, wireless	.	.	106
rapport	report, bulletin	.	.	216
rapportera	report	.	.	236
redan	already	.	.	128
regel	rule	.		46, 51
regera	reign, rule	.	.	185
regn	rain	.	.	112
regna	rain	.	.	158
ren	pure	.	.	77
ren	reindeer	.	.	184
resa	go, travel	.	.	100
resande	traveller	.	.	185
resväska	suitcase	.	.	214
rinna	run, flow	.	128, 149
rinna upp	rise	.	.	184
rita	design, draw	.	.	214
ro	row (vb.)	.	.	107
roa	amuse	.	.	157
rock	coat	.	.	90
rolig	amusing	.	.	158
roman	novel	.	.	172
rum	room	.	.	58
rusa	rush	.	.	128
rå	hold sway	.	.	107
rädd	afraid, careful	.	70, 196
rädda	save	.	.	93
röka	smoke	.	.	100

S

sadel	saddle	.	.	44
sallad	lettuce	.	.	168
salt	salt	.	.	49
samt	together with	.	.	179
samtlig	all	.	.	236
sann	true	.	.	70
Schweiz	Switzerland	.	.	185
se	see	.	.	113
sedan	then, after that ; since	135, 179
sedel	note	.	.	169
segel	sail	.	.	45
sekel	century	.	58, 111
sekund	second	.	.	82
semester	holiday	.	.	141
servera	serve	.	.	219

Page

sida				page, side				82
siden				silk				44
sill				herring				233
sist				last				73
sjuk				ill, sick				90
sjukdom				illness, disease				48
sjukhus				hospital				90
själv				self				157
sjö				sea, lake				48
sjöfart				navigation				184
skaffa				procure, get				93
sked				spoon				60
skepp				ship				214
skidor				skis				214
skina				shine				23, 129
sko				shoe				51
skog				forest				184
skola				school				66
skott				shot				235
skratta				laugh				182
skrika				cry, shriek				120
skriftställare				writer				185
skriva				write				120
skrivelse				letter				109
skyldig				owing, guilty				169
skynda sig				hurry up				195
Skåne				Scania				185
skåp				cupboard				53, 58
skär				skerry				184
skära				cut				149
skärgård				archipelago				184
sköta				tend				99
sluta				conclude				141
slutligen				finally, in conclusion				135
slå				strike				113
smula				crumb, trifle				205
små (pl.)				small				68
smör				butter				118
smörgås				sandwich				223, 234
snaps				schnapps				232
snart				soon				135
snyfta				sob				196
snäll				kind				167, 226
snälltåg				fast train				117
snäsa av				snap at				205
snö				snow				35
snöa				snow (vb.)				158
sol				sun				223
soldat				soldier				96
som				who, which ; as				77, 117

KEY TO EXERCISES
Exercise 1

(*a*) A horse is an animal. The horse and the saddle. The bird and the feather. The house and the temple. The sign in the sky. The camp is in the desert. The paper and the silk.

(*b*) Rodret i vattnet. Hästen och fågeln. Regeln och medlet. Templet och lägret. Fågeln i öknen. Fingret; observatoriet; metern; exemplet.

(*c*) The horses. The lice. The men with the geese. The fishermen. The rudders. The soldiers are in the camps.

(*d*) Tecknen. Vattnen. Huvudet. Männen och hästarna. Rodren och seglen. Ögonen och öronen. Mössen är i huset.

Exercise 2

Pojkarna, flickorna, männen, hustrurna, mödrarna, döttrarna, sönerna, bönderna, läkarna, prinsessorna, botanikerna, studenterna, lärarinnorna, resandena, negrerna, konstnärerna, professorerna, agenterna, barnen, djuren, hästarna, korna, getterna, bina, broarna, dikena, husen, sjöarna, träden.

Exercise 3

(*a*) Have you a clock in the room ? She has a table, a cupboard and two chairs. Have you a carpet ? He has four rooms. Eight horses and nine cows. Nils has a pen and a book.

(*b*) De har ett hus. Har du (ni) tolv stolar och tre bord ? Har rummet två fönster ? Nej, det har ett fönster. Männen har sex hästar. Modern har två söner och en dotter.

(*c*) The farmer has twelve goats. Two cupboards and a lamp. The century. Three centuries. The house has seven rooms. In the room (there) are two beds. The goat has horns. Man (the human being) has two eyes, and two ears. We have four cushions.

(d) Du (ni) har tre kuddar och fyra stolar. Två sekel. Har han en (blyerts-)penna ? Nej. Har du (ni) en kopp och två kakor ? Ja, tack. Tre sängar. Fyra mattor. Åtta stolar och fem bord.

Exercise 4

(a) Here's father. There are father and mother. Where is the woman ? Where is the staircase ? Are the children in the garden ? How many doors and windows has the house ? Where is Nils ? Has the farmer (got) twelve goats and six horses ? Where is the bread ? Here is a plate for you.

(b) Kudden är på golvet. Knivarna och gafflarna och skedarna är på bordet. Huset har fyra väggar. Är du där, Nils ? Här är ett ljus. Mor, var är glaset ? Har barnet en tallrik ? Har barnen tallrikar ? Där är trappan. Mattan på golvet. Mannen på hästen.

(c) Here are the carpets. The cups and the glasses are in the cupboard. The children are in the room. Where are the glasses ? Thirty cups. Have you a knife, a fork and a spoon ? The house has twenty-eight windows and sixteen doors. How many carpets are on the floor ? Have you much bread ? Thirty-eight plates. Father, have you a pen (pencil) ?

(d) Är mattorna på golven ? Är glasen i skåpet ? Hur många barn är i trädgården ? Sex glas och sju koppar för nio män och fyra kvinnor. Har huset många dörrar och fönster ? Ljusen i rummen. Ett hus har fyra väggar.

Exercise 5

(a) Min bok är i skåpet. Hans böcker är på bordet. Vem har hennes kopp ? Nils, var är våra gafflar ? Ditt (ert) rum är nära mitt. Hennes hus är nära skolan. Bordet är mitt. Nej, det är hennes. Är skedarna dina ? Är detta din (er) kniv ? De är hennes vänner.

(b) The cupboard is mine. No, it is hers. Is your friend at school ? Mine is at home. I have my book and his too. Are the knives yours ? No, they are theirs. Are your parents here ? No, they're at home. Is his cup on the table ? Yes, and hers too.

(c) Nils är en god vän till mig (en av mina vänner). Är han hemma ? Nej, han är i skolan. Är huset ditt ? Nej, det är hans. Hon har sin bok. Ja, och han har sin. Professorn har studenternas böcker. Han har deras.

(d) Their children are (at) home. Ours are here. The professor's children are not here ; they are in the country. This is one of my pupils (a pupil of mine). Are the pupils (schoolchildren) at school ? No, they are at home. Their children are here ; where are yours ? They are here too.

Exercise 6

(a) En liten hund. Ett litet barn. Små barn. Ett nytt vitt hus. Ett rött hus. En blå fågel. Ett blått märke. Ett vilt djur. Bladet är grönt. Flickan är söt. Vinet är sött. Hästen är trött. Hundarna är trogna. Grå ögon. Hårt bröd. En lång gata. Är det sant ? Sanna ord.

(b) A round table. Many (a lot of) red and white houses. A wild horse. Raw (and) cold weather. Warm (and) mild weather. A little girl. We have red and white wine. The wine is good. The apples are ripe. A free country. Showy colours. A wide (and) long street. How wide is the table ? Two metres. The floor is hard and smooth. I am warm. Are you warm ? A Merry Christmas and a Good (Happy) New Year.

Exercise 7

(a) Sweden is a large country ; but it is not so large as Russia. The city of Gothenburg is smaller than Stockholm, but the port of (harbour at) Gothenburg is larger than that of Stockholm. Sweden has a cold climate ; the winter temperature is much lower in Sweden than in England. The English climate, however, is not so dry as the Swedish (climate) ; the air is clearer and purer in Sweden. Sweden has many large lakes ; (the) largest is (Lake) Väner.

(b) Ryssland är mycket större än Sverige. Norge är

precis lika stort som Finland. Dagarna är längre på sommaren än på vintern. Guld är tyngre än järn ; men bly är tyngst. Island är mindre än Norge ; men Danmark är ännu mindre. Vintern är mörkare i Sverige. Sverige har många öar ; störst är Gotland. Gotland är större än Öland. Malmö är inte så stort som Göteborg.

Numerals

Sjutton, aderton, tjugotvå, fyrtiotre, femtiosju, sextiofem, sjuttioåtta, fyrtio, femtio, åttioåtta, (ett) hundrasjuttionio, femhundraåttionio, niohundrasjuttiotvå. (In the last three examples a space may be left between *hundra* and the following word).

Exercise 8

(*a*) My brother is older than my sister. My father is the oldest man in our town. Bread is nourishing. Meat is more nourishing. Eggs are most nourishing. Mount Everest is the highest mountain in the world. The largest Swedish lake is (Lake) Väner. England has many more towns than Sweden. How many pages are there in his book ? Two hundred and twenty-five. A year has three hundred and sixty-five days. A month is four weeks. A week is seven days. A ' dygn '[1] is a day and a night. A ' dygn ' is twenty-four hours. An hour is sixty minutes. A minute is sixty seconds.

(*b*) Jag har ett större hus än du. Min bok är nyare än din. Din cykel är dyrare än min. Bladen är grönast på våren. Ett sådant fult hus ! Det är det fulaste huset i sta(de)n. Storgatan är den längsta gatan i vår stad. Hennes bok är tjockare än hans. Hans har två hundra sidor, men hennes har mera än trehundra. Ja, men papperet är mycket tunnare. Han hade mycket mera papper än jag. Ju mera pengar du (man) har, dess bättre. Min äldsta bror är lika lång som min far. Min mor var fattigare än hennes syster. Här är det nyaste paraplyet i huset. Få människor ; färre barn.

Exercise 9

(*a*) Mrs. Afzelius is an old friend of ours. I call her "Tant." Aunt Greta has many (lots of) brothers and

---

[1] No English equivalent.

sisters ; she lives here in the town. I must write a letter to Grandma ; she is ill. My sister is going to sew a button on to my new coat. Their parents are not at home. I must be home soon. Miss Norén is her aunt ; she lives in the big house in the country. Grandpa has fallen down on the stairs ; he is very ill. My brother-in-law was wounded in the war ; he was operated on (underwent an operation) at the hospital. My cousin Ingrid is at school now ; but she is going to be a teacher one day. What do you want ? I want six good Swedish books. The roofs on (of) the houses in our town are red.

(b) Jag skall snart skriva ett brev till min svägerska. Karl har blivit farfar. Bor din (er) syster i London ? Bor dina syskon också i London (or : i London också) ? Nej, de bor på landet. Vad vill han ha ? Var kan jag skicka ett telegram ? Sjukhuset har etthundra nittiotre sängar. Februari är en kall månad. Det är vinter ; det är mycket kallt. Sommaren är mycket varmare i Sverige. Jag kan inte gå till sta(de)n nu ; jag har inte tid. Men jag skall gå snart. År nittonhundrafyrtiofem. Tolv små svenska städer. Sjunger (ni) Fröken Andersson ? Nej, inte mycket.

Exercise 10

(a) She stayed here. We shall (are going to) stay here a week. My sister cycles to the office. The soldiers fought like heroes for their native land. I called him ' Brother.' He fell ill yesterday. Look, there's your father ! Have you looked at the book ? A week is seven days. The first day of the week is Sunday. How many hours is a ' dygn ' ? My birthday is the 24th December. The 24th December is Christmas Eve. April is the fourth month of the year. How many days has February ? Shall we pick (some) mushrooms to-day ? Will you get me a kilo of coffee. Ask him how much it costs. How much is the coffee ? It costs four kronor per kilo.

(b) Stanna här. Tåget stannar inte här. Ni (du) måste stanna hemma. Varför ? Jag är inte sjuk. Den lilla flickan kallade mig ' Farbror.' I morgon är min födelsedag. Varför är din bror så lat ? Han är inte lat, han är sjuk. Vintern är den kalla årstiden. Hur många månader har ett

år ? Hur många dagar har januari ? Veckans tredje
dag är tisdag. Plåga mig inte nu ! Har du (ni) plockat
svamp ? Pojken kastade stenar. Vi badade i sjön. Jag
vaknade. Vill du (ni) borsta min rock ? Jag tvättar hän-
derna. Soldaten räddade mannens liv. Jag önskar att
skicka ett telegram ; hur mycket kostar det att telegrafera
till London ? Jag väntar (ett) brev från min kusin. Gustaf VI Adolf är Sveriges kung (or : konungen av Sverige).

Exercise 11

(a) I felt the cold. Can you hear me ? Yes, I am hearing
(=can hear) you well. I read (*past tense*) many books
about Sweden. She bought the book in (the) town but
forgot it (=left it behind) in the tram. Nils drives the car
well. My brother is seeking an appointment as a teacher.
He has read modern languages. We changed (trains) in
Hallsberg. The trains passed each other there. I have
bought the tickets for the theatre this evening. Thanks !
Will you have a cigarette ? No thanks ; I only smoke a
pipe. The students went abroad. I am thinking of going
to Sweden after the war. So shall I. I hear the wireless
programmes from Sweden. It's a good way to learn the
language. When do you want to be called ? At 7 o'clock
sharp. I must get my hair cut soon.

(b) Jag kände mannen mycket väl. Jag mötte far i går.
Han hade köpt blommor åt mor. Förlåt, hur sade ni ?
Det har jag inte sagt. Jag känner kölden, jag måste lägga
mig. Jag lade boken på bordet. Vem har gömt min penna ?
Jag tycker om att läsa. I går läste jag om Anders Zorn.
Han var en känd målare. Boken är tryckt i Lund. Vad har
du (ni) gjort ? Jag har bara rökt en cigarrett. I dag glömde
jag min näsduk, men jag köpte en ny. Jag valde en stor.
Jag har klippt gräset. Han satte väckarklockan på precis
kl. 7.

Exercise 12

(a) Is this his boat ? Yes, I think so. I like that answer.
You can row and I'll fish ; and when you have rowed for a

while, we can change. Yes, we will (let's do that). My sister didn't want to go to the pictures ; in the first place she was very tired, and in the second place (secondly) she wasn't keen on it. I have been (staying) with my parents for some time. Oh, how were they (keeping) ? Not particularly well, thank you. They have been ill. When the day dawned, the prisoners fled. The peasants who lived near the frontier helped them. They made (stitched) their clothes. There was (prevailed) cold weather all the time. The farmer forecast rainy weather. This prisoner was arrested.

(b) Det här äpplet är mitt ; det där är ditt (ert). Är detta din (er) penna ? Detta är mina böcker. Läser du (ni) den här boken ? Ja, naturligtvis. Läs inte den där boken. Den är inte bra. Den där hunden är ful. Är den där hunden din (er) ? Nej, det är hennes. Den lilla är min. Far köper sin tobak i den här butiken. Är den här tobaken hans ? Nej, den är min. Är detta vägen till Uppsala ? Är detta tåget till Stockholm ? Är den där långe herren din (er) lärare ? Nej, han är min far. Vad gör du (ni) i det här rummet ? Ingenting. Stanna inte här. Här är kallt. Fångarna flydde till Sverige. Bonden har sått sin säd. När gror säden , om vintern ? Nej, naturligtvis inte. Jag trodde inte, vad han sade. En olycka har hänt nära huset.

Exercise 13

(a) Please may I have (=I want) a quarter of a kilo of butter. May I have a score of eggs ? No, we cannot sell so many eggs (as many as that). May I trouble you for the salt ? Yes, certainly ; here you are (it is) ! Thanks very much. When do we get lunch ? At about one o'clock. What's the time now ? It will soon be twelve. Oh (is it) ; then we must be going. Yes, I'll ask the waiter for the bill. May I have the bill ? How much does it come to ? The person you're thinking of is not the one I mean. What did she say when she caught sight of him ? How much is two thirds of three fifths ? It's two fifths. Have you received your salary ? Yes, and now I must go to the bank. Have you seen the new film ? No, I have not been to the pictures lately. I saw him in the street half an hour ago. There were dozens of bottles on the floor.

(*b*) Filmen varade halvannan timme. Här är en bok, som du måste läsa. Var fick du (ni) den ? Jag måste lämna tillbaka den bok, som jag lånade. Regnet varade två och ett halvt dygn. Jag såg allt, vad han gjorde. Jag stod på gatan mera än en halv timme. Min bror stod på bryggan och såg mig på båten. När går du (ni) upp ? Jag går upp klockan halv åtta. Och när lägger du dig (ni er) ? Vid elva-tiden. Min gamle lärare är död. Han dog i lunginflammation. Hur gammal var han ? Han var sextio. Är detta tåget, som går till Uppsala ? Ja. När går det ? Om en halv timme (timmes tid). Och när är vi i Uppsala ? Strax efter fem. Är detta den man, som du (ni) menar ? Jag såg honom på gatan för en kvarts timme sedan. Det är en kvart över två nu. Kan jag få en kopp kaffe till ? Den man, som du (ni) menar, bor fem och tre kvarts kilometer från stan. Vi fick gå halva vägen, vilket gjorde mig mycket trött.

Exercise 14

(*a*) Falling snow. A sewn case. A (sewn) piece of needlework. An estate (which has been) purchased. A germinating (grain of) seed. Soft-boiled eggs. A crying child. A loaded cart. The commercial traveller's name. All (the) rooms have running hot and cold water. The wounded soldier I spoke of (mentioned) is dead. My beloved mother. The horse is already sold. How is that written ? The word 'come ! ' is called the imperative. The table was laid by the daughters of the house. The princess is rescued by the hero. When is the subject placed after the predicate ? The children we spoke about (mentioned) are ill. Your words were heard by all of us. Shave or haircut ? A Merry Christmas and a Happy New Year is wished by the Tamm Family.

(*b*) I peep (look) out of the window. Evening is near (at hand), and the rising moon is shining over the lake. The fallen leaves cover the ground. It is autumn and the street is nearly empty (deserted). Only a watchful policeman walks to and fro. Now and then (occasionally) a car is heard hooting as it rushes past. From the house I (can) see across the street a barking dog is heard.

(c) Spännande historier. En döende krigare. Den hotande stormen. Flygburna trupper. De fallnas namn. Pengarna som jag fick för de sålda husen. Skalade potatisar[1]. Stekt kyckling. Ett fallande träd. Hur stavas det här ordet ? Det slott, som du (ni) ser i fjärran, äges av kungen. Han är inte längre den man, han var. Jag är trött. Ja, det syns på dig (er). Ingen märkte, att kungen var där. Det är samma person, som jag såg i går.

Exercise 15

Stockholm, 18th July, 1940.

(a) Dear Nils,

Thanks for the (=your) letter. I have been in Stockholm a week, but I haven't had time to write to you before (this). I am very pleased with the boarding house you recommended. The rooms are very nice and the food is excellent. We are getting on very well here in every way. Yesterday the whole family was out bathing at Lidingö. The weather was radiantly fine (splendid) and there were a lot of people out there. This evening we are going to the theatre, and to-morrow we are thinking of going for a trip to Drottningholm, if it doesn't rain. Now I must conclude, but next week I'll write to you again. Kind regards from all of us.

Yours sincerely

Gunnar.

(b) Malmö den 22 juli 1940.

Bäste Gunnar !

Hjärtligt tack för ditt sista brev, som jag fick för en vecka sedan. Det var roligt att höra, att du trivs så bra i Stockholm. Förra året (i fjol) bodde jag hos några vänner, som har en stuga på en liten ö nära Lidingö, så jag vet, hur det är där. Vi badade varje morgon från bryggan och gjorde utflykter i en motorbåt. Det var en härlig semester.

I år stannar jag hemma till början av augusti. Då skall jag göra en fotvandring i Småland.

Din tillgivne

Nils.

---

[1] The plural form *potatis* is also possible.

(c)   **The Swedish National Anthem**
             " Du gamla, du fria."
             English version, translated freely.

Thou ancient, thou free (land), thou mountainous North,
thou silent, thou joyous fair (land). I hail thee, fairest land
upon earth, thy sun, thy skies, thy verdant tracts.

Thou art enthroned on memories of times of former
greatness, when honoured thy name sped o'er the world.
I know that thou art and wilt remain as of yore. Oh ! I
would fain live and die in the North ; yes, I will live and
die in the North.

Exercise 16

(a) There is someone (who is) ringing at the door. Did
you hear anything ? No I heard nothing (didn't hear
anything). There is no one at home. Is there any tea left ?
Which of these books have you read ? Can (may) I have
another book ? What sort of book do you want ? We
haven't got any others. Can (may) I have another (a
further) copy ? Have you any more books of that sort ?
No, all the others are sold out. We were each given (each
received) a book as a present. Trains leave every twenty
minutes. She talked about everything under the sun. Tell
me in a few words how you got on in the country. Who was
Strindberg ? Strindberg was a well-known Swedish author.
What's the time ?

(b) Har någon sett min bror ? Vilken bror ? Min äldsta
bror. Nej, jag har inte sett någon här. Vem ringde du (ni)
till ? Vad sade [va sɑ:] han ? Ingen vet någonting därom.
Träffade du (ni) någon ? Kan ingen hjälpa mig ? Vilken
väg skall jag [ska ja] ta ? Det finns inget (coll. for intet)
vatten i glaset. Har du (ni) något kvar ? Det här glaset är
smutsigt. Var snäll och ge mig ett annat. Kan ni säga mig,
vilket tåg som går först ? Jag vet inte, vad han sade.
Hurudant var vädret i går (or : gårdagens väder) i Stockholm ? Hurudan hatt vill du (ni) ha ? En sådan (dylik).
Kan jag få sex sådana ? Någon annan gång. Varannan
vecka. Vartannat år. Var tredje vecka. En annan stad.

(c) I drank (had) a cup of coffee. He didn't get time to read any more; he had to run to the station. He is always in time for (catches) the train. He ran for all he was worth. When Adam ploughed and Eve span, everyone was then a nobleman. Who has stolen my bracelet? Near the house there ran (flowed) a small river. Fortune comes and fortune goes. The glass burst into a thousand pieces. Did you sleep well (have you had a good night)? Yes, thank you. I slept like a log. His (the) thoughts do not let him find any (give him no) rest. A sharp (piercing) sound went through the air and grated on his ears. An old man used to go around in the country.

(d) Jag har skurit äpplet i två bitar. Han föll nedför trappan. Jag fann din bok på bordet. Hästen kommer nedför gatan. Den drar ett tungt lass. Flickorna satt på bänken. Tala om för (säg) mig, vad du (ni) har givit honom. Jag har ätit för mycket frukt. Han svor, att han skulle hjälpa henne. Han höll paketet under armen. Jag tog min semester i augusti. När skall vi äta lunch?

Exercise 17

(a) **Mrs. Svensson gets up.**

Mrs. Svensson begins the day early. She gets up at 7 o'clock and puts on the coffee pot. Whilst the coffee is boiling, she goes into the bathroom and makes her morning toilet. Then (after that) she has a cup of coffee in the kitchen. There is a ring at the door. It is the milk-girl[1] with 2 litres of milk, (and) 2 decilitres of cream together with fresh (newly baked) rolls for breakfast. At 8 o'clock Mrs. Svensson listens in to the news on the wireless. Then the postman arrives with the post (letters). Then it is time to wake the children and get the breakfast ready. To-day there is porridge and milk, boiled eggs, strips of pickled herring, coffee, butter and several sorts (kinds) of bread, such as rolls, spiced bread and crisp bread. By about 10 o'clock the tidying and washing up is finished, and Mrs. Svensson is ready to go out shopping.

[1] -bud means a messenger or bearer; here it could mean 'man, boy or girl.'

(*b*) Han satte sig på en bänk. Jag lägger mig kl. 11 varje kväll. Jag känner mig inte riktigt bra. Han rakade sig mycket fort. Hon gifte sig för pengar. De kände sig ytterst lyckliga. Jag känner mig bättre nu. Jag bryr mig inte om, vad han säger. Jag kunde inte föreställa mig, att det var sant. Du (ni) måste skaffa dig (er) ett exemplar av den här boken. I själva verket har jag ett sådant. Jag själv såg kungen.

Exercise 18

(*a*) **Mrs. Svensson goes to (the) market.**

It is a fine Saturday morning in August. Mrs. Svensson goes to the market early.

Mrs. Svensson :	Good morning ! What have you got (to offer) to-day, Mrs. Andersson ?
Mrs. Andersson :	Good morning. I've got plenty for you to choose from to-day. What would you like ?
Mrs. Svensson :	I want half a kilo of tomatoes, six crown artichokes, two litre of pears and a litre of chantarelles. Have you got a nice firm lettuce ?
Mrs. Andersson :	Yes, certainly (I have). Will this one do (suit you) ? It costs 20 öre.
Mrs. Svensson :	Yes, please ; it looks nice. How much do I owe (you) now ?
Mrs. Andersson :	The tomatoes come to 1 crown 50 ; the crown artichokes are 25 öre each ; that comes to (makes) another 1 crown 50. The pears cost (are) 50 öre, the chantarelles 60 öre and the lettuce 20 öre. That'll be 4 crowns 30 (all) together.
	(Mrs. Svensson tenders (hands her) a 5 crown note and receives 70 öre change).
Mrs. Svensson :	Goodbye, Mrs. Andersson.
Mrs. Andersson :	Goodbye ma'am, and thank you (very much).

(*b*)   London den 3 augusti 1945.

Svenska Turistföreningen,

    Stockholm.

Jag vore tacksam om ni godhetsfullt ville skicka mig ett
exemplar av er broschyr " Semestrar i Sverige."

På förhand tackande

Högaktningsfullt

N. N.

(*c*)

Stockholm den 30 augusti 1945.

Kära Faster !

Bara (endast) några rader för att låta Faster veta, att jag
anlände hem i går kväll efter en god resa. Det var mycket
folk på båten, men jag fick en bekväm plats.

Ett varmt tack för den underbara tiden i Kolsvik.
Pappa och mamma hälsar.

Fasters tillgivne

Henrik.

Exercise 19

(*a*) **The Geography of Sweden.**

Sweden comprises the broader eastern and southern
parts of the Scandinavian peninsula, together with the
islands of Öland and Gotland in the Baltic. It extends
fr[o]m north of the Arctic Circle to about the same latitude
a[s] Edinburgh. The country is very rich in (has a multitude
of) lakes and forests. The largest lakes are Vänern, Vättern
a[n]d Mälaren.[1] Stockholm, the capital, is situated at the
point where Norrström, the outlet of Mälaren, flows out
into the Baltic. The Swedish coast is strongly (extremely)
indented and is fringed by many thousands of islands, which
are called skerries. An entire group or chain of skerries is
called an archipelago, e.g. the Stockholm Archipelago, the
Bohuslän Archipelago.

---

[1] These names can scarcely be used in English without the final -*n*
of the Swedish Article.

In the northern part of the country there are mountains and sparsely populated regions which are covered with snow (during) the greater part of the year. Here (there) live about 7,200 Laplanders, who tend their herds of reindeer. Most of the rivers rise in the mountains and flow into the Gulf of Bothnia or the Baltic. They have a swift course and are not suitable for navigation but are used for floating timber. The numerous waterfalls in the North of Sweden are exploited (harnessed) to provide industry with water power (approx. 1.5 million H.P.); and all the important railways are electrified.

The southern part of the country comprises the fertile lowlands. Here much agriculture is carried on, especially in Scania. The lowlands are comparatively densely populated. The largest towns in Sweden are Stockholm (approx. 1,160,000 inhabitants), Gothenburg and Malmö.

The northern part of the country is called Norrland, the central part is called Svealand, and the southern part is called Götaland.

Det svenska kungahuset.

Kung Gustaf VI Adolf föddes (år) 1882 och besteg tronen 1950. Hans far, Gustaf V, föddes 1858 och regerade i nästan 43 år.

(År) 1905 gifte sig den nuvarande kungen med prinsessan Margaret av Connaught. Barnen i detta giftermål var: prins Gustaf Adolf, prins Bertil och prinsessan Ingrid. Prins Gustaf Adolf omkom vid en flygkatastrof 1947 ; hans son, Carl Gustaf, är nu Sveriges kronprins. Prinsessan Ingrid är gift med kungen av Danmark. Hennes mor dog 1920, och tre år senare gifte sig den dåvarande kronprinsen igen (ännu en gång) med en engelska—Louise av Mountbatten. Drottning Louise dog 1965.

Kung Gustaf V hade tre bröder. Den äldsta var prins Bernadotte. Hans näst äldste bror var prins Carl. Denne hade tre döttrar. En av dem lever ännu. Den äldsta prinsessan Margaretha, gifte sig med en dansk prins; den andra, prinsessan Märtha, var gift med Olav, den nuvarande kungen av Norge. Den tredje var prinsessan Astrid, ex-kung Leopold av Belgiens första hustru. Hon omkom vid

en bilolycka i Schweiz 1935. Kung Gustafs tredje bror,
prins Eugen, dog 1947. Han var en berömd konstnär.

Exercise 20

Cinderella.

(a) Once upon a time there was a girl whose name was
Cinderella. She had two sisters who were much older than
she was and so ugly that the mere sight of them was
terrifying. They were not only ugly, but spiteful and
unkind, too, and they bullied their little sister a great deal.
Cinderella was very pretty, that is, she *would* have been
pretty if she had not looked so pale and unhappy. For her
sisters compelled her to perform (do) all the roughest
tasks (work) and to stay all day by herself in the dark,
unpleasant kitchen. She had no nice (beautiful) clothes but
was always dressed in a ragged brown dress, and on her feet
she had (wore) a pair of worn-out slippers. And since she
always had to clean the grate and see to the cinders, she
was called Cinderella.

One day when Cinderella was working in the kitchen as
usual, there was a knock at the door. " Hurry up and see
who it is ! " shrieked her sisters ; and Cinderella opened
the door. There stood a page from the (very) court. " An
invitation from H.R.H. the Prince " he said, handing her a
letter with a low bow. " Hand over the letter this very
instant ! " screamed the ugly sisters ; and when they saw
that it was an invitation from the Prince himself to attend
(go to) his ball the following evening, they quivered with
excitement. " How lucky that we bought the new material"
said one (of them). " Now Cinderella will have to sit up
all night and make us each a ball dress."—" Can't I go
too ? " asked Cinderella wistfully ; but her sisters only
laughed mockingly at her. " *You* go to the ball, you
fright ! " they cried. " Why, it's ridiculous ! Hurry up
with our dresses." So Cinderella had to sit all day and all
night in order to get the two dresses finished. When the
evening of the ball arrived, the sisters drove gaily off. They
looked uglier than ever.

(b) Den stackars lilla Askungen satte sig sorgset framför brasan. "Om jag bara finge vara med" snyftade hon. Bäst som hon satt där, hördes en röst : "Var inte ledsen ! Du *skall* få vara med på balen !" Till Askungens stora förvåning stod en besynnerlig liten gumma nära brasan. "Var inte rädd, kära du (kära lilla vän)" sade hon. "Jag är din fégudmor, och här är jag för att hjälpa dig." Askungen log blygt. "Jag skulle så hemskt gärna vilja gå på balen, snälla gudmor" sade hon, "men jag har bara den här utslitna gamla klänningen." I stället för att svara viftade hennes fégudmor med trollspöet, och se ! hennes trasor förvandlades till en glänsande vit sidenklänning och hennes tofflor till små glasskor. Innan hon visste ordet av, bad hennes gudmor henne att hämta en pumpa och sex små råttor, som hon hade fångat i en fälla. Askungen hämtade dem genast, den goda féen viftade med spöet, och vips ! pumpan blev en gyllene vagn, medan råttorna förvandlades till sex små vita hästar. "Nu kan du gå på balen, mitt barn," sade féen leende. "Men kom ihåg, att du absolut måste lämna balen före klockan tolv, för då förvandlas dina kläder till trasor igen."

(c) Min syster är lärarinna. Hon känner en svenska, som heter Tora och som arbetar som maskinskriverska i Stockholm. Hon bor hos sin faster (moster), de har en våning på Östermalm. Hennes faster, som är danska, är författarinnan till flera utmärkta romaner. Min syster var studentska vid universitetet i London. Hon hoppas kunna resa till Sverige efter kriget och besöka Tora.

Exercise 21

(a) **A Scotch Story**

Two Scottish brothers bought a bus and began to drive passengers between two towns in order to earn money. One was (the) driver and the other was (the) conductor. But the experiment did not prove a success. And why ? Well, the one who was the driver died within a short time— of a dislocated neck.

(*Note.*—This story requires a little reflection.)

(b)   **Cinderella** (*continued*)

Cinderella stepped into the coach. " I'll be sure to remember. But how shall I be able to thank you enough, my dear godmother ? " she cried, waving her hand excitedly as she drove off (away). The golden coach soon stopped outside the palace. Cinderella got (stepped) out and timidly went up (climbed) the stairs. Inside the hall there was a crowd of courtiers (lords) and ladies, all beautifully dressed, but she had never seen anyone as handsome as the prince in his white and silver-coloured uniform. He, too, thought she was the most beautiful girl he had ever set eyes on. " Who can it be ? " he thought. He walked (went) up to Cinderella and bowed low. " May I have (the pleasure of) the next dance ? " he asked, and Cinderella curtsied gracefully. Then he took her hand and they danced together while all the court stood and looked on. The ugly sisters looked green with envy, but little did they suspect that it was Cinderella. The prince danced every (single) dance with her and didn't even cast a hasty glance at anyone else.

Suddenly the clock began to strike. It was almost midnight ! " I must leave at once " cried Cinderella, and before the prince could speak (knew where he was), she began running away. In her haste she dropped one of her glass shoes on the stairs ; but though the prince cried " Stop ! ", she only ran faster and faster. Just as she got outside the palace, the clock struck twelve. Her coach vanished, and her clothes were turned into rags again. She ran all the way home, and soon afterwards her sisters arrived in a very bad temper.

(c) Under tiden stod prinsen och såg tankfullt på glasskon. Ingen kunde tala om för honom, var han skulle kunna finna den förtjusande flickan, som han hade dansat med hela kvällen. Plötsligt fick han en härlig idé. " Den unga flicka, som denna sko passar åt, skall bli min brud," förklarade han. Nästa dag kom den ena damen efter den andra och provade glasskon, men förgäves. Sedan kom de fula systrarna. En sådan syn det var, när de försökte klämma sina jättestora fötter in i den näpna lilla skon ! Just då kom Askungen blygt fram. " Låt mig försöka " bad hon.

"Du ! Usch ! Det är löjligt ! " snäste de av henne och grät av ilska, men prinsen sade vänligt : " Låt henne försöka." Och så provade Askungen glasskon och den passade henne precis, förstås. Och i samma ögonblick (i ett nu) förvandlades hennes trasor till en vacker vit brudklänning.

"Äntligen har jag funnit dig ! " utropade prinsen, tog henne i sina armar och kysste henne ömt. Alla klockor började ringa. De gifte sig samma dag och sedan levde de lyckliga i all sin tid.

Exercise 22

(a) He is very good at drawing. He is very good at translating. He didn't know where to go. I can't afford to buy such a dictionary. The maid is preparing the food. The captain had very little hope of being able to save the ship from foundering. Is there any hope of (my) being able to meet you again ? Her daughter was never allowed to be up late. It's (there's) no use trying. A play by Strindberg is well worth seeing. I am very busy packing my suitcase. Eric is coming to the station to meet us. I am afraid of meeting him. Please (step this way) ; dinner is served ! I don't want her to find me here. He sat writing. Seeing is believing.

(b) Mina bröder tycker om att ro och fiska. Har vi någon chans att få en plats ? Jag tycker om att läsa. Hon är trött på att vänta. Vi blev förvånade över att höra, att han var sjuk. Att lära sig att åka skidor är inte lätt för äldre nybörjare. Jag är ledsen över, att jag glömde att besvara ditt (ert) brev. Han har sparat (pengar) för att kunna köpa den här boken (denna bok). Det är för bra för att kunna vara sant. Vi vill, att du (ni) skall komma till en liten supé. Vi kan inte låta bli att tycka om honom. Farbror (morbror) är den första som gruffar, när något (någonting) går galet. Är du (ni) färdig[1] att gå ? Vi längtar efter att se dig (er) igen. Kan jag lita på, att du (ni) är mycket rädd om pengarna ? Jag är rädd, att bilen blir stulen i min frånvaro. Matroserna räddade livet genom att

[1] *färdiga* if the *ni* represents a plural.

simma till stranden. Han skrev ett brev och talade om,
att han var gift. Han gick ut ur rummet utan att be mig
om ursäkt. Efter att ha bott på landet i tio år, flyttade han
plötsligt till Stockholm. Han fick mig att skriva brevet
för honom. Jag är ledsen över att ha låtit dig (er) vänta.
Hans far gillar inte, att pojkar har en massa pengar. Han
klagade över, att de hade tagit så mycket betalt för ett glas
konjak.

(c) **A weather report**

The weather report of (from) the Meteorological Bureau
has (gives) the following forecast(s) for land districts :

For the West Coast (district) and district around Lake
Väner : moderate to fresh wind, gradually (by degrees)
decreasing ; for the most part fair weather[1] ; temperature
in the main unchanged.

For the rest of Götaland, N.E. Svealand with (including,
and) Gotland : light to moderate wind ; unreliable for
(= risk of) some rain ; temperature unchanged.

For the Bergslagen district (and) the entire inland
district and mountain regions of Norrland : moderate to
fresh wind, initially (first) increasing somewhat (slightly) ;
occasional rain or drizzle (at times) ; temperature falling.

For the entire coastal region of Norrland. . . . Rain
has fallen during the day in several parts of the country ;
thus 3 mm. were recorded in Stockholm, in Gothenburg 4,
in Karlstad 3, etc.

Forecast for sea districts :

For west coast waters : fresh to stiff wind, backing. . .
(A) gale warning has been issued this evening for the
coastal region between Hälsingborg and Landsort for a stiff
to strong (persistent) wind.

---

[1] *uppehåll* indicates that the rain is holding up, i.e. no precipita-
tion (*nederbörd*).

Exercise 23

(a)   At the Restaurant

Mr. Svensson rings up his friend Mr. Johansson and asks (him) whether he would care (feel inclined) to have dinner with him at the Victoria Restaurant. They agree to meet at 6 o'clock outside the entrance. At 6 o'clock they meet as agreed.

Mr. Svensson :   Good evening, my dear fellow ! I hope you have (got) a good appetite. I'm as hungry as a hunter.

Mr. Johansson :   Yes, so am I. It'll be fine to get something nice and hot (into oneself).

Mr. Svensson :   Well, let's go in.

They leave their outer garments in the cloakroom and enter the dining room.

Mr. Svensson :   Shall we sit at the window over there ? I think there's a table free.

They sit down and the waiter comes and receives (takes) their order.

Mr. Svensson (to the waiter) : We should like a large schnapps each and two (bottles of) light ale. And perhaps we can (have a) look at the menu.

Waiter (handing them the menu) : Here you are, sir !

————————

The gentlemen have finished their meal with punch and coffee and wish to settle up (pay the bill).

Mr. Svensson :   May I have the bill, please ?

Waiter :   Certainly, sir. (It was) two dinners at 4 crowns, spirits, beer, coffee, and a half-bottle of punch. That comes to 21 crowns all together.

Mr. Svensson hands (him) three 10-crown notes, and when he has received his change, he puts 3 crowns on the table as a tip. Then the gentlemen go out.

Mr. Johansson :   Thank you very much for a splendid dinner ; next time it will be my turn to invite you.

(b) Flyget avgår först i morgon, alltså får du (ni) övernatta här. Vad vill du helst bli, när (då) du blir stor ? Jag vill resa. Men jag talar inte franska så värst bra, ej heller kan jag mycket tyska. Han frågade, om jag ämnade komma. Hon ville absolut inte följa med, utan ville stanna hemma. Jag hade knappt lagt mig, förrän jag hörde ett skott. Så snart som jag hörde bullret, väckte jag mina kamrater. Medan vi låg där, hörde vi flera skott till. Bullret blev så starkt, att vi inte kunde sova. Vi låg där en lång stund, innan vi märkte, att bullret inte (ej) kom från gatan utan från nästa hus. Om jag vore som du, skulle jag anta hans anbud. Jag kan inte (komma och) hälsa på er i kväll, för jag har massor av brev att skriva. Det är så många, att jag inte vet, var jag skall börja. Men du kan (väl) komma och hälsa på oss, så snart som du (har) slutat din brevskrivning. Ja, det skall jag göra. Jag stannade hemma, tils jag (hade) skrivit alla breven. Sedan var jag så trött, att jag somnade i stolen. Jag skickade av brevet i god tid, så att han skulle få det tidigt nästa morgon. Nu måste vi börja äta, vare sig han kommer eller inte. Jag gav kyparen en femma, därför att han hade passat upp sällskapet så bra. Jag sprang så fort jag kunde, fast jag inte hade stort hopp om att hinna med tåget. Ju mera han arbetar, dess mindre tycks han lära sig. Ju mera han hörde, dess mindre sade han. Nästa morgon var vädret mycket dåligt, så jag stannade hemma. Eftersom vädret var så dåligt, stannade jag hemma. Hon både sjunger och spelar mycket bra. Mina händer var så kalla, att jag inte kunde hålla i pennan. Jag kände mig som om jag skulle få en förkylning. Han talade om Stockholm, som om han hade bott där länge. Sedan vi (hade) ätit lunch, tog vi en lång promenad. Tala inte om det, förrän han (har) kommit hem. Jag skall inte ge upp allt hopp, förrän jag hör från hans kamrater.

(c) Evening news from the Newspapers' Telegram Bureau.

According to a Moscow communiqué Russian troops on the northern front are now in the outskirts of Riga.

On (concerning) the fighting in Italy Allied Headquarters

state that great (heavy) losses have been inflicted on the German army.

The British Air Ministry reports that Munich was exposed to a severe (violent) air attack last night.

———————

We now proceed to this evening's telegrams :

The Russians' attack on the Germans on the Baltic front is increasing in violence. They have succeeded in driving a wedge into the German defensive positions and have made an advance of nearly (getting on for) 8 km. All (the) German counter-attacks have been repulsed.

The German Supreme Command reports from the eastern front that in severe defensive battles the Fifth German Army has repulsed repeated Russian attempts to penetrate into the German positions. Several Russian groups were liquidated.

The Allied High Command in Italy reports that yesterday the British Eighth Army successfully landed troops from landing craft at three places on the west coast. Attacks from the landward side were started (initiated) several hours before, and the Germans are said to be surrounded (it is claimed that . . . surrounded). Reports from Reuter's correspondent indicate (suggest) that all aerodromes in the district had previously been put out of action (rendered unserviceable). The Americans have succeeded in establishing bridgeheads north of Angelio. Further to the east German resistance has stiffened.

On (concerning) air activity of the past twenty-four hours it is reported from London that Southern England was exposed (subjected) to an air-raid this evening. The "raiders passed" was given (sounded) after a short time.

British Lancaster bombers make a heavy (violent) attack on Munich last night. During the morning American heavy bombers attacked military objectives in Northern France. . .

That is all to-day from T.T.

Exercise 24

(a)   **A Commercial Letter**

Messrs. Spik and Bult[1], Ltd.,
    7, King Street, Gävle.

                         Stockholm, 3rd January, 1944.

Dear Sirs,

                 R̲e :   Luleå Office.

As intimated in previous correspondence we intend to
open a branch office in Luleå. We are taking this step
primarily with regard to (in view of, in connection with) a
rather large building complex (block of buildings) which
we have undertaken (to erect) in the Luleå district ; but
we hope that future developments will show that we are
justified in retaining the new office (branch) as a permanent
link in our organisation.

Within the next few days we intend to write to (approach)
you again with an enquiry for sundry material in connection with the Luleå contract. Moreover unforeseen needs
(requirements) of (in regard to) tools, etc., will probably
arise during the course of the work (while the work is in
progress). As far as we know, you have no branch in Luleå ;
but perhaps there is an agent who keeps your goods in
stock.

It is principally on the latter point that we are at present
in need of information from you.

                    Yours faithfully,

                    BUILDING CONTRACT, LTD.

[1] Note.—*spik* ' nail ' ; *bult* ' bolt.'

(b)   **The Reply**

                         Gävle, 5th January, 1944.

Messrs. Building Contract, Ltd.,
        Stockholm.

Dear Sirs,

                 R̲e :   Your Luleå Office.

We thank (you) for your esteemed favour of the 3rd inst.,
on the matter quoted above (in the heading). It is quite

correct that we have no branch office in Luleå. Our interests there are watched over by Messrs. E. G. Karlsson's Iron-monger's Store, which keeps a fairly well-assorted stock of our goods. We beg to suggest that your representative should call on Mr. Karlsson, the manager, to discuss his possibilities of satisfying (ability to cover) the more urgent requirements foreseen (indicated) in your letter.

We look forward with great (much) interest to your enquiry for the iron and steel items specified for the building complex in question.

Hoping that the pleasant collaboration which has always characterized our business relations will prove fruitful in the Luleå project, too.

We are, Sirs,

Yours faithfully,

Spik and Bult, Ltd.

(c)   **Supply and Demand**

Let us consider, for example, the process by which we are all provided with our needs (requirements) of fuel for heating and cooking. In large parts of the country we now make fires with coal or peat, of course ; but wood is un-doubtedly a better and cleaner (form of) fuel ; and it is undeniably (certainly) best of all to be able to pile up one armful of wood after another on an open hearth, as was customary in olden times. Such a flaming fire on (in) the grate, round which the whole family gathers in the even-ing(s), outweighs (is worth more than) scores of the amenities of civilization ; it is invaluable (a priceless gift) both from the aesthetic and the hygienic point of view. But nowadays it is almost (practically) only in the remotest forest districts that people can still afford such a luxury ; we others, both wealthier and poorer, have long since been obliged to have recourse to slow combustion stoves, etc. Why should this be so ? Is not the growing forest a free gift of Nature ? Why then should not anyone have a perfect right to cut

down and carry home as much wood as he (himself) can, or
let others do this for him for payment ? The answer is, of
course, obvious : under such a regime (system) all the
forests in the country, at least all those south of the Dalälv,
would be cut down within a few years. Thus it is absolutely
necessary for some limitation to take place (be made).

Exercise 25

(a) Sunday arrives. And now every fisherman remembers
that there is a church here. It is remarkable how full the
church gets. There come the fishermen one by one along
the narrow paths in the snow. And to-day they have not
got (are not wearing) sou' westers, but broad-brimmed hats.
But one or two (some) of them have sea-boots (on) because
otherwise they would only have had slippers to have (put)
on. The ringing (sound) of the bells rolls out over hill and
sea, and the men enter (step into) the church with snow on
their boots, and since they are all used to the back seats in
the church at home, here, too, they begin to pack themselves
into the last (rearmost) seat (pew). But when it is (gets)
impossible for any more (of them) to squeeze in there, they
sink down (drop) into the next ; and so it creeps forward,
(pew by pew).

(b) Anna Svärd was certainly made for going round with
(hawking) goods. She had an eye for what should especially
be offered to customers. It had never happened to her that
she had put any goods that wouldn't sell into her bag.
If she came to a place where they wouldn't do business, she
went away without being unpleasantly obstinate. If she
came across (the kind of) customer(s) who liked to bargain
(haggle), she let them have their way and looked rather sad
(crestfallen), so that they should think they had done a
good piece (stroke) of business. Moreover she was quite
honest. She never offered a piece of damaged material for
sale.

(c) The princess was spoilt and beautiful. The king, her
father, could scarcely deny her anything. Only in one
thing (respect) was the king severe. He wanted his daughter
to become (be) the most cultured princess in the world.

And for this purpose he had engaged three awfully learned ladies-in-waiting, who gave her difficult lessons. The princess had to learn much (a great deal) that was good and useful but quite a lot that was unnecessary. Four hours of the day were set apart for learning lessons and four for hearing her say them. But for the remaining four the princess was free and was allowed to amuse herself with her maids of honour. While she was under the sway (in the thrall) of learned ladies-in-waiting and lessons, the young maids of honour would embroider or go for a stroll and feel rather bored. But when at last the princess was free, they made up for the loss (it).

(*d*) When the hen saw that the perches had gone, she flew up in the air and nearly hit Svante in the face with her wings. Next minute she was out in the yard. Mama came out. And the two (both the) maids came out. And there was a terrible to-do. The hen flew through the flower beds, dashed off across the hedge, flew back again and finally landed (arrived) on the verandah, where she started to fly against the window panes. Svante ran after her all the time, with his heart in his mouth, and felt (feeling) like a real little imp (of mischief), until the hen had been caught and was well and truly stowed away in the coop again, for it was he, of course, who had let her out. And now he promised Mama that he would never do it (so) any more.

(*e*) Far off (away) in the forest, where the roads are narrow and shut in and the trees stand (have stood) untouched for hundreds of years, there lies a castle which belongs to a noble fairy. Its wall rises steep and grey. A passer-by could (might) take it for the face of a rock. And the gate is not very conspicuous. But high up above the dense crowns of the trees (tree-tops) rears the castle; and up there in the light the roofs of the towers gleam and the windows shine (glitter) like crystal. Only the birds in their journeys (passage) across the forest get an idea of the magnificent form (outline) of the fairy castle. The birds— yes—and the little boy who one fine day proceeded to climb up (in) one of the highest trees to search for the way home, which he had lost during one of his excursions (rambles) in the forest.

(*f*) Erik Gustav Geijer who was born in 1783, had six younger brothers and sisters. They lived simply but pleasantly in the little single-storied building with its dark hall and its rooms with small leaded window-panes and heavy furniture; massive oak cupboards, deep armchairs and long sofas. And there was method and order in the entire house, for the father of the house (pater familias) was very severe and would not tolerate any untidiness. Woe betide anyone who had hung up any (one) of the keys in the wrong place or mislaid the clothes brush ! The father did not really become (get) angry, but derisive and crushing. Nevertheless (all the same) everyone in the house was warmly (devotedly) attached to him, both his gentle, good wife, the children and the servants, for they knew that he was striving to do his best for all of them.

(*g*) There once lived in Marstrand a poor fishmonger, whose name was Torarin. He was a feeble and humble man. One of his arms was paralyzed so that he was neither fit for fishing nor rowing. He could not gain his livelihood at sea but travelled around selling (and sold) salted dried fish to folk on dry land (people on shore). One day in February he came driving along the highway. Beside him on the load (his loaded cart) he had a good friend with whom he could chat. It was a little black dog with a thick (bushy) coat, whom Torarin called Grim. For the most part (generally) he lay still, with his head pressed down between his legs. But if he (got to hear) heard anything that did not please him, he got (would get up) on the load, pointed his nose up into the air and howled worse than a wolf.

(*h*) Hulda was kind and splendid (a jewel) and good in every way ; but she had to go out into the world too early, poor child. She had passed her telegraphist's examination, and as she needed to earn an income as quickly as possible, she had accepted the first situation she had been offered, as a postal and telegraph assistant far away up in Norrland. It was difficult (hard) for the (her) mother to let her only child go so far away alone ; she had always dreamed of a post for her in Gothenburg or its neighbourhood. But as regards Hulda herself, she seemed rather to be glad to go so far away. She was young, of course, and what was new and unknown attracted her—and then, too, she probably found (felt) life rather monotonous (living) with her mother and grandmother, who were both of them (both of whom were) aged and infirm.

(*i*) In China calligraphy has always been very intimately connected with the (art of) painting ; and an eminent calligraphist has always been esteemed as highly and (always) met with (been the object of) the same admiration and respect as an eminent painter. Just as we decorate (ornament) a room with paintings, so in China they ornament it with literary quotations, written in large bold characters on white canvas, and executed by some eminent master. A Chinaman can go into ecstasies over a fine touch (piece of brushwork) just as much in a written character as in a picture. Now the intimate connection between writing and painting results in the Chinese artist (who is, as a rule, both a calligraphist and a painter) often introducing into his picture a line or two of writing, which he knows how to place and execute in a masterly decorative manner.

(*j*) In his exterior (outward appearance) Johan Rydberg was a handsome stately man. In spite of the unkind vicissitudes of fate he is said to have preserved his erect tall figure up to the last ; and the military bearing which his youngest son possessed even in the evening of life was inherited from his father's side of the family. But, like so many great men, Viktor in his inner qualities probably took after his mother, who was the most outstanding (influential) personality in his parental home—its good angel. According to pronouncements (statements) from the most varied quarters she was by common consent a woman of rare qualities : gentle, kind-hearted, of warm emotions and sincere, as well as active and winning (easily gaining friends). She superintended her household and carried out her vocation (duties) with extraordinary efficiency. To all her milieu she served as a splendid pattern : a pious, energetic and loyal (dutiful) woman.

(*k*) Erland rose and followed the brook into the forest. He wandered in the shade of the fir-trees, clambered over boulders and ledges of rock, and then came to a spot (which had been) cleared by the wood-cutter's axe but (which was) still uninhabited. Only a hut of dried boughs and twigs, one such as charcoal burners build, stood there near (beside) the remains of a kiln ; heather, fungi and bracken were growing round about. Here there were stakes driven into the ground ; and while he was wondering what they had served (been used) for, Rasmus, the marksman, came wandering across (through) the glade and told the young nobleman that a crowd of strange people, men, women and children, with swarthy skins and black hair and eyes, wearing strange clothes and speaking a strange language, with horses, waggons and a great deal of baggage, had had their tents pitched on the cleared ground (in the clearing), had stayed there a day and then wandered (gone off) to the north. Rasmus could tell nothing more about them, but he pointed out the tracks of their wheels, winding along where the trees stood farthest apart. And as Erland looked at the wheel-tracks and thought (realized) that Singoalla must be one of (belong to) these people, he found a red bead on the ground, like those that ornamented the girl's arms and ankles. He picked this pearl up and kept it nearest his heart.

INDEX

(The numbers refer to pages)